COURSE CORRECTION

Yale University's first national championship women's crew, 1979 (from left to right): stroke Mary O'Connor, Anne Boucher, Elaine Mathies, Cathy Pew, Ginny Gilder, Lisa Laverty, Sally Fisher, bow Jane Kraus, and coxswain Joyce Frocks. Courtesy Yale Athletics Department.

Course Correction

A Story of Rowing and Resilience
in the Wake of Title IX

Ginny Gilder

Beacon Press

BOSTON

Beacon Press
Boston, Massachusetts
www.beacon.org

Beacon Press books
are published under the auspices of
the Unitarian Universalist Association of Congregations.

18 17 16 15   8 7 6 5 4 3 2 1

This book is printed on acid-free paper that meets the uncoated paper
ANSI/NISO specifications for permanence as revised in 1992.

Design and composition by Wilsted & Taylor Publishing Services

Library of Congress Cataloging-in-Publication Data

Gilder, Ginny.
Course correction : a story of rowing and resilience
in the wake of Title IX / Ginny Gilder.
pages cm
Includes bibliographical references.
ISBN 978-0-8070-7477-0 (hardback) — ISBN 978-0-8070-7478-7 (ebook)
1. Rowing—United States. 2. Women rowers—United States. 3. College sports
for women—United States. 4. Gilder, Ginny. 5. Women rowers—United
States—Biography. 6. Sex discrimination in sports—Law and legislation—
United States. 7. Women athletes—Legal status, laws, etc.—United States.
8. United States. Education Amendments of 1972. Title IX. I. Title.
GV796.G55 2015
797.12′3—dc23   2014037358

TO C. D.

ad te veni, per te me inveni

CONTENTS

Prologue
Changing Course
ix

PART I
Catch

CHAPTER 1 · 3

CHAPTER 2 · 12

CHAPTER 3 · 26

CHAPTER 4 · 41

CHAPTER 5 · 56

PART II
Drive

CHAPTER 6 · 73

CHAPTER 7 · 89

CHAPTER 8 · 102

CHAPTER 9 · 116

CHAPTER 10 · 125

CHAPTER 11 · 136

CHAPTER 12 · 151

CHAPTER 13 · 164

CHAPTER 14 · 177

CHAPTER 15 · 190

PART III
Release

CHAPTER 16 · 201

PART IV
Recovery

CHAPTER 17 · 215

CHAPTER 18 · 224

CHAPTER 19 · 234

CHAPTER 20 · 239

Epilogue · 244

Acknowledgments · 248

Bibliographic Essay · 251

Changing Course

A well-rowed shell is art in motion. It moves smoothly. Stroke after stroke, oars drop in the water and come out together. The rowers' bodies swing back and forth in sync, performing the same motion of legs, backs, arms at the same instant; no extraneous shrug of the shoulders, flick of the wrist, turn of the head, shift of the seat. The result—perfectly spaced swirls of water trailing the shell's wake—offers the only visual cue of the speed these on-water dancers live to create.

It's a deceptively pretty picture, because an all-hands-on-deck battle rages deep within the head of every rower. Forget the wind and the weather; ignore the crew in the lane next door; the real fight pits your single-minded desire against the trio of your physical limitations, your intellect, and your fear.

During a race, the question always boils down to this: How badly do you want to go fast? How much pressure can your body tolerate as the pain crescendos past uncomfortable to excruciating? How completely can you ignore your rational self, which chooses this moment to conduct an in-depth analysis of the importance of rowing and the imperative of speed? How much fear can you stand when its loud voice shrieks of losing and losers, reminding you how hopeless your dreams are and empty your future?

Depends how desperate you are. Because you *love* this stupid sport.

When it came to rowing, I was a sucker from the start. The heart wants what the heart wants.

The first time I saw a shell in motion, I was sixteen, a high school junior who had slipped the chains of my fancy boarding school life for the briefest of respites. I stood on the Boston shore of the Charles River watching a meandering race, the synchronic back and forth of the rowers' bodies; the fluid, controlled motion; the play of light on rippling water and polished wood; and I was a goner.

I can easily imagine what I looked like, a landlubber standing by herself. A brown-haired girl with hazel eyes that sidestepped direct contact, dressed in drab thrift-store clothes and a torn, faded blue-jean jacket. My second-hand clothes disguised an upper-middle-class background, and my usual scowl suggested I was just one more defiant, troublemaking adolescent; only a careful observer would see my face already trained in the practice of worry, the sadness in the downward cast of my mouth, and recognize how out to sea I was. Lost and floundering.

Yellow leaves swished through the air as I watched the boats. The river sparkled in the fall light as they rowed by, dark streaks in the star-studded water. The well-varnished wood hulls were nearly submerged, but none of the rowers seemed to notice. A driver hunched in the back of each boat, issuing orders through a small megaphone held by a thin canvas strap wrapped around his ears. He steered with white plastic handles attached to thin wires that disappeared into the boat's interior and connected to the rudder in some manner both mysterious and invisible to me on shore. Occasionally he rapped the sides of the boat with the handles, as if for emphasis. Eight rowers faced him, sliding back and forth within their allotted spaces, dropping their oars into the tannin-stained water at the same time, pulling to the end of the stroke, and popping them out.

How do they make it so beautiful? I wish I could do that.

Follow the person in front of you, do what they do, hands extend out in front here, legs compress against your chest there, oars arc into the water now, and you can create beauty. Not just beauty, but harmony, too, reliably predictable. You can count on the future, stroke after stroke, as long as you repeat the same set of motions. An endless circle of perfection. Safe and secure in the knowledge of what will come next.

The calm of the scene washed over me, muting my internal drumbeat of anxiety. I had lived with the constant jibber-jabber of my insides, like a hamster scuttling around scenting hidden danger, for long enough not to notice it anymore. I'd have stoutly denied I was uncertain or anxious if you'd asked. But now, desire pierced me with a stabbing suddenness. I didn't think about who I was: an asthmatic, uncoordinated city girl with the briefest of sports résumés, on the run from my family story. I wanted in to the world flowing by me: peaceful, controlled, synchronized. Give me a big helping of order and routine, splashed with sunlight dancing on water and everyone pulling together.

A careful observer might have noticed the slow ignition of a new passion as I stood in the autumn sunshine, staring at the oars flicking the water. No jumping up and down, no diving into the water and swimming out to claim a seat; just the creep of anticipation across my face as I turned to the sunrise of a new possibility.

In my delight, I missed the pain etched on the rowers' faces, and overlooked their labored huffing and puffing. Maybe they were too far away. Or maybe the sunlight shimmering on the water obscured the full picture. Perhaps the constant yelling of the coxswains distracted me: *Power ten . . . hard on starboard . . . give way . . . ten for concentration . . . we're moving, gimme their two seat . . . we're open water up.* The phrases lifted off the water like fog, a foreign language crafted from familiar words. I may not have understood what I heard, but I was mesmerized by the beauty in motion.

It didn't take long for me to discover the hidden story of that beauty, even though I never thought I'd have a chance to step into a shell, no matter how smitten I was that day. It was 1974. Title IX was barely two years old; the federal legislation mandating equal access hadn't yet forced open the gates to sports complexes of all sorts to girls and women, commonly viewed as the gentler sex, a euphemism for fragile and weak. Although I didn't see myself that way, I saw only guys on the river dancing in the sunshine. I didn't know rowing could be for girls, too. Besides, I had dreamed of escaping my family for years and nothing ever happened to set me free. I had no reason to think the dream of rowing would end any differently. I didn't know yet that dreams precede reality, a precursor to creating something from nothing.

Six months after that afternoon by the river, I tore open my college acceptance letter from Yale. Weeks later, I mentioned my interest in rowing to my father; maybe I could try it in college. He responded with an offer to buy me a pair of rowing shoes for my upcoming birthday. Neither of us knew that rowers come barefoot to their shells, sliding their feet into shoes bolted into place, a standard feature. We knew so little about what lay before me.

Rowing's truths were out by the end of my freshman year at Yale. By then I had stumbled into its demanding embrace, succumbed to its brutal glamour, and accepted its preeminence in my life. I was in a full-blown love affair with the sport. I wanted it all. I would do whatever it took to be great.

It took me a long time to understand what propelled my leap into this hard, wet world. Initially lured by unfamiliar beauty, I stayed because I found myself in unexpectedly familiar waters: like the world I came from, this one trumpeted the picturesque, easy on the eyes, but hid the pain, hard on the heart.

I grew up among experts in deception who lived one way behind closed doors and another in open spaces. I knew how to buck up and shut up. I knew all about swallowing hard and putting on my game face. I knew how to swim the oceanic emptiness between private terror and public confidence.

Ornery, brash, successful at keeping the world at bay, yet I felt helpless to defend against the endless internal incursions that undermined my poise. I set myself on course to learn how to be tough, how to protect myself. Best defense: strong offense—that was my life, until rowing launched me on my journey of eventual discovery. Rowing taught me toughness, but it turns out I had much more to learn to row my own race.

Looking back, I see the sirens calling from those flimsy boats. I see why I dedicated ten years to going fast.

It wasn't about winning or Olympic gold. It was about survival.

Of course, at the time I thought it was all about rowing. And really, for a long, long time, it was.

PART I

Catch

I

I endured my first three days of college surrounded by budding Nobel Prize winners, already-published authors, and nonchalant geniuses speaking multiple languages in the course of a single conversation. I crept into my bunk bed for three nights straight, plagued by panic and vivid dreams of walking naked on campus. I woke every morning to a crowd of thoughts clamoring to present more evidence of my mistake. Too young. Not smart enough. Unprepared. Not Ivy League material. Whatever delusion of adequacy my admission to my father's alma mater had encouraged evaporated like morning dew, and I was left to panic before the stark, unblinking truth: I was an interloper.

I was trudging across Yale's Old Campus to the Branford Dining Hall for lunch on my fourth day when I saw a long wooden object inside the High Street gate. The shape looked vaguely familiar, although it seemed out of place. I walked up to take a closer look. Several metal triangles poked out from its middle. Its smooth, rounded bottom rested in a pair of scruffy canvas slings. Another fish out of water.

A rowing shell.

For the first time since I arrived on campus, my chattering anxiety quieted. I reached out and touched the varnished wood, ran my hand along the grain and felt its glistening smoothness. I closed my eyes. I could hear the splash of oars and imagine flecks of water cooling my skin as the boat rocked me gently.

A tall man with a faded John Deere baseball cap perched high on his head was handing out fliers and cheerfully calling out to passersby, "Hi there, you want to learn to row?" He had a long regal nose, proportionately prominent, matched by broad fleshy lips. His clean-shaven face was tanned to a burnished red, proof of time served in the weather. His blue jeans sat loosely on his hips and his long-sleeved, fraying denim work shirt was stained with oily grease. He talked only to girls, and only some. He spoke warmly and respectfully, inviting without pushing. He seemed to go for the taller ones and avoided the heavier-set girls. Most people stopped and listened politely, took the flyer he offered, and walked on.

I introduced myself and smiled. "Hi, I want to learn to row."

His warmth evaporated; his forehead creased as he tugged his base-ball cap down to hood his eyes. His sudden, sullen retreat surprised me.

"Uh, you do?" he replied.

Hearing his reticence—not exactly the first no-confidence vote I'd ever heard—I felt something inside lock me into place, defiance click-ing into determination. The universe had finally nudged my way and I was not going to squander this chance. I remembered sunlight dancing on water, the rush of calm that surrounded me as I watched those boats glide up the Charles River, like a soft embrace that I could lean into without falling. Nor did I forget the smoothness of the strokes and the orderly repetition of the rowing motion. Again I felt the stirring of an alien feeling: was this hope?

I said, "Yeah, I do want to row. So how do I start?"

He took his cap off and ran his hand through his thinning hair, then plopped the hat back on his head and adjusted the brim down-ward again. "Um, let's see . . . ," he said.

Nat Case, the varsity women's crew coach, behaved entirely in character that first meeting. At 5′7″, I was a runt as a rower. Nat as-cribed to the belief that mass moved boats: in choosing recruits, he sought out the advantage that height conveyed. I would discover he prized it above other, less obvious but more valuable traits.

I pried out of him that learn-to-row sessions had already started in the gym and would continue every afternoon for the rest of the week. I gave him my name and made sure he wrote it on the schedule for the following day. I held out my hand for a flyer until he gave me one.

"Thanks," I said. "I'll see you tomorrow." My voice, perhaps, but the universe had spoken.

Of course I didn't go to my first rowing lesson alone: fear and anxiety held my hands, tugging me to slow down and rethink matters. Remind me why you think you can do this? Since when are you a jock? But eagerness and excitement had hold of me, too, and they were flying. Nothing could bring me down. I felt like skipping as I walked.

Payne Whitney Gymnasium towered thirteen stories at the edge of campus. Its Gothic design mimicked the majesty of a cathedral; this building meant business. As I stepped into its cavernous entry for the first time, I had no idea what my future held. I would attend more practices in this building, and hear myself utter more pleas for mercy within its walls, than the most devout religious convert would attend services or pray for deliverance.

I found my way down to the dank basement, home of the rowing tanks. There were three, each identified with a spare, utilitarian designation, A, B, and C, side by side in separate four-story-high rooms that resembled airplane hangars. I found my way to the one assigned to the girls, in the basement's west corner. Dingy yellow brick covered the walls. Half windows, cut high into the back walls, allowed in slits of natural light. Plain light fixtures with bare bulbs hung from the ceilings. The machinery propelling the water in the tanks hummed. I had entered a factory, noisy and purposeful, whose workers focused on maximal productivity, efficient use of resources, consistent effort: a blue-collar haven in the bowels of an Ivy League world.

Tank C looked like a giant bathtub sunk about four feet into the gym floor, with a narrow island bisecting its entire length. The bottom was painted a graying white, with cheery pale blue walls: gazing into the tub was like looking at a watery reflection of a cloudy tableau, with blue sky horning in at the edges of dour weather. Safety railings surrounding the tank had mirrors attached to their insides to allow rowers to check and correct their technique.

Eight stations were dug into the tank's island, one behind another, each with its own equipment. A small wooden backless seat with wheels slid back and forth on a pair of narrow metal tracks. Directly in front lay the foot-stretcher, a simple mechanism comprising a heel cup at the bottom and an adjustable leather flap on top that accommodated all foot sizes, angled at forty-five degrees.

Oarlocks were bolted on strips of wood that ran the full length of the island along both edges. They looked ancient: rusty metal holders with gates that locked into place to prevent oars from bouncing out during a stroke. Each station had one oar, alternating port and starboard sides. The wooden oars had thick handles, smoothed by many hands, blotched with blood and stained by sweat, and collars attached at the same place along the shaft of every oar. When the oars were extended through the oarlocks to row, the collars rested against the locks, preventing the oars from sliding too far into the water. The oars' narrow blades were painted in two horizontal stripes: Yale blue on the water edge, pristine white across the top.

The actual tank snared only about one-third of the floor space in each room. Swedish bars climbed the back walls. Cracked gray mats covered square chunks of the floor, with weights and barbells scattered on them. A pair of odd-looking machines—movable wooden seats perched on top of a sturdy steel base, which connected to wooden handles that looked like wings—occupied a far-off corner. A sixty-minute clock with a prominent second hand was bolted to a stand behind the handles.

A few girls lounged against the railing, observing the rowers in the tank. I wondered who they were. Perhaps more newbies like me? They were talking and smiling among themselves, whereas I knew no one. Several other girls were rowing in the tank, following the person in front of them. Their movements looked a tiny bit like the rowing I remembered from the Charles River. I watched them for a moment and then spied the coach I'd spoken with the day before. He was holding a clipboard, had a pencil tucked behind his ear, wedged under his baseball cap, and had hiked up one of his long legs against the outer wall of the tank. He leaned against his bent knee as he closely watched the rowers.

"Hi, I'm here to learn to row."

He glanced my way, responding gruffly, "Hmmm, hi. What's your name?" I told him and he scanned his list. He didn't find it; this seemed impossible, as I'd watched him write it down. But no matter. I stood and waited until he added my name to the sheet.

"This group is just finishing up. You can join the next session."

My turn finally came to step in. I walked up the short flight of steps and down to the strip of seats. I wanted to shriek and do a victory dance, but everyone else was just choosing a place and sitting down, so I said nothing. Heart pounding, thoughts buzzing, ready to dive in, I sat in the first available seat, behind three other people, and did what they did. How am I going to hold onto my oar with such sweaty hands?

The foot-stretcher's thongs were way too big for my bare feet, so I slid my sneakered feet under the cracked leather straps. I cradled my oar handle in my lap and rolled back and forth a couple of times on the seat. Is my butt ever gonna get sore sitting on this skinny thing. I shoved the oar out toward the side of the tank and grasped the handle, keeping the blade free of the water. Rough wood met my soft, damp palm. The coach was talking gibberish. What the hell am I supposed to do? I kept my gaze glued to the person in front of me.

Holding my oar, I maneuvered my blade so that its edge was perpendicular to the water and thrust my arms straight out in front of me. I crept up the slide on my rolling seat and when there was no place else to go, suddenly my oar dropped into the water. How did that happen? What did I do? I tightened my grip and pulled against the oar. It followed my lead and suddenly fantasy yielded to reality.

We were indoors, confined in a crummy half-lit basement. The scenery didn't change. There was no boat to move, only the sound of motor-driven water. The wind wasn't blowing lightly through my hair; no sunshine beat down, sparkling the water running along the boat's hull; the air smelled slightly stale. But I didn't care. I was rowing.

The oar felt heavy in my hands. I had to concentrate on gripping firmly with both hands to pull it through the water, let it turn in a looser hold as it exited the water, hold it flat until the next stroke was about to start, then reposition its blade edge perpendicular to the water and drop it in at the right time at the right depth, in sync with the person in front of me.

There was nothing flawless about my first attempts. But I learned how to feather and square up, and heard about the different parts of the stroke. I figured out the girls on the perimeter of the tank were the varsity rowers, muscular, oozing confidence, experienced and expectant, and on the hunt for new teammates. I watched them surreptitiously while tussling with my oar. Perhaps their standards were different from the coach's. Maybe they would welcome unbridled enthusiasm. Maybe they would recognize themselves in my show of raw desire, instead of being sure at a single glance that I had nothing to offer and lacked the prerequisites for success. I had no idea. All I could do was focus on the girl in front of me and try to follow her, sliding back and forth on my moving seat, putting my oar in the water and taking it out, dancing to the new rhythm I heard that day on the Charles and finally had a chance to make my own.

"Okay, we're done for today." Nat spoke through the megaphone above the rushing water. "There's a sign-up sheet for practice times tomorrow posted on the board. Make sure you write your name in an open time slot."

Okay, made it through that. Do I have to get out now? I glanced up to see another group of girls waiting for their turn. When can I do it again? My turn over, I pulled my oar across my seat, leaving the blade balanced high above the moving water. I slid my shoes out from the leather thongs and walked down the tank's stairs to the floor.

As I waited behind a couple of other girls to pick a practice time, one of the observers came over and introduced herself as the team's captain. Her name was Chris Ernst.

"How'd you like it?"

She was short, but there was nothing petite about her. Her blonde hair, cut close to her head but not styled, played to its own tune, with random strands curling in defiant tufts. Blue veins ran down the insides of her arms from her shoulders to her wrists. I had never seen such bulging biceps on a girl before. I could feel intensity seeping from her skin like sweat.

Her blue eyes, framed by rimless round glasses, looked right into mine. She seemed to be searching for something. I wanted to give it to her, whatever it was.

"It was good. I'm ready for more. There's so much to think about . . . how do you put it all together?"

She smiled, but the intensity didn't disappear. "Just keep coming back and you'll figure it out."

"Don't worry, I will." I said it lightly, but I could feel my determination stirring again.

"Wait until we row outside. It's so much better when you're in a real boat. We'll go to the lagoon next week."

We! Did you hear that?

I'd spent my first several days of college over my head, gasping for air. Now, down in the basement of Payne Whitney, a shrimp of a powerhouse tossed me a buoy. Maybe I could find my niche among a new band of sisters, fit in without having to talk about myself, and make friends by sharing the challenges that rowing seemed to promise.

I penned my name in one of the available slots on the sign-up sheet and left the tanks swinging my arms happily.

I gloried in the late summer heat as I left my dorm room for my morning class. New Haven was wrapped in a comforting, muggy embrace. As I walked across campus in a T-shirt and shorts, I turned my face to the sun, closing my eyes and basking in its affectionate warmth. I could tolerate anything on a day like this.

Hours later, I had no one to complain to as I jogged at slug speed in the heat, sweat soaking my brand-new women's crew training gear, heading to my first outdoor rowing session on the lagoon two miles from the university's main campus. Yellow school buses regularly departed from outside Payne Whitney to drive students on the football, soccer, and cross-country teams to the athletic fields that lay just beyond the lagoon: for some reason, however, none of the rowers were allowed to ride them.

I zigzagged through dilapidated New Haven, past houses with shutters hanging off hinges, peeling paint, and rusty chain-link fences. People peered at me from the safe shade of their front porches. What the hell was I doing, running through this neighborhood, in this heat? They may have been wondering, but I wasn't. A chance to row in a real shell awaited me at the end of my slog.

My legs felt like lifeless logs. My arms were ten-ton steel beams. My breathing sounded like the chug of a steam engine. I arrived at the lagoon just in time for practice, aching for a drink and a rest, but ready to row.

The lagoon was part of a public park, but it looked like a war zone. The metal boathouse, covered with graffiti, thick chains securing the boat bay door handles, and surrounded by hard-packed sandy dirt and sparse grass, looked defenseless and alone.

Nat squinted at the group, divided us into port and starboard rowers, then into groups of eight, with four ports and four starboards, adding a coxswain to round out the crews. We entered the boathouse empty-handed: we came out with a three-hundred-pound wooden shell digging into eight novices' shoulders. My first encounter with the task of hoisting and carrying a sixty-foot-long boat tempted me to drop it and walk away.

But we reached the splintered wooden dock a few hundred feet away without anyone abandoning ship. Following Nat's precise commands, we thrust the boat off our shoulders and up above our heads, grabbed the outriggers, turned the boat over, brought it down to our waists, and placed it in the water. Then we managed to stuff nine people into a shell less than twenty-four inches wide without anyone putting her foot through its bottom, where the wood's thickness measured less than a quarter of an inch.

The lagoon water was murky and smelled faintly of chemicals. Trash lay submerged at the water's edge, caught in the tall reeds that crowded the shore. I tucked my feet into the shoes in front of my seat and smiled at the memory of my dad's birthday gift offer. I shoved my oar into the oarlock and closed the gate. The blade smacked the water. At the coxswain's command, eight hands pressed on the edge of the dock and shoved the boat away.

I found myself in another world, far away from the stench and trash. The wheels under my seat squealed and whined as I slid back and forth. I tried to mimic the person in front of me, to remember when to push my legs down, how to feather and square my blade, how to get the oar out of the water. I heard the coxswain's commands and worked to translate them into English. Perhaps my sweat dried up or clouds covered the sun, but I no longer felt hot, bothered, or quarrelsome.

We worked on technique drills: blades squared during the recovery to feel how high the oar had to travel above the water without snagging it; pausing after the release, with our hands pushed away from our bodies and our backs angled forward to feel the boat run underneath us; rowing gingerly by pairs, then fours, with our eyes closed to sense our bodies moving together. Nobody knew enough yet to pull hard.

I was determined to figure out all the things I was challenged to do at once: the correct technique, the right body motion, at the exact same time as the person in front of me. Following involved more than just looking. I had to develop a feel for when one stroke was over and it was time to release my blade and start up my slide on the recovery.

My brain was bursting with questions. My frustration mounted, but it wasn't a "forget this, who cares?" desire to return to shore and bail on the whole damn thing: I had to figure this out.

I returned to my dorm exhilarated, with my first set of blisters sprouting on my palms and fingers: slender shoots of green bursting through the soil in the first sunny day of late winter, harbingers of better climes. As I fingered the rising watery welts, preoccupied with my memory of my first row and hopes for what lay ahead, I discounted the tingle of pain.

I hadn't taken one hard stroke yet. And I didn't know the challenge of rowing would extend well beyond my body.

2

When you think of sports, vocabulary likely doesn't spring to mind, but every sport has language that defines and describes its physical requirements. Using cognitive skills to build physical skills is a no-brainer; language augments the power of observation by providing an avenue to break down a physical act into its component parts and add detailed nuance to pinpoint distinctions.

When I stepped into this new world, I stumbled into its language, too, and began to learn a new set of terms and expressions, many of them stolen from everyday usage and angled slightly off their normal meanings to coin technical phrases. I loved discovering new meanings and learning to associate them with new sensations. I sprinkled rowing jargon like an old pro, name-dropping technical terms that mere months earlier I didn't know existed and couldn't have used in a sentence.

Start with the "catch." What a word. A noun and a verb. Play catch; catch the bus. It can convey aggressive action or passive reaction. Catch a thief; catch a cold. It can describe a hindrance: what's the catch? It acts upon the physical domain or the senses. Catch fire; catch her eye.

Within a rowing shell, "the catch" defines both a moment in time and an action. It marks the instant between forward and backward, a hovering between two states. In that brief transition, the boat flows under you as your body and breath poise for the next stroke. The controlled ease of the recovery is about to yield to the explosive effort of the drive.

The catch begins with the oar's blade seizing the water, initiating the transfer of your body's energy into boat speed. The oar serves as the medium. It starts with a deceptively simple motion: at the top of the slide, just raise your hands to drop your oar into the water. Catch that precise moment when your body changes direction. From your roll toward the stern, against the boat's forward momentum, reverse to move with the boat as you begin pulling backward toward the bow.

This moment, combining timing and technique, is fraught with opportunity for mistakes. The oar can enter the water too early, before the recovery ends; too late, once the drive has begun; or badly, at the wrong angle. Poor timing and bad technique, alone or in combination, can kill your speed.

Rowing well requires the development of boat sense, the capacity to feel your own body and discern the boat's rhythm. Where are you on the slide? When is the moment of convergence when all the rowers catch the water with their oars and pick the boat up together? How is the boat flowing underneath you? Choppily, with a back-and-forth stagger? Smoothly, soothingly consistent?

The ability to position your body correctly, to use your various limbs and muscle groups in optimal order, determines technical proficiency. The techniques to negotiate an oar in and out of the water—squaring up, feathering, releasing, catching—can be taught. Practice and focus develop the muscles' cellular memory to the point that thinking is not required. But what about timing? Coaches can't teach it: they can only notice its presence or absence. They can point out what to look and listen for, but they are bystanders, outside the experience.

Spending time in the boat, paying attention to its inner workings, teaches timing. Listen to the gurgle of the water flowing by. Hear the whoosh of the shell gliding forward beneath the recovery. Notice the jolt at the catch when the crew's change of direction jerks the boat backward for the barest instant. Feel how the boat responds to the energy transfer—like a lumbering backhoe or a streamlined Mercedes? Sense the quality of the crew's cadence; is it rushed or relaxed? Twenty-eight strokes per minute can feel breathless and scattered, while thirty-five can feel controlled and light. Consider the impact of the oars' finish on the boat's momentum—does the boat slow and sink at the end of the stroke, or run out smoothly as the rowers gird themselves for the next?

Rowing is a combination of attacking and yielding, of aggression and acceptance. You expend huge effort to create an outcome, and then you must let it unfold. You can't make it all happen; you have to obey the established rhythm, even though you're the one responsible for its cadence. Boat speed and boat sense come from your physical effort and your internal awareness combined. Boat sense emerges from practice; you learn what rushing means, develop the feel of a heavy catch, and discover the right ratio of drive and recovery that establishes a balanced cadence.

How do you develop boat sense about your own inner world? How do you discover what you need to see when it's hidden, without a coach to guide you?

One stroke at a time.

It's hard to discern the precise moment of the catch, the change in direction that pivots between the two extremes of the recovery and the drive, between indifference and head-over-heels, gotta-have-it determination, the instant that stirs the feeling that lies at the heart of any attraction.

Like water in the curve of the oar's blade, I was caught by my desire to row.

But, at seventeen, a novice rower, and barely an adult, I lacked boat sense and personal sensibility. I knew rowing had caught my interest, but I couldn't acknowledge my life was caught by my past. My attraction to rowing seemed like a non sequitur, a break in the continuity of my life story that I welcomed with open arms. To me, rowing was completely different from anything I'd ever done before, and that fact alone increased my desire.

I'd already been on the run from my family story for over five years, determined to leave the details and influence of that saga forgotten on some far-off street corner. I thought rowing gave me another opportunity to distance myself, to swerve off the expected route and run in a new direction. Turns out, I was as ignorant of the deeper motivations propelling my attraction as I was clueless about the lingo of rowing.

Sometimes you have to go backward to go forward. All rowers know that, as they sit backward facing the stern. Every single stroke is followed by a complete reversal of direction, a gliding return to the top of the slide against the boat's forward motion. That's the only way to prepare for another stroke.

Here, too, there's only one way to understand why my decision to start rowing made sense, and that's to go backward. Just as the separate components of a rowing stroke are linked together, so was my choice to take up this grueling endeavor anchored to my past. My denial didn't negate its influence.

Whether or not my teenaged self knew it, rowing also offered me a route back to myself. My foray into the world of pencil-thin boats, rock-hard musculature, and near-divine requirements for endurance may have been an accident, but it provided rescue.

I wasn't supposed to be that sixteen-year-old girl standing by the Charles River, yearning for escape from my life, already sad and sorry enough to resemble a defeated grown-up. My life's trajectory had veered off its initial arc, catching me unprepared, leaving me anxious and uncertain. I was too young to learn about the fragility of love and the pain of loss, but absorbed those lessons as they came nonetheless, without the benefit of gentle introduction or wise guidance.

For the longest time, as far as I knew, our family was normal, happy, and healthy. Our family photos boasted the usual suspects: a father and a mother, with four kids entering the picture over the course of an action-packed six years. The second oldest, sandwiched between my two sisters, with my brother the caboose, I was a preadolescent living the high life on Park Avenue with no second thoughts. I knew we were lucky. I saw my share of beggars shaking their tin cups outside the Plaza Hotel on Central Park South. I knew everyone didn't live in an Upper East Side penthouse apartment with elevator men and doormen opening doors and carrying packages, or go to a private school that taught its students to curtsey along with math and science, or spend summers out of town, away from the hard concrete and sodden heat of the city.

Like any kid who knew only one way of life, I took my family and our circumstances for granted. But I knew the past didn't hold all happy endings. Mom was a first-generation immigrant who traveled all the way from Sweden, via England, when she was only eighteen years old, determined to reinvent her life. She left her entire family behind—a younger sister, a baby brother, her mother, grandparents, cousins, aunts, and uncles—to escape not poverty, but her father. I couldn't imagine hating my parents enough to run thousands of miles away, and Mom didn't give me much to go on. She put me off with a tight-lipped, vehement sideways shake of her head whenever I ventured toward the subject of her father, but I heard enough bitterness about her not being the pretty one—that was her sister, Evy—but the smart, thick-lensed-glasses–wearing, disappointing one, to give me a hint.

I didn't find out until years later that my *Morfar* (maternal grandfather) was a heavy drinker and an abusive drunk, and by then I also knew the wallop that parental disappointment, regardless of its legitimacy, delivers to the hapless children who don't live up to expectations.

When she first arrived in this country, Mom worked as a masseuse, a waitress, and a nanny. She moved up to secretary in an office when she and Dad were first married, then quit when she got pregnant because the doctor told her she would lose the baby if she walked up stairs. Her office was on the fourth floor of a brownstone in Queens, and the elevator was reserved for the executives. One day, many years later, she confided to me, "I didn't tell my boss I shouldn't use the stairs. I didn't tell your father about the elevator. I wanted him to take care of his family, earn the money. He had to do his job."

From then on, she and Dad divided their duties along traditional lines. Mom took care of all things household and kid-related. Not much for warmth, with a record short on kisses and hugs, she conveyed her love by honing her family management skills. She was in charge of it all, from laundry, dusting, and vacuuming to hosting parties and serving the nightly dinners she concocted.

Meanwhile, following his graduation from Yale and a one-semester fling with law school, my dad landed a job in the investment business. To me, my father's world was a box of mystery, filled with taking care of clients, hiring secretaries, traveling to visit companies, reading boring paperbacks called prospectuses, and buying things called stocks. Occasionally we four kids accompanied him to check out the companies he invested in. Denny's and Dunkin' Donuts were my favorites because Dad never skimped on product testing.

But when we behaved badly, he morphed into the bad guy who wielded the belt and strapped us bare-assed or knocked our heads together to thrust us back on course. I learned the importance of staying in line and keeping him happy, whether that meant whispering on Sunday mornings to let him sleep undisturbed or doing what he told me to avoid an argument.

By the time I was eleven, Mom had relocated us to our fourth—and most lavish—apartment, edging us out of Queens' Forest Hills neighborhood where I lived as a baby into progressively larger abodes, landing us on the southwest corner of Park Avenue and 81st Street on the topmost floor, in what I assumed would be our family's permanent home. A toddler when we moved from Queens to Manhattan, I didn't register my parents' march up the wealth scale. Moving to the Upper East Side, right off tony Park Avenue, didn't mean anything to me. The next move didn't mean much more, but of course my father was successfully making his way, building a base of clients and figuring out how to negotiate the stock market, buying long, selling short. With the last move, once Mom was done with her remodeling, the evidence of his financial success beamed from every room of our new apartment.

By then, Mom had mastered running our family, ruling with a sure hand and occasionally an iron fist. Collectively, we were a well-oiled operation, our days ordered, the details addressed. She did a bang-up job crafting a home from the maze of nineteen rooms, linked by hallways and connecting doors, she had convinced Dad to purchase.

Although I got lost the first several times I ran through the empty apartment, chasing my big sister Peggy, by the time Mom finished knocking down walls and decorating rooms, I knew exactly what was what and where I belonged. In attending to the myriad of minutia that effects the transformation of space into safety, Mom created magic. From the décor of our home's most public spaces to our family's most private nooks, she made room for all of us. We ended up with a home that impressed the snootiest of guests, secured privacy for her husband, and allowed us kids to roam freely, a refuge filled with sparkling sterling silver, a baby Steinway grand piano, Oriental rugs, European paintings, and durable furniture that could survive pummeling and spilled milk. She paid equal attention to the design of my father's closet with its row of neatly pressed suits and folded underwear, dark socks with garters, and multiple versions of his trademark V-necked navy cashmere sweaters tucked into built-in dresser drawers; the wallpaper design and paint colors of the private bedrooms she selected for each child; the polka-dotted couch in the kids' sitting room; and the gym at the back of the apartment with Swedish bars, a trapeze, and a rope ladder.

Our home was made for the high life, for preening and partying, strutting and showing off, and my parents took full advantage. Thanksgiving, Christmas, and Dad's birthday offered ready-made excuses to stage fancy celebrations to showcase their home and broadcast Dad's growing success, and Mom manufactured additional reasons to party. Holidays included children, but not the other occasions. I spent my share of evenings peeking out from the kitchen, awed by the formal table settings, heavy with ornate sliver and linen waiting for their moment to shine, watching the waiters serve drinks and hors d'oeuvres from fancy trays, ogling the parade of colorful dinner dresses, and tracking our mother's regal progress from room to room, cigarette smoke enveloping every huddle she joined as she kept the party's excitement going. Glitz and glamour governed my parents' social life; they were the king and queen, and it all looked so good.

But, my mother found herself in the wrong world at the wrong time. Postwar America in the 1950s was eager to live happily ever after, which translated into a renewed focus on family and domesticity. While many women had worked in traditionally male jobs during the war as mechanics, engineers, and factory workers, once the men returned from overseas, women were fired or pressured to quit so their male counterparts could resume their proper roles as breadwinners. The smartest choice for an intelligent woman was to find a husband who would be successful and focus on raising a family, as her career options were nearly nonexistent.

In 1952, in an environment marked by nonstop tension with the Soviet Union as the Cold War escalated, Dwight Eisenhower, a World War II general and hero, won the presidential election. The world's entry into the atomic age, with the ever-present threat of nuclear attack, as well as the rabid anti-communism that pervaded the American political sphere, helped promote a cultural emphasis on security and family. It was patriotic, the American ideal, to raise resilient and prepared children who could handle the uncertainty that pervaded the world. This was not the best time for a single woman to pursue her own dream, and no wonder my mother capitulated, not even realizing at the time what was happening, as the power of a cultural imperative washed over her and pulled her into its current.

My mother fell in love, hard and long, to the point that when she woke up over a decade later in the waning 1960s, she had given her future to a man who was steadily making his way in the world, expected she would handle all the child-raising as a solo act, and yet demanded her full attention. Somehow, her private dreams for her own life had slipped away somewhere, a package that couldn't be held in arms that were already overloaded.

I was too young to understand the bargain my mother had to make, forced by an era that preceded the birth of the women's movement. Ten years following the end of WWII, American culture embraced women who used their smarts for interior decorating and party planning, who dedicated their energy to tackling challenges no more daunting than clean rooms, sparkling silver, and well-behaved children. By the time the sixties arrived, my mother was in deep, and her private dream had faded into the dining room's woodwork that had to be kept polished along with the silver.

Thankfully, I knew none of that. I loved my life. I loved my siblings, divided since time immemorial into the Littles and the Bigs. My baby brother, Dixie, and my younger sister, Britt-Louise, nicknamed Miss Muffet, constituted the younger pair. Peggy and I were the Bigs. Three years separated me and Britt-Louise, a divide I regarded with pride tinged with haughtiness and a sense of responsibility, as the Littles deferred to us Bigs who called the shots. Peggy lorded her twenty-two months of seniority over me and christened me her sissy sidekick. I tried to stay out of trouble, an extremely tough balancing act given my big sister's penchant for mischief; outright disregard for anything that smelled like a rule, instruction, or prohibition; and her relentless attempts to inveigle me to follow her lead.

Then, there was school, all-girls, replete with stodgy, vomit-green uniforms, bloomers included. So much to love: diagramming sentences, learning about gerunds and dangling participles, and listening to Mrs. Clauss read us *The Yearling* in English class (I couldn't stop sobbing at the end); unwinding the trail of details in just the right order to solve complicated word problems in math class; and competing with

Fritzi Beshar and Dorinda Elliott for a nod of satisfied approval from stern Miss Trembley. I belonged there, known by all my teachers and accepted by my many friends.

Mom and Dad even took us abroad to Sweden, where I met my only female cousin, Annica, along with aunts and uncles and, of course, my rumpled *Mormor*, Mom's mom, so gently welcoming with her soft folds and warm embrace. No one mentioned the MIA *Morfar*, Mom's dad, and by then I knew my questions would yield only irritation. Everyone spoke mostly Swedish, while I could speak only English, but hugs and smiles translate across all cultures.

All mighty fine, but our summers trumped everything. According to family lore, Mom and Dad met just off the beach in the Atlantic Ocean one summer day, when Mom was swimming and her bathing suit top came off. Dad was the on-duty lifeguard, his summer job in Ocean Beach, Fire Island, during his college years, and, misinterpreting her distress, swam to her rescue. The rest, as they say, is history.

Our lives may have been orderly and matter-of-fact during the school year, but when school ended for the summer, our daily routine evaporated without a trace. Mom transformed into the queen of laissez-faire, dropping our city life rules like a handful of graying coals on the barbecue. She squeezed our entire household—four children, luggage, bicycles, and Chocolate the cat—into Blackwood, our sturdy Pontiac station wagon, and headed to Long Island, leaving school, homework, early bedtimes, and Central Park's postage-sized concrete playgrounds and the grubby dirt of the Great Circle in the dust. We left Dad to fend for himself during the lonely workweeks and grab a train on Friday afternoons to join us every weekend for his own hit of summer.

We spent our first summers in Ocean Beach where Mom and Dad first met. Cars were banned and rusting red wagons reigned, so I ran barefoot everywhere, often stubbing my big toes on the concrete slabs of sidewalk so badly they bled. My usual attire was a bikini bottom sans top. I learned how to ride a bike on the narrow walkways and helped my dad tend his row of tomato plants that lined the sunny side of the house; I controlled the hose at watering time and helped pick the juicy ripe balls when they turned orange red.

But just as she had in her quest for the perfect city home, Mom didn't settle for good enough, setting her sights beyond Fire Island. She took years to locate the perfect summer corollary to our Park Avenue apartment, which she found on the far eastern end of Long Island, in East Hampton. Heaven turned out to live at the end of Briar Patch Road, where the road dwindled to a narrow single lane and the asphalt petered out to a scruffy mix of dirt and sand. There, Mom set us free to scamper unfettered in the sunshine, nose about in the woods, explore the abandoned barn and catch baby mice, play in the meandering field below our graveled circular driveway, and splash in the shallows of Georgica Pond, tucked in front of the endless stripe of the Atlantic Ocean, which extended across the far horizon like an ear-to-ear smile. We claimed the seemingly endless acreage that comprised the property, where we all ran free like gazelles, speckled brown by the sun and gaily light-footed as we danced through the freedom that defined the season in our household.

We ventured away from our rental property daily, passing countless hours at the beach, riding waves, building sand castles, prowling for shells. We frequented the duck pond, where we sprinkled molding bread on water dappled by pollen, and we wandered the aisles of the public library, seeking books to browse and borrow. But many of the best moments occurred at the end of Briar Patch Road, and Mom made them possible. A master at finding the right ingredients, she created the conditions for summer perfection. Yet, for all her researching and planning, seeking and finding, when it came time to enjoy the fruits of her labors, she missed the boat. Spending time with us wasn't at the top of her list. Expert at the logistics and details, setting the stage for action, she remained behind the scenes she created. She was long on duty, short on presence, and it all worked just fine, until it didn't.

Although the rest of the family loved the ocean and she found a house that allowed easy access to its waters, Mom was not a beach person. She loathed sand. She found the perfect solution, college-aged mother's helpers to ferry us there and to our many other adventures, guaranteeing fun for us and peace for her. Coming home, usually tired, damp, sandy, and hungry, we nearly always found Mom in her favorite sunny corner on the far end of the big wraparound porch, lying on a chaise lounge in her two-piece bathing suit, her wrinkled tummy, courtesy of four children and one emergency appendectomy, lying flat and exposed. She would be smoking one of her trademark Lucky Strikes, eyes shaded by a pair of enormous dark glasses, deep into one of her beloved mysteries.

Once bathed, we would spend the end of the day nipping at her heels, as she prepared our supper, often grilling steak and burgers on the back porch behind the kitchen. After dessert, as twilight ushered in the day's end and the stars twinkled their first hellos of the evening, she occasionally treated us to her own version of games. Sometimes she devised treasure hunts, hiding wisps of paper scrawled with age-appropriate clues around the property. She sat in a rocking chair on the front porch smoking, a gleam in her eye as we scampered here and there, sorting through her meanings and solving her riddles. When we presented our crumpled clues for inspection, Mom meted out our just rewards: trinkets from Woolworth's and miniature chocolate bars.

More rarely, Mom herded us onto Blackwood's opened back gate and gave us her version of a joy ride, bouncing the station wagon onto the grassy field and driving slowly over the rutted ground. I loved her homemade roller coaster. As I clutched Peggy beside me while we flew over the bumps and occasionally lifted into the air, my joy of speed commingled with my terror of falling off.

The summer I turned eleven would be our last on Briar Patch Road, but no one knew that at the time. Peggy's and my usual ten weeks of summer freedom got cut to two that year. I could always recount the names of our mother's helpers, starting with the first, dark-haired BG, who worked for Mom two consecutive summers; followed by Julia and Francie, a package deal; and then Susan. But I didn't know that summer's girl, with long, wavy dark hair and heavy thighs, well enough to remember her name. Mom sent us to Camp Four Winds in who knows where, way too far away, in northern Maine. Being packed off provided us the first obvious clue that something was off, but we missed its significance while we slept in unheated cabins, swam in frigid lakes, learned how to paddle canoes, and ate institutional food, pining for our usual summer routine of waking up and doing whatever we wanted.

When we finally arrived in East Hampton for the last two weeks of August, the night air had lost its softness, replaced by a crisp note of chill, an early calling card of fall. The time was too short to cram in all our favorite activities, and, vaguely unsettled, I bid adieu to summer.

"Peggy, Ginny, Miss Muffet, Dixie, come here!"

It was late September, mid-afternoon on a Sunday, and I sat in my bedroom at my desk with my sixth-grade math workbook open, solving extra-credit word problems. My first impulse was to hide, but I knew that would solve nothing. If Mom wanted to find me, she would. Had she found the mutilated Barbie doll Muff and I stashed in the cabinet or maybe the broken plate I hid in the garbage? Nothing seemed major enough to match the volume and tenor of her voice.

Peggy appeared at my doorway. "What we'd do?" I started to ask, but saw her bewildered shrug and stopped.

"Come on, let's see."

I followed Peggy down the hall to the master bedroom. Miss Muffet and Dixie sat scrunched together at the foot of the bed, their feet dangling above the carpet. Muff's eyes were downcast and her forehead furrowed, and Dixie leaned right up against her, as if to shield himself. Mom wordlessly pointed us to take our places beside them, brandishing the hairbrush she held in her hand.

Peggy and I snuggled close to the Littles. It was as if the four of us made a silent pact; if one of us was going down, we'd all go down together.

We sat for a long moment, waiting, watching Mom glare at us. She looked furious, madder than she'd ever been, and, being kids, we made her mad often. Her face was a giant snarl. Even her hair seemed wild. I wanted to cower and hide behind Peggy, and could feel my body trying to shrink itself into extinction. Peggy, however, showed her big-sister colors.

"Mom, what's wrong? We haven't done anything." Her defiance wavered at the end of her sentence as Mom took a menacing step toward us and raised the hairbrush.

"I have told your father to leave." Mom's voice was so strained, her accent so thick, it sounded almost as if she was speaking Swedish.

Leave? Leave where? He often departed on Sunday evenings, flying out the night before a Monday morning visit to a company in another city. Fear trumped confusion. I said nothing.

"He's having an affair with BG. That slut."

Peggy slumped beside me as if she'd been shot. "No way!" Her words suggested disagreement, but I heard disbelief. Muff and Dixie, only eight and not yet seven years old, respectively, unsure of Mom's meaning but not immune to her upset, started whimpering.

Mom leaped to defend herself. "I told him he had to choose between that whore and me and . . ." She gestured at us with the brush, including the entire family in Dad's rejection.

Shocked into silence, no one moved. I stared hard at my lap, overwhelmed, not wanting to see anyone else's reaction. I felt dizzy, watching my life detonate so suddenly. A rogue wave had washed in and wrecked our solid family like a sand castle. Now I really didn't want to look at Mom, because I heard her sniffling. She had started out sounding so angry, but when I snuck a look at her—still waving the brush, smacking the air—her makeup was smudging.

I had never seen my own mother cry.

Now Miss Muffet was leaning into me, sobbing.

"Not my dad!" I said.

Mom started yelling at me, "He's gone! Ask him yourself. You'll see."

I tried to square all I knew about my father, everything I had learned, with the new information from Mom. I couldn't do it. I was so confused. He had left? And with BG, our old mother's helper? I barely remembered her. Didn't Dad hire her as his secretary? What was she doing in this conversation? I wanted to shake my head and knock out all the pieces floating around that didn't fit into my age-old picture of our family.

No one said anything else. Everybody cried. I suppressed my contrary impulses to defend Dad and give Mom a big hug: she didn't look like she wanted to hug anyone, but to kill someone.

It was a few nights after Mom's explosive announcement before Dad finally showed up to see us kids. He met us in the lobby and didn't even bother to come upstairs to say hi to Mom. We went out for hamburgers and milk shakes. It was quite a treat midweek, but it felt all wrong.

Dad didn't really say anything about anything, just asked about school. None of us kids had the courage to raise the only subject we wanted to talk about. But I couldn't stand the silence, so I offered to walk him back to his hotel, the Stanhope, on the corner of 81st Street and Fifth Avenue, just him and me. As we crossed Madison Avenue, I took a deep breath, clenched his hand, looked up, and asked, "Dad, won't you please come home? It's not the same without you."

He stopped, dropped my hand, and looked at me. I looked into his eyes and saw his sadness well up, but when he spoke, he sounded more determined than sad.

"No, Ginny, I can't. I don't think I can ever come home. I don't love your mother anymore."

"Can't you try?"

He sighed. Although he started out sounding sad, he ended angry. "No, Ginny, I'm sorry. It's too late. No more questions. Enough, okay?"

The sudden edge in his voice warned me not to push further. My instinct to ask, "What about me? Do you still love me?" fought with, "Don't make him mad. Then he really won't love you anymore."

I walked with him the rest of the way down the street, kissed him goodnight, then turned and ran the two blocks home. My eyes stung—was it the wind or my tears—but pouring my heart out through the pounding of my feet on the sidewalk offered brief relief. Flying up the street, legs stretching to their limit, arms pumping to maintain my momentum, my sprint occupied my full attention, and I stopped noticing how badly I felt.

3

At Yale, running and endurance training assumed center stage in my life, no longer an avenue for escape, but a means to a desired end. Never before had I strung together more than three consecutive days of physical activity. I occasionally jogged a couple of miles around my high school campus, attempted basketball, played tennis desultorily in physical education classes, and warmed the bench for my school's volleyball and softball teams, but the payoff from those efforts didn't trigger any increased desire or fiery commitment.

This time, things were different. I should have noticed I was entering the deep and murky waters of insistent passion. But that's what love does; it blinds us to the full picture, painting only the promise, never the pain.

Nat scheduled the team's first timed run at 7 a.m. on a Saturday morning in September, but I got off to a slow start. I had slept through my alarm. It was a jolt to open my eyes and see the time. I leaped out of bed, threw on shorts and a T-shirt, laced on my running shoes, and blasted down the stairs and out of the dorm, running full tilt to the gym.

Great start! Now you'll never make the team. You've handed him just the excuse he needs.

I arrived huffing and puffing, fifteen minutes late. Nat stood alone on the sidewalk with a clipboard tucked under his arm, a stopwatch cradled in his hand, and a pencil snuggled behind his ear, peeking out from under his ever-present baseball cap. The sidewalk beyond him was empty as far as I could see.

"You're late."

"Can I run anyway?"

I was prepared to beg, but he nodded his head up Tower Parkway toward the Grove Street Cemetery. "Do you know the route?"

"Past the cemetery, left on Prospect, up Science Hill, right on Highland, first right onto St. Ronan, all the way to the end of the street, right on Edwards, left on Prospect, and back to the gym." I was already breathless.

"Yep, okay, go on." He pulled out his clipboard, wrote my name down, and noted the stopwatch reading.

I set off at a dead run. I couldn't remember how long the course was, and I didn't care. I thought nothing of pacing, only of redemption.

Stupid, stupid, stupid! Recrimination pounded into my head as my feet pounded on the pavement. To the extent a seventeen-year-old couch potato could muster speed, I flew.

Within the first mile, I arrived at the base of Science Hill—Mount Everest to my novice legs and flabby pulmonary system. No matter. My pride was on the line. I bullied and scolded myself up the hill. Don't stop. This is your own fault. The goading kept time with my pacing. You have no one to thank but yourself.

At the top of the hill, I saw a cluster of runners several blocks ahead of me. Perhaps they were fellow crew members. Invigorated by the chance to catch up, I sped up. Within a few painful minutes I reached the group and recognized some of the faces as I drew even. They were plodding with slow deliberation.

Okay, so you're not going to be last anymore. Good!

"Hi, you guys," I huffed as I stepped into their rhythm. A couple of wheezy "hi's" greeted me. I didn't know the team etiquette here, whether to stay with them or speed on ahead, risk making them mad, or go for it and see what I could do.

It felt as if someone else decided. I didn't get a chance to protest. I just kept running without slowing down and left my teammates in my wake. I focused on running, not thinking.

Periodically, I'd see other team members a few blocks ahead of me. Each time, I caught up to them, passed, and maintained my pace.

I heard increasingly loud and insistent pleas for mercy from various body parts—feet, calves, quadriceps, lungs—that turned into throbbing hot spots and eventually merged into an all-over full-body burn.

Don't stop. You're making progress. See if you can catch that other girl.

I did not keep track of how many team members I passed, nor did I know the size of the crew that had set out from Payne Whitney on this timed adventure. I had no way to calculate where I was in the pack.

I didn't waste any energy on the math. I was no longer dead last; I could have slowed down. I wasn't going to bring up the rear in a sorry-assed state of humiliation. But somewhere along the way, my goal grew.

I reached the run's halfway mark at the back side of the loop that led to the gym and saw a solitary runner several long blocks ahead of me. Come on, move it! You can catch up to that girl. By now, the furious pace I had maintained throughout the run, well above my predictable capacity, was taking its toll. Although I valiantly attempted to ignore the crescendo of my pain, I was no athlete. I knew my body was not up to this competitive challenge that had come out of nowhere. But . . .

You can take her. I heard it loud and clear.

I turned onto Edwards Street. A horribly steep incline greeted me. No time to die; I put my head down and dug in. Of course I slowed, but I didn't stop, although I was gasping for air, my legs felt like concrete, and the sidewalk ahead wavered as my vision blurred. As I crested the hill, I tripped on an uneven section of sidewalk and staggered a couple of steps, but I recovered. No quitting!

I ignored the dizziness as I turned the corner to run the downhill section. Keep on going! I didn't recognize the inner voice that was calling the shots, and I didn't think to ask. I kicked into an alien gear and started to sprint.

I chased the girl ahead of me the entire way down Science Hill, about two-thirds of a mile. As we turned onto Grove Street right outside Woolsey Hall, with about a quarter of a mile to go, I pulled alongside her.

This girl knew something about responding to a challenge. I could hear her breathing, fast and rough. She glanced at me, but I couldn't tell if she was wincing or glaring. Ten steps later, it seemed as if she'd sprinted a mile ahead.

The race was over. The timed run ended less than a minute later, as I crossed the last street and ran all out past Nat, who represented the finish line. He noted the time on his stopwatch and made an entry on his clipboard.

Stopping abruptly didn't end my physical pain. For several minutes, I battled competing sensations of nausea, exhaustion, and exhilaration. I wanted to lie down, close my eyes, and let my respiration rate return to normal, but I was standing on a concrete sidewalk in the middle of a city while my insides bucked like an angry horse. Instead, I stepped off to the side, out of the way of incoming runners, breathless, waiting, unsure what came next. I heard Nat tell the fast girl her finish time and ask her if it was a personal best. She nodded yes.

Then she introduced herself to me. Turns out I had challenged an up-and-coming Olympian. Anne Warner wasn't going to let some upstart freshman pass her. No fucking way.

Two members of the Yale Women's Crew were Olympic aspirants. I had met Chris Ernst, the captain, at my first practice, and Anne Warner the day she kicked my butt at the end of the timed run. They had rowed in the US women's eight (eight-oared rowing shell) the previous summer, earning a silver medal at the World Championships in Nottingham, England. The following summer, women's rowing would join the roster of Olympic events for the first time in Montreal. Chris and Anne intended to make the US team and row for gold.

I hadn't yet figured out how to drop my oar in the water in sync with the other rowers. I hadn't taken one hard stroke. But what I felt for rowing was for real: so real that when I discovered that women who were going to the Olympics in less than a year's time were going to be my teammates, I decided I wanted to make an Olympic team, too. If they could do it, I could do it.

I was smart enough not to voice my impulsive desire. Even though I knew my instantaneous decision would stick, I also knew anything I said out loud would sound totally ridiculous. Besides, I had no one to tell. I barely knew my teammates. My coach already thought I was a loser. My father would be unimpressed; hell, Mr. Skeptical would tease me out of the room.

What business did I have getting serious about sports? I knew how my dad would answer that question, and any rational person would agree with him. Starting with my past and ending with my physique, there were reasons aplenty. But I knew rowing and I were made for each other.

So much so that I could ignore the obvious, my skimpy athletic background, my shrimplike stature, my nonexistent conditioning, minimal strength, and, oh yes, my asthma. I barely registered its existence, as I'd not suffered an attack since I was a high school sophomore, an eternity in teenage years, and I no longer used medication. I was fine. I could do this.

I didn't know why rowing held so much allure. It just did. It gave meaning to every day, structured my time, and helped me focus. I didn't have all afternoon to fritter away after attending my classes: I had to finish my homework so I could hoof it to practice for two to three hours. I didn't have to talk to connect with other people; I just had to show up and learn. I didn't embarrass myself academically and maintained my grades, and my heart leaped at the chance to get into a rowing shell every afternoon, rain or shine.

As the fall progressed and the leaves tumbled onto the surrounding streets, and into the lagoon's disgusting water, I finally took my first hard strokes. I caught my first crab—losing control of my oar when I was late getting it out of the water—just a split second after everyone else. The blade stuck fast in the water while the boat kept moving forward, and the oar handle punched me in the stomach. It hurt, but not for long.

I learned to row as the late afternoon sunshine turned to rosy dusk progressively earlier, as autumn moved toward winter. I learned the feel of the boat when we closed our eyes with our oars balanced during the recovery, skimming the water like geese, letting the boat run out. I secretly reveled in the sense of shared purpose that slowly emerged among the girls on the team. There were no cuts that fall, no varsity or junior varsity rankings; everyone who wanted to row was welcome.

Six weeks into college, I was competing. Nat entered several crews in the Head of the Charles regatta that had sucked me in the previous year in Boston. That day, I had unknowingly witnessed the tenth anniversary of the biggest one-day rowing event in the world, a three-mile race whose course wended its way upstream under six bridges, with four major turns.

This year, instead of watching starstruck on the shore, I rowed starboard in a women's eight, a mixed crew of experienced and novice rowers. I wore a Yale Women's Crew sweatshirt over a simple cotton racing shirt. I felt the chill of the autumn air spike the sunshine as we rowed downriver to the widest part of the Charles, known as "the Basin," to warm up. I listened to the commands filling the air as dozens of shells organized themselves single file according to bow numbers, and followed my coxswain's directions as we headed in the long line of string bean boats to the starting line, marked by big yellow buoys. In keeping with the format of a head race, we maintained a distance of several boat lengths behind the crew in front of us as we worked our power up to full pressure about ten strokes in advance of the line.

The starting official, Ed Singer, greeted us in a deep voice that boomed across the open water: "Yale University, please approach the starting line. Coxswain, bring your crew up to full power. You are crossing the line. Have a good row, ladies."

We're off! I matched my timing with the rower in front of me, but it was hard to contain my excitement and not rush up the slide or yank my oar through the water with giant rip-roaring jerks of glee. The race was going to be long, over fifteen minutes, maybe as long as twenty, and I reminded myself I had to pull hard the entire way.

Less than a quarter mile into the race, our coxswain pointed us through the first bridge, a double challenge: a combined railroad bridge, with tracks going at one angle, and a roadway bridge at a different angle, each with its own pair of pillars standing different widths apart. Not only did she have to avoid the bridge obstacles, our coxswain had to exit the bridge without crossing the line of buoys that started on the other side of the bridge on the shore side. We came through cleanly, our blades touching nothing but water, and the coxswain set our course just off the starboard buoys as we rowed past Magazine Beach.

Things got serious right after that because I started to feel winded, which helped calm me down. Can I do this? Although the wind was not a factor, all the boats rowing ahead of us rippled the water's surface, creating unsettling wakes. When our shell rocked side to side, I had to think about how to adjust my hand height to help steady it. Thank goodness for our coxswain, who reminded the starboards to pull in high and the ports to lower their hands.

The first big turn approached. The port rowers rowed extra hard to help the coxswain power the boat around the corner that ended at Riverside Boat Club. This steering adjustment put us into the Powerhouse Stretch, a three-quarter mile section of race course devoid of turns. We passed uneventfully through two low, arched bridges with spectators leaning over the sides, snapping photos and cheering loudly.

The first mile marker bobbed between the bridges, and our coxswain took note. "We're a third of the way through! Let's take a power ten for the legs! On this one . . ." I made sure my next catch dropped in with extra crispness and my legs powered through the stroke in spite of the tiredness that had already crept into the edge of my consciousness.

As we came through the bridge near the end of the straight stretch, we overtook our first crew, forcing its coxswain to steer away from the buoys and take a wider path along the course. We cruised by them like they were standing still. Seeing the effect of our collective effort was thrilling. I felt reenergized. I wanted to pass someone else.

A giant turn lay ahead, where the river swerved hard to port under the Weeks Footbridge, the race's halfway point. Our coxswain maneuvered us into perfect position at just the right moment, and the crew we overtook veered into the middle of the river while we took the shortest route. Our boat felt strong as we headed into the second half of the race, but I could feel my legs tiring. I concentrated on keeping time with the rest of my crew.

We rowed under the Anderson Bridge, near Harvard Square, and caught another crew. Our coxswain warned us as we started to pass, "This is going to be tight on port." Sure enough, our port blades clashed with their starboard ones as our coxswain fought for the course she wanted, asserting her right as the overtaking crew to choose her line: "Don't stop! We're almost by them." The boat rocked unsteadily as the port rowers struggled to hold on to their oars and keep rowing. My left hand banged on the starboard gunwale. Ow!

We finished passing and won a clear shot to the start of the next big turn, a full 180-degree, half-mile-long curve to port. The entire starboard side would need to help pull the boat around for a couple of minutes, just as I was starting to flail. I concentrated on pushing my legs down and finishing each stroke. But I couldn't block out the rising desperation as my muscles cataloged their aches and broadcast repeated requests to ease up, warning of imminent breakdown. I struggled to keep my focus and not to speculate about how much longer I could pull hard.

One more bridge to get through and one more big turn, and we would be done. As we emerged from under the Eliot Bridge, I heard cheering for Yale. That was for us! I heard, "Go Gilder!" and almost smiled. My first-ever cheerleaders! I hunkered down and kept my eyes on the back in front of me, even though my arms were ready to fall off.

We rounded the last turn and took our last forty strokes. That minute-plus took forever . . . but we finally crossed the line. Because the crews in a head race don't start or end at the same time, determining race results requires time to tally, especially without the benefit of computers. I had no idea how we'd fared against the competition, but I felt like a champion.

Everything hurt, including my butt. My hands sported new blisters, my lungs felt like they had been rubbed with sandpaper, and I wondered if I would be able to stand up when we docked. The race officials posted the results hours later, and we found our crew's time in the middle of the pack, a nothing-special outcome. I had never felt happier.

So much had changed in the year since my first encounter with rowing on the banks of the Charles. I jumped shore into a new adventure, found my own boat, and was learning its ropes. I could see the future beckoning, where I could speak like a rower and maneuver my oar like an experienced hand. My body was starting to slim down and thicken up, as my extra cushion of chubbiness melted away and new muscles emerged. My hands were already toughened; my first set of blisters had thickened into calluses that covered my palms and spiraled up the insides of my fingers. They looked like warts, but they were mine and I was secretly proud of them.

As autumn yielded to the inevitability of winter, chill winds blew over New England's open spaces. Rivers froze from Princeton to Hanover. There would be no more rowing outdoors until spring.

The start of indoor training coincided with the end of fall semester. By now, wending my way around campus, I often recognized and greeted various members of the group of twenty-five-plus regulars with whom I'd rowed through the lagoon's murk. There were several freshmen to get to know, among them tall, lanky, brownish-blonde-haired Elaine Mathies, sporting a faintly Svenska look, thanks to her shoulder-length braids, whose 6'1" frame must have caused Nat to salivate; stocky Sally Fisher, another shrimp, albeit a tad taller at 5'6" than Chris Ernst; strong-looking, medium-tall (i.e., above my pathetic 5'7" but not cracking the dreamy 6' mark) Margaret Mathews, with an abundance of wiry auburn hair whose growing up in Europe and Turkey intrigued me; and another super-tall goddess in training, Cathy Pew, a pre-med smartie who projected an air of self-assurance I could only hope to fake. Besides the team's Olympic aspirants—our captain Chris, whose natural charisma and quick wit got me liking her immediately, and Anne, whose obvious sense of disdainful superiority got me wanting to keep my distance—there were sophomores Jennie Kiesling and Lynn Baker, aka Bakehead. Both these upperclasswomen seemed more at ease than I felt, not just around the boats and all the associated accoutrements, which made sense, but with themselves. I hoped that in another year I would feel more comfortable in my own skin, like Bakehead, as she swaggered around, looking a bit like the bulldog of our team, with powerful shoulders; proud of her bulk and the power it gave her, she claimed it shamelessly. I found myself gawking with amazement at Jennie K, first because of her utter fascination with and deep knowledge of military history, and then because of her habit of counting every single stroke she took, whether in a practice or a race. Now there was a woman who could not be distracted!

I also knew my roommates by now—Maria and Gwen—and I had figured out we weren't going to be best friends, although I liked them well enough. I knew the names of the girls in the suite across the hall and recognized most of the students on the lower three floors of Lawrance Hall, my dorm. I spent most of my free time in the early weeks of college with several of them, but my involvement with crew gave me an easy pass on forging lasting friendships, allowing me to step out of the social swirl without looking like the loner I was.

Aside from the press of my dorm's social scene, I liked my new home, which reminded me of my hometown. I felt comfortable in New Haven, despite its well-earned reputation as dangerous, given its record of student muggings off campus. Although the city shared a grittiness with New York, the university's private campus police force and focus on security kept fears of crime to a minimum. The campus was located squarely within the city and stretched several blocks in many directions, so the university's attempt to maintain a separate identity was difficult. The dozen residential colleges that lay outside the Old Campus, with their ornate architecture, locked gates, and quads with lush green grass and low stone walls, served as oases of green peace from the city's concrete and less savory elements.

Lawrance Hall, affectionately nicknamed "Lousy Lawrance" in my father's era, was sandwiched between two other dorms, Farnum on one side and Phelps on the other. The row of brick buildings nestled shoulder to shoulder, like Manhattan brownstones, with their stairways leading up from the public sidewalk to the front doors of private homes. A slew of these buildings, including Wright, Durfee, Battell Chapel, Welch, Bingham, Vanderbilt, Street Hall, Linsly-Chittenden, and Dwight Hall, served as the boundaries of the quadrangle known as the Old Campus. Broken by four major sets of wrought-iron gates and another three or four smaller gates, they comprised the bulk of the freshmen's living quarters, along with some buildings serving as office and classroom space.

Lawrance's entry doors opened onto the Old Campus, whose graceful elm trees scattered among its sprawling open space and walking paths crisscrossed the green lawn. The dorm's back windows looked out onto College Street and the New Haven Green. I lived on the fourth, and top, floor of my entryway. Another suite housing three more students was directly across the hall from my suite. A dank, cramped bathroom with a moldy shower and a single toilet stall opened into the hallway opposite the stairwell, shared by everyone on the floor. Nothing fancy, but certainly serviceable, with a hint of history in view everywhere, starting with Connecticut Hall, at the interior of the quadrangle, which was erected in 1752 and was the oldest building on campus.

I had entered a skewed new world, in which having officially been co-ed for the last 5 percent of its 275-year history, Yale's men occupied way more than their share of every classroom's seats, but this aspect of the surrounding culture neither informed nor deterred me. Self-absorbed in my own private transition, I didn't think one way or another about the implications inherent in the situation. In fact, I was much more comfortable with my classes since discovering rowing: my fellow students weren't all geniuses; my professors weren't supercilious tyrants gunning for my failure. And the 24/7 presence of boys brought some advantages: I plunged into the dating scene, had some fun without getting entangled in the drama of romance, and slept with a couple of guys in my dorm. Even though the sex was just fine, I discovered that the physical intimacy I shared with them couldn't compete with the thrill of stepping into a shell.

The upperclasswomen fretted about the onslaught of winter training—something about difficulty and intensity—but I nodded happily at their grumbles about weightlifting, running, ergometer pieces, stairs, circuits. I didn't know what they were talking about, but by now the unfamiliar was no deterrent. I would be there, come hell or high water.

Ignorance was bliss.

Winter training stripped away the best of rowing and exposed its worst, magnifying the drudgery, monotony, and pain. There was no scenery to distract, weather to enjoy, boat to feel, or rhythm to seek. Instead, I spent every day in the dank basement of the cavernous gym attempting whatever marching orders Nat scrawled on that day's torn piece of notebook paper pinned to the bulletin board. The experienced rowers translated the mysterious phrases for the novices, all synonyms for torture: stairs, 1–9b, 5–9b × 5; tanks, 3 × 15 min. @ full pressure/5 min. off; Edwards Street run; Nautilus, free weights, body circuit × 5; 6 minute ergometer; wind sprints.

As newly fit as I felt in November, by December I discovered I was an out-of-shape blob. I lacked strength and fitness, as well as the knowledge of how to build either. As for mental toughness, I'd never heard of it, so surely I needed to develop it.

Regardless of the methodology, the goal of weightlifting for rowers is to build muscle, whether it is a bicep, hamstring, tricep, glute, lat, quad, or ab. These muscles have to be strong, and their strength has to last at least as long as a two-thousand-meter race—which takes somewhere between six and seven minutes in an eight-oared rowing shell, depending on weather conditions and a crew's competence. Assuming an average crew rows about thirty-five strokes per minute, factoring in the starting twenty to forty strokes at the beginning and end of the race, when the rating can exceed forty, the average race requires nearly two hundred fifty strokes. If either a rower's muscles or pulmonary system fail to deliver, the result is the same: her power production diminishes, her ability to maintain the cadence and synchronicity with her teammates decreases, and the boat slows down. A crew is truly only as fast as its weakest link.

I learned how to lift free weights: cleans, squats, dead lifts, bench presses, clean-and-jerk. I used nautilus machines: leg extensions, hamstring pulls, lateral pull-downs, and leg presses. The bench pull was a homemade torture device designed especially for the rowers: a bench raised four feet above the ground with a slot for a weight bar notched at hanging-arm length below it on one end. It resembled a sturdy ironing board made of wood, with a rectangular surface long enough to hold a person's body. The exercise consisted of lying face down on the bench, chin hanging over the edge, and raising the weight bar—anywhere from forty to seventy pounds—to the underside of the bench, then lowering it to full arm extension. Repeat thirty times per minute for up to six minutes.

During a stroke, a strong rower can shove her legs from a compressed position to straight legged in well under a second; accept without hesitation the transition in load from the legs to the lower back, supported by the abdominals; link to the arms via the latissimus dorsi (the muscles under your arms that wrap around your back); and finish the stroke with a crisp pull of the biceps. Many of our weightlifting exercises mimicked a single element of the rowing stroke to isolate and strengthen those particular muscles: that way, leg strength could be built without being limited by wimpy arms, and individual rowers could focus on strengthening their own particular weakest links. Leg presses recreated the leg drive; dead lifts engaged the lower back to open up at the end of the stroke; bench pulls evoked the finish, where it was all up to the arms.

To build muscular strength, we lifted the heaviest weights we could muster. To build muscular endurance, we slogged through weight circuits, which lasted anywhere from fifteen to thirty minutes, depending on Nat's mood, and never included a second of rest. Sometimes the goal was to perform a set number of repetitions of different exercises; other times, to complete as many repetitions as possible in a set amount of time. A circuit consisted of ten repetitions at each of several stations, which could include dead lifts, cleans, sit-ups, burpees, pushups, bent-over rowing, arm overhead splits, squat raises. Nat manufactured homemade weight bars out of heavy plumbing pipes with cement-filled coffee containers glued to the ends: they ranged from thirty-five to forty-eight pounds.

Circuits, stairs, rowing, and running combined to tax and stretch the rowers' cardiovascular systems in supremely vicious ways. Mere minutes into any of these endeavors, lungs begin to lag in producing oxygen to meet the muscles' needs, and the muscles express their displeasure, immediately and emphatically. Without sufficient oxygen, a muscle will fail to deliver: and to a muscle, failure to perform as instructed by the brain spells disaster. So when muscles work hard enough to outstrip the available supply of oxygen in the bloodstream, they resort to backup mechanisms that are less efficient, but stave off disaster for a little bit.

In these moments, the muscle will manufacture its own oxygen anaerobically, which literally means "without air"—within the muscle itself. This shortsighted solution comes at a painful price: the production of lactic acid as a chemical by-product of the muscle's desperate fix. The acid creates a burning sensation in the overworking muscles. Within two to three minutes of continued anaerobic oxygen production, the lactic acid level increases to the point that it diminishes the muscle's effectiveness. The acid's burn can progress into severe cramping, triggering a decrease in output and athletic performance. At this point, the muscles have no choice: they slow their production to match the oxygen aerobically available through the pulmonary system—through good old-fashioned breathing.

Developing cardiovascular fitness requires pursuit of a two-pronged goal: increase the amount of oxygen the pulmonary system can distribute to the muscles, and increase the muscles' ability to work at maximal output in the presence of lactic acid. Athletes need lungs that can provide more oxygen and efficient muscles that can tolerate acidic discomfort. Nat proved a merciless expert in developing both kinds of fitness.

I forced myself to run outdoors in cold, slick weather, torrential rain, and wind-whipped sleet; to race sprints around the indoor track; and to leap endless repetitions of interminably long flights of stairs. I felt my breath quicken and shorten, my lungs ache with constant over-drive exertion, and my leg muscles seize as I pushed them beyond their capacity to sprint one more step, lift one more weight, row one more stroke, jump one more circuit, or run one more stair. I heard my body protest the workload, beg for a break, whine with the pain, and refuse to continue. And I learned to listen to the voices that communicated without words below the complaining: hope and desire.

I intended to survive this endless test. I wanted to get back outside into a rowing shell. I didn't want to lose my chance to glide across pristine waters in the company of my teammates, our bodies arcing through the drive into the recovery, safe and controlled, predictable, an endless circle of magical motion. All that mattered was to live to fight another day, to get out in a boat one more time and feel the sun on my face, the water splash on my back, the pressure of the oar in my hand, the success of one more stroke.

Rowing had trapped me with its promise of beauty in motion. Winter training delivered nothing but ugly. Stinking sweat, heaving lungs, breathless exertion, endless effort, and exhaustion. Nothing of beauty to love, just the chance to toughen and test myself. That was enough.

I had never suffered from an all-over deep body ache before, with every major muscle throbbing. I had never been so tired that reading could put me to sleep in the middle of the morning. I had never struggled to get out of bed, hold a pencil, walk up stairs, or carry a loaded food tray.

Evenings after supper I lay on my bed, muscles stiff and sore to the touch, my body so coated with Ben-Gay that the pungent smell drove all visitors away. It hurt to sit up, to turn over, to cross my legs or raise my arms. Propping a book against my chest demanded more energy than I could muster. Staying awake past 9 p.m. proved impossible, regardless of my need to study.

Yet, somehow I successfully completed my first semester. I passed my exams and finished my papers, avoided academic embarrassment, and headed home for the Christmas holidays. I took my running shoes and sweats with me; I wanted to be ready to resume winter workouts in early January.

4

Second semester began. Although I had been a reliable regular on the team since early September, it took both time and circumstance for me to claim full membership on the women's crew. To qualify as a team member, I only had to show up and do the work, without sharing stories or secrets about myself. I liked that what I did mattered, not who I was.

As drawn to rowing as I was, past experience taught me to be wary of relationships: trusting people felt riskier than relying on a skinny sliver of wood to hold my weight. But no novice could survive winter training alone. Chris Ernst's tough-minded, slightly impatient encouragement that buoyed me enough to approach impossible challenges with a shrug, Anne Warner's not so subtle putdowns that somehow galvanized me to push through excruciating pain, Jennie K's casual mentions of military history tidbits that lightened my mood, and my fellow freshmen's various states of disbelief, determination, and exhaustion from the tortuous nature of our daily workouts, which made me feel like I was part of something bigger than myself, all combined to keep my head above water.

We came from such different backgrounds—Sally Fisher from a conservative small town in Connecticut; Elaine Mathies from the puddles of Portland, Oregon; Cathy Pew from a fabled Philadelphia oil family, whose wealth she did her best to ignore; me from urbane and sophisticated New York, where the doorman shoveled the sidewalk when it snowed (Lynn "Bakehead" Baker, hailing from the snowy

Midwest and a family on a tight budget, never let me live down my request to shovel the boathouse dock one day after a snowstorm, a novel challenge for me)—yet when it came to practice, we were united in our sense of purpose and refusal to be bested by the daily posted instructions or by each other. The companionship and competitiveness of fellow rowers are as fundamental to success as oars to boat speed: there is nothing like the edge created by training companions who are slogging through the same workouts and trying their hardest to score the best running times, erg scores, stair-climbing speeds, circuit repetitions, and lifting maximums.

In the bowels of Paine Whitney, I learned my first rudimentary lessons about counting on those who kept showing up when the fun faded and the going got tough. Inevitably, our Olympic wannabes set the bar high for the nearly thirty girls who showed up daily and ticked off the required elements of every workout. As Anne and Chris trained for the spring collegiate racing season and the summer Olympics, I did the same exercises and drills they did—granted, they had better technique, did less huffing and puffing, and showed more speed. I could run with them (well, usually behind them), lift weights with them (okay, substantially fewer pounds than they did), and race up stairs with them (staggering several flights behind them). I watched them with awe, listened to them taunt and goad each other, and admired all of it. I fancied myself in their seats, slipping my feet into their foot-stretchers one day.

There were no secrets at the gym or on the water. The number of seats in a rowing shell was a fact: only eight people would row in the varsity. Competition among teammates was necessary, normal, and openly recognized.

For me, it was also deeply uncomfortable. I hailed from a different world, where jostling for position among my siblings was routine but unspoken, and yet somehow unsavory and wrong. I didn't understand why I had to fight so hard for a bit of space, why there was never enough room for me to be myself and loved as I was. I had dedicated years to securing a place for myself beyond my older, stronger, funnier, smarter, and more likable sister's shadow. I had alighted on a goody-goody strategy—good grades and good behavior to please my parents.

But aiming to please came at a high price: in the shuffle of figuring out what they wanted, I lost track of what I needed and pleased no one. My mother was impossible to satisfy because she had dropped out of full-time parenting and spent much of her time abroad; who knew what she expected or wanted? My father proved tough not because he had high standards—although he did—but because he wanted everything to go his way. Even Peggy complicated matters: whenever I beat her, inevitably in the domain of grades, her irritation ruined any satisfaction I gleaned from gaining my parents' attention. Win or lose, in my family I often felt as if I lost.

In signing up for the crew, I knew what I was getting into. Making the varsity was the goal. I welcomed the gauntlet that rowing posed: the chance to prove myself, whether a quitter, a wimp, or someone I could be proud of. I told myself I could drop out any time if I couldn't handle the pressure to perform, the jostling for position, the reality of my rank staring me in the face every time the varsity launched without me. I told myself that if I couldn't cut it, life would continue and I would move on.

Without my training companions, I may well have quit that first winter. Luckily, during those dark and dreary afternoons, there was no dearth of compatriots ready and willing to tackle the posted workout. Although I depended on my teammates to help me stay the course, I hesitated to embrace the team as mine, to declare my loyalty. I had learned the hard way that for all the feel-good moments of connection I got from friendship and relationships, in the long run trusting others brought me disappointment and sorrow. My job was to make myself tough and reliable enough so I would never need others or disappoint myself.

Yet, the power of teamwork was impossible to ignore or refute. Within the first several weeks of winter training, I had to concede I was stronger as part of a functional unit than as a loner. I could get myself to practice every day, but the companionship of others, sweating and grunting beside me while they both did their best and tried to best my efforts, got me through. But I was a reluctant learner and needed an abundance of evidence to sway me.

An ordinary practice, a weight-lifting day, offered some. I was

lucky. Chris was my workout partner that afternoon, the perfect partner it turned out, who, along with spotting me while I hoisted bars
loaded with iron, taught me about sparring and standing my ground.

"Hey, what are you doing? That's our equipment!" echoed an irritated voice from the far end of Tank A. I looked up from the weight
rack, suddenly uneasy. I felt my gut do a back flip. I saw several heavyweight male rowers stretching on the mats staring at me and Chris,
scowling.

Chris didn't stop her calculations as she loaded the weight bar. "We
need a twenty-five and a ten on each end to start. We'll go up from
there," she continued.

"Hey!"

"Hi, guys. You have a problem with our using the equipment?"
Chris's question hung in the air. She stepped in front of the weight
bar, adjusted the protective weight belt that rested above her slim hips,
and positioned herself to start her first set of cleans. She knelt in front
of the bar, feet hip width apart, grasped it from above with both hands
shoulder width apart and took a deep breath, as she prepared herself to
lift the weighted bar straight up to her chest in one explosive motion,
flick her wrists up, sink down into a squat, absorbing the bar's weight
as it reversed direction and settled into her palms.

"This is our equipment. Not for girls." The voice was closer now, as
the men's crew captain stalked toward our lifting station, hands balling
into fists.

"Oh," Chris stared him down, standing taller than him even
though she was a foot shorter. "I see, boys. So you must pay more
tuition than we do, right?"

No one moved for a long moment. Veins protruded from the captain's neck. His fists remained by his sides. He glared at Chris . . . then
finally shrugged and returned to his teammates, stiffly uncurling his
fingers. The men continued to stare as if they could shrink us to nothing. But I was no longer afraid: Chris buoyed me with her aggressive
confidence.

"There aren't any girls on our team," she told me between sets.
"We're women. It's the Yale Women's Crew. They don't call the heavyweights the Yale Boys' Crew, do they? Don't let anyone diminish you
by calling you a girl."

We belonged in that weight room. We deserved consideration and respect. I basked in the familiarity of an older sister looking out for me, leading the way. My own inner resolve edged forward, my confidence infused with Chris's.

We completed our sets, unloaded the weight bars, and put the equipment away.

"Bye, boys," Chris said as we walked across the room. As I swung the door open and stepped safely across the threshold, the dam of silence behind us broke.

"See ya, cracks."

"Good riddance, sweat hogs."

What? Chris had to tell me what the epithets meant. My sister, Peggy, had called me names, but a stranger never had. It stung.

These heavyweights were Yalies; they were supposed to be smart. I was shocked by their apparent belief that their gender granted them a valid claim of superiority. It was 1976, but the Dark Ages prevailed in New Haven, Connecticut.

The weight room incident was not the first or last attack: verbal skirmishes with the guys continued all winter. Maybe the men were tired of indoor training too, as the brutality and intensity of daily workouts increased. Maybe their longing to return to open water and rowing in real shells clouded their judgment. Maybe they were big babies who didn't want to share. Whatever, by winter's end, their words no longer hurt: I'd moved on to anger and disgust.

Women undergraduates had first matriculated at Yale as transfer students in 1969, not a moment too soon for my purposes. In 1967, I had started fourth grade at my new school, white-gloved Chapin located on East End Avenue, four blocks south of Gracie Mansion, the home of New York's mayor. The all-girls student body was a change for me, coming from the co-ed P.S. 6 on 81st and Madison, but I had no trouble adjusting to the fact that girls held every position of leadership. I never gave it a second thought, coming from a family where my big sister ruled, and I settled into the protected environment without realizing my good fortune.

I set my sights on attending Yale University that first autumn at Chapin. Miss Proffit, my homeroom teacher, assigned Fritzi Beshar as my desk mate and positioned us smack in the first row, directly in front of her desk so she could keep an eye on us. I wasn't a troublemaker, but she didn't know that yet. Nine-year-old Fritzi, however, already had developed a reputation for outspokenness. She and I traded tidbits of our family history the first time we met and became fast friends. Both of us had two sisters and one brother, first-generation immigrant mothers, and fathers who were Yale graduates. Upon discovering this common ground, we confided in each other that we, too, planned to attend that venerable institution when our turn came. We sealed our friendship with an agreement to room together, ten years in the future.

Luckily, no one told us that Yale wasn't open to women undergraduates. My father taught Yale fight songs to the entire family and regaled us with stories of his freshman year on the Old Campus, his upper-classman's life at Branford College, and his tenure with the radio station, but he somehow neglected to mention that the school was only for men. Of course, I knew nothing about the status of girls and women beyond my school's front door. It was normal for mothers not to work. I didn't wonder why mine didn't. Fritzi's mom was a lawyer, but I knew she was special, especially because she passed the New York State bar exam without ever attending law school.

I didn't know that in those days, marriage automatically excluded women from employment and educational opportunities; even Luci Baines Johnson, the daughter of President Lyndon Johnson, was refused readmission to Georgetown University's School of Nursing following her marriage, as the school did not permit married women to matriculate.

I didn't know that Billie Jean King won her first Wimbledon title in women's doubles as a seventeen-year-old in 1961, long before she turned pro in 1968, and was never offered a college scholarship. I didn't know that women were considered too weak to run as far as men and were, in fact, barred from doing so. In 1966, a woman secretly ran in the Boston Marathon for the first time, although she didn't enter the race. Bobbi Gibb hid in some bushes near the starting line and waited until about half the entrants passed, then jumped out and ran without a number. In 1967, the first woman formally entered the race, but because she used her initials on her entry form, "K. V. Switzer," her name slipped by the race officials. Around the four-mile mark, one of the race's cofounders, Jock Semple, recognized Kathrine Switzer for who she was and physically accosted her, yelling, "Get the hell out of my race." After escaping from his grasp, she managed to complete the full 26.2-mile course without further incident.

I didn't know that colleges all over the country were closed to women. For example, Virginia state law prohibited women from admission to the College of Arts and Sciences of the University of Virginia, the most highly rated public institution of higher education in the state: only under court order in 1970 was the first woman admitted. Yale was not the only Ivy League school that reserved its hallowed halls for half the educable population. Princeton University was for men only, while Brown, Columbia, and Harvard maintained affiliations with women's colleges (Pembroke, Barnard, and Radcliffe), but remained single-sex institutions. Only Cornell and University of Pennsylvania were well ahead of their Ivy League brethren, accepting women beginning in 1870 and 1880, respectively.

I was too young to notice the sea changes rippling through American culture at the time. The Civil Rights Act of 1964 expanded access to the Constitution's promise of equal opportunity and represented a national commitment to end discrimination. The legislation prohibited discrimination in employment based on race, color, sex, national origin, or religion, but didn't address access to education. In 1965, President Johnson extended the antidiscrimination laws when he signed Executive Order 11246, which prohibited federal contractors from discrimination in employment on the basis of race, color, religion, or national origin. He amended the order, effective October 13, 1968, to include discrimination based on sex, thus preparing the legislative soil for the passage of Title IX.

Against this backdrop, all the Ivies began accepting women. Yale accepted its first female undergraduates as transfer students in 1969 but capped the number of admits to satisfy its restless alums, who doubted the wisdom of such a monumental change. That same year, a part-time lecturer at the University of Maryland, Bernice Sandler, became the first complainant to invoke Executive Order 11246 to fight for her job and equal pay. In applying the rationale that higher institutions of learning, as recipients of federal funding, could not legally discriminate against women, she planted the seeds for Title IX.

From there, the first flakes of change coalesced rapidly, and the growing clamor for legislation snowballed over the next three years. Representative Martha Griffiths (a Democrat from Michigan) gave the first speech in Congress focused on discrimination against women in education on March 9, 1970. Only three weeks later, Harvard University gained the dubious distinction as the site of the country's first contract-compliance investigation of sex discrimination.

During the following summer, Representative Edith Green, a Democrat from Oregon, in her capacity as chair of the subcommittee that dealt with higher education, took the first legislative steps that resulted in the passage of Title IX, overseeing the first congressional hearings on the topic of education and employment for women. She partnered with Representative Patsy Mink, a Democrat from Hawaii, to draft the legislation that would prohibit sex discrimination in education.

The first woman of color elected to Congress, Mink had extensive and relevant personal experience. Turned down by twenty medical schools, she completed law school instead, only to discover no law firm would hire her. Motivated to fight to remove the barriers she encountered, she entered politics.

In 1972, Mink and Green introduced, and Congress passed, the legislation whose preamble reads, "No person in the United States shall, on the basis of sex, be excluded from participation in, be denied the benefits of, or be subjected to discrimination under any education program or activity receiving Federal financial assistance." With his signature, President Nixon enacted Title IX of the Educational Amendments, codified as United States Code, Title 20, Chapter 38, Sections 1681–1686.

Title IX applies to all educational institutions receiving federal financial assistance, from kindergarten through graduate school. It addresses ten key areas, including access to higher education, career education, education for pregnant and parenting students, employment, learning environment, math and science, sexual harassment, standardized testing, and technology, and extends to all of an institution's operations, including admissions, recruitment, educational programs and activities, course offerings and access, counseling, financial aid, employment assistance, facilities and housing, health and insurance benefits and services, and scholarships. And athletics.

The first women who enrolled as freshmen at Yale graduated in 1973, a year before I submitted my application. I started my freshman year with a student body that was still two-thirds male. When I started rowing, I had no idea I was entering a cultural battleground, where the fight to define femininity commingled with the fight for equality. Only four years earlier, a Connecticut judge had rejected a high school girl's petition to join the boys' indoor track and cross-country team because there were no girls' teams, declaring, "Athletic competition builds character in our boys. We do not need that kind of character in our girls."

The women's rowing program at Yale started as a club sport in the fall of 1972 and retroactively earned varsity status in 1974, after only two years, thanks to a strong showing that spring racing season. That year also marked the establishment of the Eastern Association of Women's Rowing Colleges and the first EAWRC Sprints Regatta in which the Yale women's eight took second behind their instant nemesis, Radcliffe. Nineteen schools participated in that spring competition, held in Middletown, Connecticut: the first championship competition for women in any sport, in any Division I conference, although back then women's rowing was not exactly on the roster of the National Collegiate Athletic Association's (NCAA) sports.

Title IX may have been enacted, but change came slowly, as did the dawning of my own awareness. Growing up, I didn't experience many sexist putdowns, other than my father's teasing that I threw "like a girl" when we played running bases and he taught me the correct arm motion. But, for the first time, I discerned new undertones in my family's comments.

During Thanksgiving break freshman year, my stepmother, BG, grabbed one of my hands and turned it over to see my palm, dotted with its unique array of healing blisters and rough-edged calluses. She recoiled in horror and, dropping it quickly, said, "What boy would want to hold your hand?"

My mom saw pictures of me with my crew and remarked with obvious relief that I wasn't "as big" as my taller teammates. Did she see the irony, wanting to squeeze my unconventional dream into a narrow definition of femininity, tugging me in the same direction of capitulation she had headed twenty years earlier, assuming the role of wife and mother, and losing her dream to travel the world, her independence, and for at least a while, her sanity?

On the Yale campus, Tony Johnson, the men's varsity rowing coach, supported the women's program. Nat, who began coaching the women in the fall of 1973, was a former Yale varsity rower himself. He'd rowed for TJ in the late 1960s and was one of his guys. TJ even contributed $600 from his budget to help launch the women's club program, but his support seemed to extend only so far, stopping at the doorway of his own crew's locker room. A handful of dollars couldn't compensate for his athletes' vocal dismay regarding the women's presence. The fact that TJ left their behavior unaddressed communicated his own ambivalence: as long as the women didn't interfere with the men, we could row. But no rocking the boat.

As a club sport, the women's program was relegated to the stinky and confining lagoon, where the men's freshmen recruits rowed for a few weeks in the fall before joining the rest of their squads at the Robert Cooke Boathouse, twelve miles off campus in the rumpled town of Derby, on the banks of the mellow Housatonic River. The real boathouse remained off limits to the women until they achieved varsity status; after all, rowing emblematized tradition at Yale, and that meant men's rowing, which dated back to 1852, the year of the country's first collegiate sporting event—a rowing race between Harvard and Yale.

Both the heavyweight and lightweight men's programs operated out of the Robert Cooke Boathouse. Reaching the three-story, three-bay boathouse, painted in Yale's traditional blue-and-white, required a twenty-five-minute bus ride from campus. Two boat bays were stacked with elegant and pristine Pocock racing shells—singles, pairs, fours, and eights—to provide a full complement of training opportunities for the men. A third bay was reserved for the full-time boat rigger, Jerry Romano, who worked to keep the fleet of shells fighting fit, repairing damaged equipment and rigging boats to suit the coaches' specifications.

History nestled in the highest boat racks: aging hulls, graying with dust, names painted on their bows that hearkened back to rowing greats from the 1920s and '30s, their equally ancient oars sporting leather collars and pencil-thin blades, clustered at the rear of the boat bays.

At the top of a rickety wood staircase in the back of the middle bay was a pair of tiny offices for the coaches. A large, airy locker room fully equipped with standard toilet and shower facilities dominated the second floor. An uncovered deck stood on the downstream side of the building and gave an unimpeded view of the finish line.

The Housatonic offered vastly improved rowing conditions compared to the lagoon. The water was clean, the surroundings safe. A dam directly downstream from the Yale boathouse limited the crews in that direction, but four miles of wide, meandering river stretched upstream for their uninterrupted use. Recreational boat traffic was scant and no other rowing programs used the waters, which kept them calm and peaceful. The gentle hills that rose and fell along the river's shores provided a visual respite from the rigors of practices.

Derby's scenery and the facilities were oceans away from the urban jungle surrounding the lagoon. When the women's program earned varsity status, the women finally gained access to Derby and the men had to make room.

To the women, Derby was heaven, but the heavyweight men protested that we made their lives hell. With limited equipment of our own, we begged boats from the men's program, diminishing the guys' inventory and storage space. We occasionally damaged boats—hitting the dock on landing, running over submerged debris during practice—just like the guys; fixing our mistakes ate into Jerry Romano's availability to repair and rig their boats. We shared dock space, imposing on their launch and return times. We rode on the bus with them to and from practice every afternoon, enduring their sly comments and obvious glares.

But we couldn't share lockers, toilets, and showers. The boathouse had one tiny bathroom on the first floor that the women could use to relieve themselves before and after practice, but there was no place to shower or change. All that had to wait, and often that wait approached two hours.

Rowing is not a dry sport. Besides the obvious source of moisture, sweat produced by aggressive exertion, the backsplash of oars entering the catch guarantees that everyone who doesn't sit in the stroke seat gets drenched at some point or another. Add to that the late winter, early spring air temperature in Derby, which averages in the mid-thirties in February and creeps up to the mid-forties in March—don't even consider the possibility of precipitation—and you have prime breeding conditions for sickness.

Fifteen to twenty minutes after the women got on the bus, sweaty, soaked, and, by now, often shivery, the men would straggle on, clean, hair freshly combed, wrapped in warm jackets, and eager to hit the dining hall for dinner. Reaching campus before the last dining hall stopped serving always proved a scramble, as the drive back took nearly half an hour, which meant that our showers had to wait even longer. No matter the weather, we waited for the men in wet clothes, we endured the bus ride back to campus in wet clothes, we ate our meals in wet clothes, and we walked back to our dorm rooms in wet clothes.

"What about taking a shower in Joni Barnett's office?" Anne joked to Chris one afternoon in late February. (Barnett was the director of women's intercollegiate sports and reported to the athletic director.) "We could bring in a bucket, sponge, soap, and a towel." Chris sneezed and wiped her nose. Only a week into rowing outside at Derby following the breakup of the winter's ice that had sheathed the river, she'd already caught a cold and Anne was struggling with pneumonia. They weren't alone; several more women rowers quickly came down with respiratory ailments after we began practice at Derby.

The university had unwittingly laid the groundwork for rebellion. Realizing the boathouse needed an upgrade, no doubt helped to this conclusion by Chris's steady complaining, the powers that be decided to transform the building's unused third floor into space for the women and shared the blueprints with Chris. However, because the expansion would require modernizing the existing structure to meet new building codes, the university deemed the project too costly and nixed it. Instead, it resorted to the solution devised the previous season: importing a temporary trailer that squeezed a triad of showers and a parking strip's worth of locker room space into the boathouse's parking lot. This year, however, the occupancy permit approval was delayed, leaving the women with nothing.

That snag, combined with her sense that the university had pulled a bait and switch regarding a more permanent solution, ignited Chris's disappointment. With the vision of a permanent locker room dancing in her head, Chris was no longer willing to settle for what had morphed into too little, too late, especially because she captained a team that relied on her and whose power to do great she not only championed, but believed in and relied on herself.

Chris followed Anne's lead. "We could go into her office and strip down. That would get her attention."

"Imagine you standing buck naked in front of Joni Barnett!" Anne started laughing. "I dare you!"

"You're on!" When this pair of Olympics-bound competitors egged each other on, there was no backing down. Chris rubbed her hands together gleefully and launched into planning our foray into Barnett's office.

I didn't hesitate to follow Chris's lead and join the protest. By March 3, I'd been rowing six months. I'd survived my first winter training. I'd accomplished previously unimaginable challenges with women I'd grown to like and respect. I was one of nineteen young women who gathered in the humid basement locker room at Payne Whitney before practice. Not everyone on the team showed up. Some had late afternoon classes, and at least one, Bakehead, citing apprehension over losing her campus job (she worked in the athletic department) and, worse, her financial aid, demurred. She could easily imagine a worst-case scenario in which the university would lash out at the participants, and she couldn't afford it: "I wish I could go, but I can't risk it," she said.

Our joking and joshing diminished as we printed "Title IX" on each other's backs in Yale-blue marker. We grew quieter as we dressed in our team-issue sweatpants and sweatshirts. We paired up and proceeded to Barnett's office in the Ray Tompkins House, home of the athletic administration, trailed by a duo of *Yale Daily News* staffers—a writer, David Zweig, who doubled as a stringer for the *New York Times*, and a photographer, Nina Haight. Barnett's secretary was surprised that Chris Ernst was accompanied by eighteen others to her appointment with the director, but she ushered us in.

We stood silently, somberly, facing Barnett, who retreated behind her broad desk. Instead of sitting down, however, she remained standing, one hand on her desk as if to steady herself. Chris turned sideways and nodded slightly. Perfectly synchronized, we turned our backs to the administrator, pulled off our sweatshirts, dropped our pants, and stood stark naked, absolutely silent. David Zweig turned his back and kept scribbling notes.

Barnett said, "Do you want this man in here?"

Chris waved her hand as if to shush a child. "Yes, it's fine. Just listen please." She unfolded a sheet of paper. "These are the bodies Yale is exploiting," she began, reading from her prepared statement. I stood there, feeling a wintry draft through the aging windows of the Ray Tompkins House. "We are using you and your office because you are the symbol of women's athletics at Yale; we're using this method to express our urgency . . ."

I felt the magnificence of the moment: standing up for myself, for all of us, surrounded and strengthened by my compatriots. Forget those rower boys who thought our beloved sport belonged only to them, who thought their disgusting nicknames for us could intimidate and dissuade us. The power of "crack," "sweat hog," and "inhuman scum" drained away, along with my sense of loneliness. I had found my place, where I didn't have to diminish my dreams or sacrifice myself to gain acceptance or affection. I could stand tall and strong without stooping to accommodate the prejudice or preferences of others, buoyed and bolstered by my teammates.

"There has been a lack of concern and competence on your part," said Chris, winding down. I felt energy coursing through me. Her words buoyed me with a new resolve. They couldn't stop me.

When Chris and Anne told Nat about the protest immediately afterward on the dock at the boathouse, he yelped, "You did what?" But he seemed proud. By the next day, however, he'd come to his senses, undoubtedly aided by the university's athletic director, who must have urged him to rein in his unruly team. Hung over and sullen, head sagging, he gathered the team together for a meeting in Jennie Kiesling's room, where he admonished us in mumbles for going around his back and making him look ineffectual. "Why didn't you let me handle this?" he said. Perhaps he'd been working behind the scenes to broker some kind of change, but that no longer mattered. This was the first time I heard my coach express his disappointment in us, which should have alerted me to his questionable judgment.

Nat's displeasure could not dent the crew's belief in either the justice of our position or the rightness of our action. As far as we were concerned, we had struck a blow for freedom, one backed up by the law of the land, and we were tired of waiting for the bureaucracy to grind out its version of progress at its leisure. The event deepened our sense of unity as a team and our willingness to rely on each other, essential qualities of fast boats.

No one on the women's crew anticipated that news of the protest would end up on the front page of the second section of the *New York Times*, picked up by the Associated Press and wired around the world, even showing up in the *International Herald Tribune*. While not all my team members' parents were happy with their daughters' uppity, ungrateful behavior, several sent clippings and congratulations, my father included. He was proud of my defiance; at least this time, I wasn't defying him. Letters poured in from alumni, some beseeching the administration to rectify the problem, others blaming the administration for creating it by admitting women in the first place. No one predicted that the publicity would shame the university into a commitment to expand the Robert Cooke Boathouse to accommodate women the following year.

5

When the Title IX protest occurred, not even Nat knew the Yale Women's varsity eight would end its season with a pair of Olympians occupying its stern pair and freshmen filling its five bow seats. He certainly didn't know an unathletic city girl with no business going near a rowing shell would worm her way into one of those seats, earning her spot the old-fashioned, sweaty, and hard-working way. I didn't either.

At the first practice after spring break, the entire squad stood in the boat bay out of the wind, surrounding Nat, waiting for his usual pre-practice announcements. Without any fanfare, he began. "I'm boating varsity and JV lineups for this coming weekend's races today." I took a deep breath. My foot started tapping and my fingers twitching.

"Anne, Chris, Bakehead, Ginny . . ." Nat's voice didn't trail off, but my ears got stuck on my name. A whoosh of energy surged through me and I felt myself swooning, walloped by glee. I only realized I hadn't fallen when no one rushed to help me. I glanced around to check the faces of my new varsity teammates. No one cracked a smile. I knew to follow their lead, but I was a crappy liar. I sang inside while my mouth struggled not to smile.

"Ok, now the JV lineup," Nat continued. I tried to keep listening to be respectful. I knew it was important to acknowledge everyone's achievement, but my happiness wanted out. I looked down at the ground, pretending to concentrate on what Nat was saying, hoping my smile wasn't too obvious.

"Here's the plan for today's workout. Let's paddle up to the quarter-mile mark and start our warm-up from there. Thousand-meter pieces today." Nat dismissed us to get ready to launch without offering congratulations or encouragement to anyone. Everyone still acted as if nothing special had happened and busied themselves with stretching and taking a last drink of water. I wanted to grab my new boat mates and hug them, swear my undying determination to die for them in the heat of battle, but no go. I tried to act nonchalant as I took my oar down to the dock, but my shoulders squared with newborn confidence and my steps hinted at a swagger. Bakehead was ahead of me, plunking a pair of blades on the dock. She turned toward me as I reached her. "We're gonna be fast," she declared as she gave me a fierce hug.

We raced every weekend from March through mid-May, beating everyone on our way to the Eastern Sprints Championships: Barnard, Boston University, Wichita State University, University of Nebraska, Connecticut College, Williams, Princeton, MIT, Cornell, Ithaca College, University of Pennsylvania, Rutgers. We raced on the Harlem River off Manhattan, on the Schuylkill in Philadelphia, on Lake Onondaga in upstate New York and the Charles in Boston.

Thanks to the Kansas branch of the Yale Alumni Association, which invited the top freshmen to visit and paid for the trip, Nat broke the varsity up for a weekend to seat a freshmen-only eight. He sent us to Wichita where we raced through the middle of the city on the narrow, winding Arkansas River and won handily, almost guiltily accepting the mustard-yellow shirts proffered by our hosts. We left the next morning and drove six hours north across the dead-flat Midwest to Carter Lake in Omaha, Nebraska, and kicked butt there, too. I rowed in the seven seat for that pair of races, behind Chris Stowe, steady and resolute, a no-bullshit athlete from tight-lipped Maine. A former cross-country running star, Chris was no stranger to pain or the demands of an endurance sport, the perfect role model for the newbie athletes following her.

Within the first two hundred meters of the Omaha race, the gate of my oarlock jiggled loose and flipped open. Our coxswain noticed the problem immediately and alerted me. Six people sat behind me, including the other three starboards, whose oars needed to stay in sync with mine.

I looked out at my rigger and saw the gate standing upright like a tiny flagpole. I couldn't help but also notice the Nebraska crew in the adjacent lane, about half a boat length behind. Damn! If the gate remained open throughout the race, my oar would likely pop out of the oarlock completely and cause total havoc—at least a bad crab, at worst a complete loss of oar control.

The intense focus of a racing start was still with me. I didn't hesitate. I snaked my arm out to the end of my rigger, snapped the gate back into place, and tightened the nut that locked it down without missing a stroke or losing track of Chris's rhythm. Steady as she goes, taking care of business. We then proceeded to walk through the Nebraska crew and win by open water.

We jubilantly called Nat, who had stayed back east to accompany the freshmen-free varsity to its weekend races, to report our successes and the oarlock incident. After asking for the crew's race times and not offering any congratulations, he observed that we should have performed a more complete equipment check before launching. Fine: I already knew that nothing we did could get a rise out of the guy. No accomplishment would merit his acknowledgment.

I didn't care. Racing swept me away. I loved the fierceness of it, the chance to test myself while hidden snugly within a crew. It wasn't all about me. Except, of course, secretly I knew it was. But I never had to admit it, because I had seven racing companions. I'm sure that every one of us contended with inner demons, but we did it together, in sync, and never discussed our private battles. Fear was nothing to flaunt, but was something shameful that had to be endured in the pre-race jitters and the first strokes of a race. It was part of the price to pay to reach the joy of rowing hard and well, to claim victory. I sure wasn't going to cop to my internal doubts; they were short-lived worries that I wasn't up to the task, showing up on race day and dissipating as soon as the starter's flag came down, but I didn't want to risk diminishing my teammates' confidence in me.

Winning felt pure and good, like an Ivory Soap commercial. I could point to our victories as proof that I didn't wimp out. I delivered.

Our season's perfect record earned us first seed for the Eastern Sprints, held on Lake Quinsigamond in Worcester, Massachusetts. The championship regatta featured heats and finals over a two-thousand–meter course. Crews raced in groups of six, with the top three proceeding to the Grand Final later in the day. We won our morning heat without expending extraneous effort, rowing most of the course at a sedate twenty-nine strokes per minute and beating second-place Cornell easily.

Then came the final.

The sun beat down with its characteristic late-afternoon, late-spring intensity as we laced our foot-stretchers and shoved away from the dock. My heart beat loudly in my throat. We were racing for the championship. The Yale women had never beaten Radcliffe or won the Sprints, but today we were the favorites. We had a chance to claim the title. All that lay between us and the trophy were five other crews who might share our dream, but not our strength or our bond.

We ended our warm-up by the starting line. The six crews in the race before ours were lined up at the starting platform, their sterns held by volunteers lying on their stomachs, arms stretched out. The rowers stared straight ahead impassively, bodies angled forward, knees tight to their chests, arms extended, oars buried in the water, ready to explode into focused aggression at the starter's command. We sat still, relaxing but not relaxed, waiting for the race to go off and the official summons to the starting dock. I tried not to think about all the things I could do wrong to blow the race. Now was not the time for fear, but I struggled to combat my inner voice of doom.

I concentrated on the real enemies, the Cliffies in their black shirts with white piping, imposing white Rs emblazoned on their backs. They looked big and mean, but we could beat them. Why not? We'd beaten everyone else all season, whether we'd been the favorite or the underdog. We would win this race.

Before I knew it, we were in the race's last five hundred meters. "All right, we're even with Radcliffe. Let's move on them," our coxswain, Lynne Alvarez, called. Now or never. Let's go! Eyes glued on Elaine Mathies, my quads pounding down through the drive in time with hers, our hands flowed out of the bow to start the recovery and reach for the next catch and kick some more ass. The boat was a little rocky, the setup disturbed by the water's slight chop, but we would not be distracted or deterred. Lynne's voice boomed through her megaphone: "Ok, you gave me two seats. I want more." Accelerated breathing, no time to gasp for air, muscles shrieking with the burn of overexertion.

"Okay, just twenty more strokes. Give me all you got. We've got those Cliffies. Let's take it home!" Lynne commanded and I obeyed, back arching with effort. "Paddle," she called. I looked up and saw Radcliffe behind us. Alright. "Way enough." We stopped rowing. Bent over my oar, now I could gasp for air. I looked across the course.

In the far lane, the Wisco crew was cheering. What the hell?

We beat Radcliffe. That was a big first, but Wisconsin sneaked by us while we were focused on passing the black-shirted crew. Our coxswain forgot it wasn't a two-boat race. Sometime in the second thousand meters, Wisconsin claimed the lead and didn't give it up in spite of our mighty final sprint. We finished second.

I'd thought we were invincible. I hadn't considered any other outcome.

"Losing sucks," I told Nat later.

He frowned slightly, but said philosophically, "You learn more when you lose."

He sounded like a professor, but I wanted a sympathizer.

Nat was right, however. The lessons would follow fast and furiously. I didn't know until then how much winning mattered. I had taken our crew's success for granted; it came so easily. Suddenly I had to contend with the possibility that I'd not done my best, not pulled hard enough, or maybe not wanted to win enough. My confidence, hard won over the previous nine months, felt suddenly tenuous again.

My freshman teammates seemed disappointed but not disheartened: we beat the hated Cliffies, our arch rivals, a never-before-accomplished feat. Captain Chris Ernst was less sanguine, noisily frustrated and disappointed. A senior with no more second chances, she couldn't understand how Lynne Alvarez had neglected the Wisco crew: that was the coxswain's job, to know the score and report our position, and help us react and adjust to the competitive situation as it unfolded. Chris knew we would've won if our crew had known what was happening during the race.

But Chris turned away from the done-and-gone Sprints, accepted her second-place medal, and resolved to rally the team to focus on the season's final race, which would also be her last for Yale. She was determined: we would beat Radcliffe again in two weeks at the historic Yale–Harvard race, which would include women for the first time in the race's 125-year history. The Harvard and Yale men's varsity crews raced against each other head-to-head for four miles on the wide and rough tidal Thames River in New London, Connecticut. The women would race two miles.

I shrugged off the uncertain thoughts weaseling into my head. We were going to do just fine. Chris had decided; she was my captain, and I trusted her.

Stormy skies. A chill wind kicking up aggressive waves. Grim water. Two miles: 3,218.7 meters. The starter stood behind us with his red flag held high, rippling. We left as the flag swept down, leaving his command to "Row" behind.

We started well, but Radcliffe did, too, and kept on going. The boat felt heavy, as if Radcliffe's speed took us out of our mental game. Our crew lost its concentration, instead focused on trying to catch our competitor. My legs were dead at the halfway mark, empty of drive. A race that started with our determination to win dwindled into a dispirited slog as Radcliffe forged into the lead and didn't give it up.

It's impossible to row a good race if you can't feel what's happening within your own crew, and if you're too distracted to focus. That afternoon we discovered that past performance is not a sure bet when it comes to predicting the future. The Radcliffe women ignored the fact that we had beaten them at the Sprints. They refuted the solid evidence that we were the faster crew. From the moment the race went off, they acted like the winners and left us in their wake.

After the race, we landed at the Gales Ferry dock. Nat greeted us silently, handed us our shoes, held onto the boat while we ungated our oars, stepped onto dry land, and laid the blades on the dock. Only our coxswain spoke, uttering familiar instructions to guide the boat safely into the shell house.

We had proven insufficient to the challenge; I had proven insufficient. I had no one to thank but myself. The sting of the moment stirred something inside, my defiant voice. Wait 'til next year. We'll show you; just you wait. Reason was bantering with me, keeping things light inside. We lost a race. It's not the end of the world.

I felt a tiny bit better. Not great. I was disappointed, yes; angry, yes; but mostly okay.

Until I saw Chris. Her college career was over, marred by unfin-
ished business. She would never beat Radcliffe head-to-head. Her scowl
started at her forehead, drove her eyebrows sharply down, deepened
into her eyes, flared her nostrils, and settled across her mouth; then
she howled at us huddled on the dock. Focusing specifically on the five
freshmen, she unleashed her fury. "You gave up! How could you? You
gave them the race! When are you going to learn how to pull?"

I had never seen Chris cry. I felt like a traitor.

When my father pricked the bubble of my growing up in a happily-
ever-after family that evening in the twilight off Madison Avenue, the
air began to leak out of my world. I didn't realize when I was eleven
that the dissipation of our family's atmospheric mix of routine, structure, duty, and affection meant the end of life as I knew it, but everything became clear soon enough.

A great divide had always existed in our family between subject
matter for adults and children, until Dad moved out. Overnight he
assumed the stereotype of a disappearing dad, and it fit like a well-
worn shoe. He didn't visit, rarely called, and saw us only on weekends.
Mom's anger moved in and filled the empty spaces he left behind. The
normal family topics of homework, dinner, clean rooms, and laundry
fell by the wayside, derailed by new, grown-up ones of betrayal and
abandonment.

Mom sniped nonstop about Dad: "You know, he left me for that
whore, that bitch. Just ask him. See what he says!"

I couldn't deny or downplay her pain, but I doubted her charges
against Dad. The tumble and turn of events seemed so sudden and
fantastic. I couldn't keep up. I felt as if I was living in a made-up story
told by a crazy person, and the shock of the new script immobilized
me. Without my father's confirmation or denial, I didn't know who
or what I was supposed to believe. My parents, who'd always served
as the bastions of truth, had blown apart into separate corners of the
universe, leaving me to sort out the facts myself.

It wasn't only the topic of family conversations that changed, but
Mom's behavior, too. The first time she ventured out of character, I
was unprepared.

The yelling sounded far away, muffled by layers of sleep. When I finally woke up, the loud noise sounded as if it was next door. Then I realized it was: in Peggy's room. "You disgusting pig. Look at this mess. No wonder he left," my mother was saying.

I crept out of my room down the hall to Peggy's open door. Light spilled from the bedroom into the darkened hall. Peeking around the doorway, I saw the cluttered floor, covered as usual by clumps of clothes, piles of dirty dishes, and stacks of books and homework papers. Peggy was in bed, halfway sitting up and looking scared. Mom stood over her, disheveled and ranting. She wore one of her flowing nightgowns, filmy material designed for allure, a flimsy cut suggesting sex. Her dirty-blonde hair stuck out in all directions, her face contorted.

Mom reached out to grab Peggy. Peggy eluded her grasp, rolled out of bed to the floor, and then crouched with her hands in front of her body. Mom lunged toward her but tripped, banged her shin against the bedpost, and fell on the bed.

"How could you do this to our family? You selfish bitch. He's not coming back." Mom started sobbing. The remnants of her mascara smudged her eyes and cheeks with black ink.

I wanted to tell Mom she had it all wrong, that Peggy was just being Peggy, messy maybe, but not a villain. I wanted to put my arm around her and comfort her, but I couldn't move. Her snarling and physical aggression terrified me. She had always been friend, never foe, even when she was angry, but she was crossing into new territory now.

She straightened up. "You pig, clean up this room completely. I've had enough of your slovenliness. Now." She bent down and picked up a book, flung it at Peggy, but her aim was off, and it thudded harmlessly on the floor.

Peggy kept her expression impassive as she reached for the clothes nearest her and began folding them. Mom watched her briefly and said, "I'll be back shortly and it better be perfect!"

She turned toward the door and saw me. Without a nod or a word or a gesture, she strode past me, her fancy nightgown trailing behind like a train. I caught a whiff of her sour smell as she sailed by. I flinched and recoiled, and felt an immediate burn of shame.

I shuffled into Peggy's room. She glanced at me, eyes brimming, and turned away. I realized we would not speak of this incident tomorrow, or ever. Half-heartedly, I reached down to pick up some papers from the floor.

Peggy waved me away as she got off the floor and sat on her bed. "She won't be back tonight, don't worry."

"How do you know?"

"Couldn't you tell? She's drunk." She saw my shocked expression. "We'll be okay, Ginny. I can deal with her. Don't worry."

Without my dad at home in those days, life deteriorated further. Mom lost her way. She stopped cooking, cleaning, and organizing on any regular basis. She stayed in bed for entire days, crying or sleeping, leaving Peggy and me to fill in the gaps where we could—making dinner, cleaning up, giving the Littles their baths, and tucking them into bed at night. Our home became a ghost town, with four shadows tiptoeing through, trying to figure out the new lay of the land.

And then, our family imploded.

One night, after we had cooked dinner, eaten with the Littles, and cleaned up afterward, Peggy and I happened upon Mom in the dining room. She sat in Dad's old place at the far end of the table. Her head bobbed gently as she slurred a hello. A depleted liquor bottle teetered in front of her, and her closed fist rested on the table.

Peggy didn't waste a moment. She ran into the room, grabbed Mom's wrist and jerked her hand to open it, but Mom tightened her closed fingers.

"Come on, Ginny, help me."

Peggy pulled Mom's hand toward me and I grabbed the clenched fingers, trying to pry them open. It took Peggy's and my combined strength to counter Mom's determined clawing, until I finally saw what Peggy had already seen: the prescription vial Mom was gripping like a life preserver. I wrenched it out of her talon-like grip.

"Ugh, Valium and vodka. Get rid of these," Peggy said.

I didn't have textbook knowledge of the risks associated with downing a giant dose of "mother's little helpers" chased by several shots of alcohol, but I knew enough to be scared. I ran through the French doors separating the dining and living rooms and stopped all the way at the other end of the room at the piano. I scattered the pills among its innards.

"No, you idiot, the toilet!" Peggy said, still battling Mom over the bottle on the table.

Reversing course, I ran into the main entry hall, through the library and jerked open the lid on the toilet in the powder room. As I flushed away the tiny blue rounds of oblivion, the phone rang. I rushed back into the library to answer it.

"Ginny, is that you?" asked Gramps. My father's parents lived three short blocks away, on 79th and Lexington, and we kids were regulars at their place. In fact, Peggy and I had run away there once when we were seven and five. Oh, thank goodness, someone I knew and trusted! "I'm just calling to check in, see how everything's going."

I replied in a rush, "Mom just drank a bunch and took I don't know how many pills. I'm not sure what they are. Baby blue, small, maybe Valium. I think that's what Peggy said."

"I'll be right over." He didn't even say goodbye, but just hung up. I stood in the doorway of the library with the phone in my hand, frozen. I didn't want to see Mom die.

She stopped struggling with Peggy and put her head down on the table. Peggy propped her up so she wouldn't slide off her chair.

Mom revived slightly when the paramedics came flying through the front door, summoned by my grandfather, who appeared shortly thereafter. Suddenly, she was fighting again, but in her groggy state, her grip was weak and she could only wave her arms around in their faces. They put her in a straitjacket to strap her onto the gurney.

Dad showed up shortly after Mom left in an ambulance. Gramps must have called him, because I sure didn't think to, and Peggy was preoccupied first with Mom and then with trying to calm down the Littles. Dad didn't say much to any of us, other than to confirm he would return home and stay with us so we wouldn't be alone.

That's when Peggy slammed her fist through a pane of glass in one of the French doors in Dad's dressing room. He cleaned her bloody cuts, bandaged her hand, and sent us to our own rooms to calm down by ourselves. His presence comforted nobody; he offered no solace.

Instead of using Mom's suicide attempt to reach out to us over the next several days, Dad fended off all questions with the same unperturbed response: "Your mother's going to be fine." As if by sweeping away discussion, he could banish our confusion and fear. He offered no explanation for what had happened, nor any concern for Mom or our reactions. We did squeeze some information from him: Mom hadn't died, although she could have. She had fallen unconscious by the time the ambulance had arrived at the hospital, but the doctors pumped her stomach. Beyond that: silence. If we asked questions, he became irritated. I could only draw one conclusion: keep your troubles to yourself, young lady. Silence is golden.

Mom returned after a couple of weeks with a pair of nurses who provided 24/7 care. Only then did I learn she'd spent those days committed to a psychiatric hospital. I felt betrayed all over again. Why hadn't Dad told us?

From the moment she returned home, Mom was different, more like a real-life zombie, tired and defeated, than a thinking, feeling person. She even had new hair, a wig that sat at an odd angle, covering her own dirty-blonde wisps.

Dad moved out the morning of her release from the hospital and left us in the hands of a recovering mental patient. Sure, she had nurses, but not even twelve hours after she arrived back, Mom left one of her stalwart Lucky Strike cancer sticks burning down in an ashtray next to the couch and started a fire. Miss Muffet, all of eight years old, woke to the smell of acrid smoke and roused the rest of us, including the night nurse, going from room to room and shaking us out of deep slumber.

Mom refused to get out of bed when Muffet came to wake her up. Instead, she pulled the covers over her head and ignored her daughter's pleas for help and comfort. The nurse called the fire department and herded us into the kitchen when the firefighters arrived. We cowered there while they extinguished the blaze in the library and stomped through the adjacent rooms to make sure the fire hadn't spread elsewhere. When they finally released us to return to our beds, I was afraid to fall asleep, sure that I could smell smoke.

In the morning, Mom got mad because the firefighters had left dirty boot marks on her precious Oriental rug. I never thought about the imprint of her recent behavior on me. Like my parents, I shoved everything that threatened the surface story under the rug. Forget about the longing for protection or rescue; don't mention the grief and shame, or the birth of my unquenchable longing for escape. Follow their expert footsteps; bury the unmentionable under the glitzy façade of our Park Avenue address, my private school education, and all the things my father's fat wallet could buy.

In my family's most desolate moments, in scene after Technicolor scene, I had learned that disappointment could crush people, even those who seemed uncrushable. Disappointment was dangerous, to be avoided at all costs. Now, here was my tough-as-nails captain, Chris Ernst, crying in front of me. She was angry, yes, but worse, much worse, deeply disappointed. Mom, Chris, Mom, Chris . . . who was devastated? For a moment I couldn't tell the difference between them.

That's when I decided I couldn't lose again; that would be deadly.

No wonder racing lost some of its lighthearted fun after this inter-action, as somehow the present became confused with the past.

As Chris ranted, a swirl of tension gathered at the back of my head and spread quickly through my body like a spiral staircase winding from a knot of tightness at the base of my skull. The tension found its way into all my nooks and crannies until I felt crowded inside, my muscles and limbs swollen, constrained by my skeleton and skin. I felt as if I'd fallen into a pressure cooker.

And then I exploded. "What do you mean?! I pulled the whole way down the course. I did everything I could. How do you know it wasn't you? We've never lost before; you have. Maybe it was you," I said.

Chris said, "Bullshit! What do you know about pulling? You're a novice. You just didn't want it enough."

I was shaking. "You're wrong! You don't know anything." I felt like throwing up. I had to get away from her. She had ruined everything. I didn't understand why she had to go crazy and get so mad. I couldn't help it. I did my best. It wasn't fair that she blamed me. "Bitch," I whispered as I walked away.

Maybe I fooled Chris, maybe I sounded angry, but I was afraid again.

My captain was gone. Things would never be the same. Just like old times. Something that started with so much promise contorted into disaster in the blink of an eye.

I had no idea that I had just been hijacked. My unrelated past had risen from its own hiding place, lunged into control, and wedged itself between me and Chris, between me and racing. That's both the nature and power of fear. It comes unbidden and when it does, it packs a wallop.

Fear isn't something you have to think about to feel. It's an independent agent, operating without the aid or assent of your cerebral cortex, jumping in to assume your controls without giving you a moment to decide if that's necessary. Fundamental to survival of the human race, fear is rooted in a primal response to change, designed to ferret out potentially dangerous circumstances and react to them literally in the blink of an eye.

The human body is sensitized to detect and process the slightest shift in the external world to keep itself safe. When you step on a stick of just the right slender proportions during a walk in the woods, your body will register the possibility that it's a poisonous snake before your thinking brain can reassure you that, no, it's really just a twig. In that unthinking instant, your body is off to the races. Your heart rate increases, heat flashes up your spine, your palms get sweaty. Blood rushes to your critical organs, causing that feeling of butterflies in your gut. Your respiration rate amps up, your blood pressure rises, and a wildly effective combination of hormones shoots into your bloodstream to prepare you to fight, flee, or freeze.

External sensory information flows simultaneously along two neural highways in your brain, transmitting both to your amygdala and your cerebral cortex for processing. The route to your amygdala is short and sweet, upping the odds of your physical survival, as that's the part of your brain that jumpstarts your body's physiological response to the external stimuli. The same information travels a more leisurely route to your cerebral cortex—all of a millisecond longer—to give your cognitive processes a shot to interpret the same stimuli, engaging your critical thinking faculties. Just as in sports, when it comes to survival, speed—not cognition—matters. A flicker of an instant can be the margin between winning and losing, champion and chump, alive and dead.

Thank goodness for fear. Without its control-freak mechanisms and autocratic interference, we would have been dead as a species tens of thousands of years ago.

When fear loses its perspective, when fear is wrong, it's no big deal. You gear up for a snake and then realize it's a stick: breathe deeply, wait for your galloping heart to slow to its normal crawl, and revel in the relief that you were mistaken. But when your fear mechanism gets hair-trigger sensitive and you find yourself reacting to much of life as if it's a snake, then you're in trouble. By the time you figure that out, you're too far down the road to reverse direction. You've done irretrievable damage. Your life has changed course.

And you may not even realize you've been hijacked by fear. That recognition requires cognitive thinking, which is permanently condemned to lag behind fear. Thinking always bats cleanup, and that sequence becomes a problem when there is way too much to clean up; by then, fear is ahead, and you have all sorts of hormones like adrenaline and cortisol coursing through your bloodstream. Those hormones don't care if you behave rationally; they want you to survive. Run, fight, eliminate the threat. Short-term results at the expense of long-term consequences. Live to fight another day.

This entire business is just a mess. No wonder when fear takes over, bad shit happens. I'm not talking now about mistaking twigs for snakes: I can live with those errors. I'm talking about the wild conclusions that get lodged in our brains following a frightening experience, the fear-spawned ideas that we never voice out loud to another person, that operate under the deep cover of our unconscious darkness. We don't question them. We don't offer them up for scrutiny to others, who might give us a more rational perspective. We accept them as the pristine, absolute truth.

Especially when we're young: it takes over twenty-five years for the average human brain to finish growing, and the area that controls critical thinking is the last to fully develop. Without critical thinking, fear disposes us to blind acceptance of any whacked-out idea that might seem convincing at the time.

When an actual trauma occurs, it is as if part of the brain takes a picture of that experience and freezes it with the kind of blindingly bright flash bulb that makes you see stars and nothing else for a while. Maybe the brain science hasn't been sorted out yet, but here's the bottom line: when your brain interprets incoming external stimuli in a way that reminds you of a past trauma, everything goes haywire, and you are screwed. When you're a terrified preadolescent in the midst of watching her entire world melt down, for example.

Or when your captain gets mad at you, blames you for losing the race, and you think the world is going to end. Somehow, you associate her with your mother, both blondes, both female, both prone to emotional outbursts. Honestly, the similarity ends there, at least to a thinking person, but you're not thinking particularly well because your captain is yelling at you, and your body has decided it's in some kind of danger, reminiscent of your mother's upsets. You remember what happens when your mother is feeling particularly devastated, at least what happened that one time. The world, seriously, did just about end back then.

PART II

Drive

6

Rowing has a way of hijacking what is normal to suit its purposes, words as well as expectations. The "drive" is another average word appropriated and rejiggered into a tidbit of technical terminology. It's another multitasker—a noun, a verb, an occasional adjective—but not as complicated as "catch." Drive a car. Drive a stake into the ground or into her heart. Do you possess the drive to become a champion? Or will you wilt under the pressure, yield to the weak and wild thoughts running through your head, driving you crazy, driving you away from that which you crave most?

The drive starts at the end of the catch. The oar has entered the water and grabbed a blade full. With arms fully extended—loose like cables, not tight like sticks—the rower grasps the oar, fingers cupped around the wooden handle, which is cross-hatched to aid the grip. All the efforts of the large muscle groups—legs, back, and arms—have to channel through those narrow digits. Strong fingers don't white-knuckle the oar; they conduct the body's transfer of energy to the blade without a strangled grip. Better be loose enough to function as a transmitter; too much tension will staunch the flow. No holding on for dear life. Gotta keep it cool.

During the drive, you pull on the oar mightily and courageously. Your tightly compressed body is positioned at the catch, legs tucked up close to your chest, body angled forward to help your arms extend to their fullest reach. With your lats you feel the oar connect with the water.

The war begins. You against yourself. Body versus mind. Passion versus intellect. Dream versus reality. Your legs launch the effort, pushing your feet against the foot-stretchers, rolling the seat back toward the bow, shoving your knees into a prone position. Meanwhile, your back remains at its initial acute angle, leaning forward, and together with the still-straight arms, follows the legs into the bow. As your hands pass over your knees, your body angle starts to change. Supported by a cast of opposing abdominal muscles, your back moves from its closed, 45-degree angle to an open one of 135 degrees.

Your legs and back reach their full extensions simultaneously, their energy spent. Your seat has slid as far back as it will go. All that's left is to finish the stroke. Without changing your body angle, shrugging your shoulders, cocking your wrist, or jerking your oar, you pull your arms to your body in one continuous motion. As you pull your hands into your midsection, you maintain a loose grip on the oar to prepare for the next transition.

That's what your body is doing. What about the rest of you? Your eyes should be focused directly ahead, transmitting information to help you mimic the body motion of the person in front of you. But you can't help yourself. You sneak a peek at your oar; is it in sync with everyone else's? You check out the crew in the next lane; who's ahead?

You'd better not be talking: it interrupts your breathing, takes too much energy, and distracts your teammates. The only person allowed to speak is the coxswain; talking to you is a key component of her job. She reports on your progress and your competitor's position, corrects egregious technique, calls the racing strategy as determined in advance, and keeps you pulling your hardest by whatever means necessary, including cheering, cajoling, commanding, demanding, demeaning, threatening, begging, and bribing.

But your internal dialogue is constant. Is winning worth this excruciating pain? YES! My legs feel like wet noodles. This sucks. SHUT UP! Is that the power twenty for the halfway mark? Are we ahead yet? LET'S TAKE 'EM! Am I skying again? I can't keep doing this. DON'T STOP! This hurts. I DON'T CARE! PULL!

All rowers are multitaskers, especially during the drive. We track our movements with the rest of the crew to maintain our synchronicity and rhythm. We need to be at the same place all throughout the drive, not just starting and finishing together.

We pull our guts out while we argue internally about whether to keep going; we keep going as long as our drive is strong. Drive comes from the heart, birthed by desire, fueled by passion, toughened by pain, fired by loss and grief. It keeps us going past the point of reasonable, and that's when we discover our greatness.

Drive was not a familiar concept in my eleven-year-old universe, given its grounding in experiences I had yet to discover. Loss and grief are expert educators, however, and I proved an adept learner.

Mom didn't ever try to kill herself so overtly again, but she never returned to her old self. She was ambulatory, but barely. Her trademark, matter-of-fact approach to life and her businesslike grip on order vanished, replaced by a plodding vacancy. We didn't starve or get evicted, as Dad continued to pay the bills. But the heart of our family beat more faintly without Mom's take-charge energy to fuel all of us.

Dad didn't ask how things were, and we knew not to offer any information. He was a big believer in the power of "don't ask, don't tell," so news flowed from the Park Avenue penthouse to his hotel home in a trickle. After several months of apparent calm, he decided the nurses weren't needed and let them go. I had grown close to Anne, Mom's day nurse, who took the time to ask questions and listen to my answers, and who understood my ache for my lost mom without trying to talk me out of how badly I felt. Watching her go, I felt abandoned again, as another grown-up I could count on slipped out of the picture and left me to fend for myself, with only my big sister to rely on.

Without an adult presence to steady Mom, we were all fully exposed to the vagaries of her moods, and our house grew more somber. Peggy and I picked up the slack when Mom couldn't go shopping, make dinner, or clean up. Yvonne, our house cleaner, continued her weekly appearances to vacuum and dust our house into a modicum of cleanliness. But despite her best efforts, a once-weekly thorough cleaning could not keep our kitchen pristine. Mom's decline was impossible to ignore once cockroaches discovered our kitchen, moved in, and started having babies. Seeing those creepy crawlers race for the dark corners, trundling their rectangular egg sacs behind them like suitcases on wheels, disgusted me so much that I stopped going into the kitchen without heavy shoes on. I made it my business to stomp as many as I could, but I never grew accustomed to the shivery shock of opening a cabinet and having one scurry away.

Loneliness descended as I adjusted to the loss of my mother. She was alive before me, yet she was gone. As for Dad, he kept a stiff upper lip, determinedly cheerful. He had escaped Mom; he could ignore her problems and pretend everything was fine. I couldn't help but hate him a little. He had left me, all of us, to fend for ourselves. He didn't ask how we were doing, and I came to equate his not asking to his not caring.

Nonetheless, I didn't believe Mom's accusation of his infidelity. I knew my father was not having an affair. He was not that guy. He never mentioned a girlfriend, never said BG's name. Mom was wrong. I never fully disputed her position, but my refusal to join in when she ranted about him told her all, and she resented my loyalty.

On a sunny Saturday morning in April, seven months into my parents' separation, I waited on the corner of 81st and Park for Dad to pick me up. He had moved into an apartment by then, four blocks away, on 84th Street, just off Madison, and was taking me to the Belmont race track, just the two of us, to figure the odds and bet on the horses. I recognized him walking up the avenue, but he wasn't alone. Confused, I focused on the person beside him. Her height and carriage seemed familiar. Suddenly the details organized themselves into an agony of cognition.

Eyes burning, fury choking my airways, disappointment ripping my faith apart, I turned around and raced back to the apartment, up the elevator, and into my room. I slammed onto my bed and buried my head under my pillow. I wouldn't answer the house phone when the doorman called to announce my father's arrival.

My mother didn't know I'd left or returned. She called down the long hall, "Ginny, your father's here."

"I'm not going."

"What?"

"She's with him."

I heard her voice on the phone, a spray of indignation splashing in my direction, as she lectured my father. I knew she was secretly happy; he had proven her right.

"Ginny, come talk to your father." I got up and trudged down the hall. I was unpracticed at defiance. I grabbed the receiver from my mother.

"Ginny, where are you? Come on down."

"I'm not coming."

"What? Why not? You've been looking forward to this. I know you have."

"No, I'm not going with her!"

"With whom? Oh . . . Why not? Come on, Ginny, try to be a grown-up."

"You said it was just you and me going. It's not fair."

"Ginny, it will be fun, I promise."

"No, I'm not going. I don't want to be with her."

"You're being selfish. I'm disappointed in you, Ginny."

The thud of his disapproval landed hard inside, smacking down much of my fury. Still, I could not shake my sense of being wronged, nor could I excuse his refusal to acknowledge the messy truth. That day, my father lost the benefit of my doubt.

As our family's ship lurched onto its side, I scrambled to hold onto something, anything, to stop from sliding into the cold murk. I caved into the external pressure to go with the program that everything was okay. In the process, I buried the truth to save myself from drowning in dysfunction and so missed a key lesson: secrets are not buoys, but flimsy plastic rings that leak air from the moment we inflate them.

My friends helped. I didn't have to lie to them about what was happening. I didn't even have to talk. All they had to do was visit our apartment two or three times after school. Mom's disheveled appearance, slurred words, and unpredictable moodiness told the story, along with my embarrassed apologies for her behavior. They stuck around anyway. They didn't pry or tease. Spending time with them was like reaching an oasis where the truth found just enough water to survive.

But still our family continued to dissolve. No one ever mentioned alcoholism or whispered mental illness. My father married BG less than sixteen months after Mom's suicide attempt, solidifying his role as a stranger to our daily lives. He never asked for details and never heard the truth about the unfolding drama in the Park Avenue apartment he had fled without looking back. Peggy and I were left alone to share our observations with each other, interpret Mom's actions, speculate about the causes of her breakdown, and justify her erratic behavior.

Peggy and Mom fought all the time. Peggy often ended up walloped by hand, smacked with a hair brush, or grabbed by the hair. One night she slathered her body with Vaseline to keep Mom from grabbing her. A glob fell on the hall rug as Mom chased Peggy in the dim light; Mom stepped in the grease and slid across the rug, skinned her knee, and opened up a raw circle on her elbow. As she lay on the floor howling with rage and frustration, I wondered if our home had become a monster's den.

Mom transformed into one of the wealthiest bag ladies around. She took no care of herself. She seemed only to want to sleep. The same scenario repeated day in, day out. Every morning, I peeked around the corner of her bedroom's open doorway to see the lump huddled under the covers. Lights still off, curtains closed.

"Mom, it's time to get up." No response.

Every morning I picked up the coffee mug in permanent residence on her bedside table and checked its contents. I always found a thick smudge of nasty dark stuff partially dried on the bottom. Leaning over her, I'd catch a whiff of old pee and long-unwashed body stink. I'd inevitably gag, then swallow hard and constrict my throat, and force myself to reach down and shake what I thought was her arm.

"Mom, you really have to get up. The Littles need to go to school." A hand would snake out of the covers, imperiously wave me away. A sound often followed it, a cross between a snarl and a groan. I would grab her empty cup and leave without waiting for another non-answer. "I'll get you some coffee, okay?"

In the kitchen, the electric coffee maker was dry but dirty, its bottom caked with scum, with coffee grounds scattered on the counter. More coffee stains decorated the counter top, artsy blobs comingling with ragged circles, marking the extent of my mother's bitter habit. Always black, sometimes hot, sometimes cold. Fresh and steaming, sludgy and decaying, no matter: she drank it however it came.

Back in her bedroom with a fresh offering. No chipped mug for her morning ablutions. I always brought her a clean cup, sunshine yellow with a matching saucer, a snippet of elegance to give a shot of prim and proper to the day. Maybe she'd take the hint. I knew better than to hope, but I couldn't help myself.

I stood above her inert body, holding the coffee. As gently as possible, as if my tone or choice of phrase or anything else I did mattered, I said, "Mom, come on. I made you some coffee. It's right here."

Most mornings, she eventually shed the covers and sat up. I looked at her, hair askew, mouth turned downward in a sour greeting, the thin strap of her sleeveless nightgown slipping off her shoulder. I held out the cup, balancing it easily with an experienced hand. She took it wordlessly, sipped her first hit, and closed her eyes.

She appeared downstairs a half hour later with the Littles in tow, shuffling out of the elevator and past the precisely attired doorman, his dark gray overcoat decorated with epaulets and shiny brass buttons marching down his front. A long winter coat buttoned up over the disarray of her flimsy nightgown, shoes without stockings, her hair uncombed, yesterday's makeup in all the wrong places, unwashed and smelling of decay, muttering under her breath, she grasped Muff's and Dixie's hands and stepped into the chill to walk them up to the Brick Church elementary school five blocks away.

Up and down, back and forth; this was our life. A little bit of good infused the great deal of bad. One night she splurged and took us all out for Chinese. We kids were all excited: Shirley Temples, eggrolls, sweet and sour pork, spare ribs, slim pancakes with Mu Shu pork, hot sweet tea, fortune cookies! Mom seemed a bit unsteady and distracted but didn't fuss. No yelling or screaming. Then after dinner, as we trailed behind her toward the door, Peggy nudged me. A dark, wet stain was spreading down the back of Mom's dress below her butt. I looked back at her chair, caught sight of the seat dripping, and saw the carpet darkening beneath it. I cringed and hurried out, relieved that at least we'd be gone when the mess was discovered.

Sometimes, though, she would straggle into the kitchen and conjure up a meal that felt like old times. Sometimes she would wash and dress and spend the day out and about, like she used to. There was no predicting her behavior. No wonder Peggy and I developed our own shorthand to alert each other to Mom's frame of mind at any given moment. "She's in one of her moods" conveyed the warning of trouble ahead and the imperative to avoid it.

Mom and Peggy continued to fight, and two years into our new life, Mom sent Peggy away to boarding school, Emma Willard in up-state New York. Just like that, I became the oldest kid in the household, with no backup or ally. I lost my partner in crime, my confidante, my fellow prisoner, and my shield. After Peggy left, Mom resurrected some sense of normality during the day. She did laundry, went food shopping, and ran errands. Life fell apart at night when she turned into Mr. Hyde—demanding, erratic, hysterical, cruel—before retreating to her bedroom and passing out.

To ward off isolation, I resorted to nightly phone calls to my friends. Then, in one of her tirades, Mom lost her temper and locked up all the phones except one: the emergency red wall phone with an extra-long cord in the kitchen.

That kitchen. A grimy field of battle. My imagination crawled with thoughts of roaches crouched in the hidden spaces behind drawers, under floor tiles, between walls, stacked on top of each other, wedged everywhere. I knew what awaited me every time I opened a cabinet, a drawer, the garbage can, even the dishwasher. Whenever I needed a plate, a spoon, a cup or glass, a pot or pan, some cereal or rice, a can opener—or to hear a friend's voice—I had to contend with the enemy. The roaches epitomized the new era in our household. Life seemed normal during daylight hours; after sunset, everything changed.

One night when Mom was sufficiently conscious and composed to prepare dinner, she stuck around to keep us company while we ate. Toward the end of the meal, as she brought the pots and pans to the sink, she saw some slim dark shadows hustle across the floor.

"Ginny, get the Raid," she instructed, dumping the dishes into the sink. She dried her hands on a dishrag that smelled like old cheese and briskly pulled out the trusty Electrolux vacuum cleaner from the broom closet.

"Back in a sec, Mom." I dashed to my bedroom and dug into my closet. I didn't want to miss a moment of Mom's display of her old, energetic self. I pulled on heavy-heeled boots and raced back into the kitchen, then passed her the tall can of poison from under the sink.

"Ready, Gins?" She snapped off the can's lid and looked at me with the intensity of a soldier gunning for battle. At the sound of my nickname, I felt a rush of warmth. Mom was back, in charge and ready to face the enemy. In my mind, she was the world champion of fighting off dirt and organizing away chaos. The roaches' take-over of our kitchen showed how far she had strayed from her normal self. She had given up, but now she was back!

Grimly happy, I positioned myself at the vacuum and picked up the hose, pulling off the rug attachment to leave the metal nozzle naked. Then I nodded, stifling my urge to run screaming from the room. Mom sprayed methodically, releasing poison in a steady stream along every cabinet at its intersection with the floor, then under the stove, the dishwasher, and the sink. She sprayed under the refrigerator, under the stools at the counter, in the broom closet, along the doorways and doorjambs, every possible point of roach entry or exit. The air stank of poison, oddly sweet in spite of its noxious overtone. It was like inhaling at a gas station; I knew the fumes were dangerous, but I couldn't stop myself from inhaling deeply.

Roaches started trickling from their hiding places and then flooded the room. Some of the weaker ones rolled over and died in full sight on the floor, but most scurried aimlessly, seeking freedom from the poison.

I turned on the vacuum cleaner and pointed the bare nozzle at the fleeing intruders, sucking them up. I relished wielding my very own weapon of mass destruction, the control I suddenly possessed, and my ability to defend myself fearlessly. To remove all evidence of disorder. In cahoots with my mother.

There were so many roaches. I couldn't look up from the floor for a long time. I didn't want to miss any. When I did pause, my mother directed me, "Gins, over there."

My glance followed her pointing finger. I shuddered, then pointed the nozzle at the wall and let it gobble the roaches crawling there. When I looked up, I saw a couple on the ceiling itself, defying gravity as they scuttled upside down, seeking a crack they could sneak into.

Repelled by the thought of a creepy crawly body falling on my bare skin, I nonetheless pointed the vacuum wand above my head and sucked them in.

We were done. They were all gone, maybe only for the moment, but that was enough for me.

———

By the end of eighth grade, nearly three years after my father's departure, both my standards and my expectations had fallen off a cliff. In spite of everything, I kept hoping that somehow Mom and Dad would patch our old life back together and we'd pick up where they'd left off. My mother was strong; she loved me. She knew it was her job to take care of us. She always had before. She would come back. And I had to help; I had to do my job.

But as time passed and nothing improved, I began to blame myself. I was a bad girl. I wasn't doing my part well enough. I didn't understand what Mom needed.

It took me those three years, day by painful day, to cave in and give up.

The final straws piled on the summer after eighth grade, when Mom decided to take the three of us kids (she didn't invite Peggy) to Europe for the summer. Two long months on Italy's west coast in the picture-perfect seaside town of Porto Ercole, with its daily fruit and vegetable market, butcher shop with feathered headless chickens hanging in the windows, and stone seawall stretching into the Adriatic. But the peaceful scenery and foreign mystique couldn't compensate for the emotional ups and downs of living with two unstable adults: Mom had acquired a boyfriend, Anton, a swarthy Bulgarian artist at least ten years younger than her, well-muscled, with prominent, well-proportioned facial features and a crown of dark curls that suggested a dark Apollo. His appearance contrasted sharply with Mom's, whose steady diet of cigarettes, coffee, alcohol, and secret swallows of unidentified pills had jumpstarted her face wrinkling and body sagging well in advance of her chronological age. We didn't know how they met, but Peggy and I speculated that Mom's wallet mattered more to Anton than her perfect looks and sparkling personality.

Day after day, week after week, we lurched back and forth between Jekyll and Hyde existences. Mom bantered and bartered with the marketplace vendors in limited but enthusiastic Italian one day, berated me for burning food she had put on the stove without telling me before passing out the next.

Living in an idyllic village, I dreamed of escape. I took long walks through the town and to the end of the pier that stretched into the harbor, but always had to come home to Mom, worried whether she would be all right when I returned and angered that I had to worry at all.

Some of my Swedish family, Aunt Evy and cousin Annica, visited for a week. On the last day of their stay, I sat on the porch of their Porto Ercole rental in the early evening, waiting for Mom, Anton, and the Littles to return from a day trip to Rome. It was late; they were late. The phone rang. Annica and I stared into the streetlights, watching the bats flit in and out of the shadows, while Evy went inside to answer it. She came out a few minutes later, visibly upset.

"Ginny, that was Anton. He's at the hospital in Rome. There was a car accident."

Instantly, my worries escalated. Someone was dead. It was all my fault. I had let Muff and Dixie go with my mother and that man, that lunatic, who always drove his fancy sports car a zillion miles an hour with my brother and sister squeezed into the practically nonexistent backseat . . . What was I thinking?

"What happened?" I didn't want to know, but I had to. It was my job to know, to blame myself, and to figure out how to solve the mess.

"I don't really know. Your mother is badly hurt. She cannot leave the hospital tonight."

Shit! "What about Miss Muffet? And Dixie?"

"They are okay. Anton will bring them back tomorrow."

When the Littles returned the next day, they were wearing the same clothes they had left in, now torn and bloodstained. They bore their share of bruises and bumps, but nothing serious. Mom wasn't so lucky. When she was released from the hospital several days later, she returned with a broken pelvis, a broken arm, a black eye, and bruises all over her body. The doctors had stemmed her internal bleeding and deemed her sufficiently stable to fly home.

By the time we arrived back in New York in late August, I was in emotional tatters, exhausted by the job of monitoring my mother and, even worse, confronted by the extent of my failure to deliver. I had not been able to keep her drug-free, to distract her from drinking, to prevent her from making a fool of herself, or to protect my sister and brother.

Then in early September, Peggy returned to New York to finish her last year of high school at Nightingale-Bamford, which she'd attended for eight years before Mom banished her from the city. "Not asked back" by Emma Willard, her boarding school, Peggy forced our parents' hand. I was stunned to discover she was not going to live with us at Mom's, but at Dad's.

Talk about an unpredictable turn of events: Mom viewed BG as the devil and had tried to keep us as far from her as possible. BG had exclaimed countless times that she didn't want any children, and Dad never stood up for us when she went off about "no kids," but just let her rant about what a pain they were. We all knew where the four of us kids stood with her when it came to Dad. She came first. We came not second, but last.

I shouldn't have been so surprised. I had heard my mother exclaim countless times on the phone to Dad, "I can't handle her, Dick. She can't come home here. It won't work." But it all sank in fully the first time I visited Peggy at the new apartment Dad had rented to accommodate her moving in with him and BG. I sat on her bed in her new bedroom, saw the private bathroom tucked into a corner, the big closet, the privacy, the peace, and I suddenly saw my own way out of life with my mother.

Until that instant, I hadn't realized the extent of my desperation. As I lay on Peggy's bed watching her unpack her moving boxes, I realized I wanted to move out of Mom's, too. Now that Peggy was back in the city, I couldn't tolerate the idea of living with Mom without her. I broached the idea of moving to Dad's too, testing out the idea of our sharing a room again, and my big sister agreed without hesitation.

We didn't have to talk about what was going on. Already discarded herself, sent to boarding school a year before, and refused reentry by our mother, she'd waited to find out where she'd get to live and go to school, while our parents tussled about her future. I figured that neither of them wanted her, but didn't know if Mom manipulated Dad into thinking he won a battle or lost one, if he viewed Peggy as the prize or the punishment.

Now all I had to do was talk to Dad. I heard my inner voice rail at me with all the reasons he would say no, but I had already decided. The possibility of one more denial or another rejection didn't faze me.

Nothing could be as bad as the unendurable at my mother's. I had nothing to lose.

Peggy agreed to back me up, to tell Dad she supported my moving in with them, and I resolved to call him that night.

I picked up the red wall phone with its long cord dangling nearly to the floor. I dialed the numbers, my forefinger turning the dial each time all the way to the right, trying not to hold my breath.

Dad answered the phone.

Now or never. "Dad, Dad, can I move in with you too?" I rushed right on by "hello" into the heart of the matter, not giving him a chance to decline. "Peggy and I figured it all out. We can share her room, just like we used to. It's okay with her. Just ask her."

I ran out of sentences too quickly.

"You want to live here too? Move in with Peggy?" He sounded surprised, but not angry. Well, that was a good start. Maybe he could imagine how awful living with Mom must be. Maybe he dredged up his own memories of his last days with her. Or maybe he just knew it was his turn.

"Sure," he answered slowly. "I think we can probably work this out. Let me talk with your stepmother to figure out the details."

I felt a faint lightening of the heaviness I had shouldered over the past three years. The guilt of fleeing would come soon enough. I would have to tell Mom, but for the moment, relief reigned.

I needed help to give Mom the news. I turned to the only one who knew more than I did about how to handle her unbridled fury and the only one I trusted to stand up to her. Peggy could take it. She wouldn't burn down. Something special ran through her veins, some kind of fire retardant that kept her cool while our mother vilified and belittled her.

Of course Peggy stepped up. Neither of us wanted to delay the inevitable. She came over right before dinner the next day, the last Tuesday of September.

Peggy and I sat Mom down in the library. Without preamble or delicacy, Peggy said matter-of-factly, "Ginny's decided to move to Dad's. She's not going to live here anymore."

Dead silence. Then Mom looked simultaneously horrified and disgusted, her eyes wide, her mouth an O of disbelief with her upper lip somehow twisting into a sneer. "You want to move in with your father and that woman?" she asked.

I nodded slowly, the first pangs of shame wrenching my innards, anxiety burning within me. I couldn't speak.

Peggy said, "She's moving out on Friday."

A switch flipped in my mother, and her face reshuffled. Her teeth clamped together, her mouth became a rigid line, and her eyes glittered darkly. She spat her words at Peggy with undisguised malice: "Who do you think you are? You're not in charge! You think you can do whatever you want?"

Her Nordic accent thickened with each successive declaration, as if marking her descent into illogic. "I'll show you what you can and can't do. I'll take your father to court, you wait and see."

She glared at me. "Fine. Do as you please. Go, just go!" She rose with dreadful composure, like royalty offended, and swept out.

Just like that, it was over. I was free to go. I didn't know how to feel: guilty or angry or sad or relieved. I looked at Peggy and shrugged. "She can go to hell," I said.

"She's already there," answered Peggy. Her voice sounded empty.

That evening after Peggy left to return to her new home, I entered the kitchen cautiously. A veneer of normalcy coated the room. Dinner smelled edible, unburned. The counter was set; the glasses were topped off with icy cold milk; Miss Muffet and Dixie were already seated. I slid onto my stool at the counter next to Muff.

Mother silently set plates down before us. I focused on the food—meatloaf, mashed potatoes, peas—eating slowly, but deliberately.

Suddenly, Mom was behind me. I wished I could shrink down, slip off my stool, and run for the door. Instead, I kept my eyes on my plate, hoping I could avoid triggering her anger. I felt her hands lightly on my shoulders. I hardly recognized this gentle touch. It had been so long.

"How could you do this to me?" she said softly. "How could you leave me?"

"Don't touch me!" I snapped and jerked my shoulders as if to fling off the guilt her words called up in me. She stepped back in surprise. I almost fell off the stool in my haste to escape.

"You don't understand anything! Leave me alone, just leave me alone!" I howled, then banged through the kitchen doors and raced to my room, finally sobbing.

Mom left me alone for the rest of the evening and never raised the subject again. Ever.

Three days later, I carted my suitcases, my stuffed animals, my record collection, and my cadre of miniature wooden Swedish horses to my father's apartment. I left much more behind, including my good memories. And worse, I didn't even notice they were gone.

Only I knew the price Muff and Dixie were going to pay. No one else, not even Peggy, understood how unendurable the previous year had been—how lonely, dangerous at times, chaotic, and slovenly, and how completely the three of us were left to take care of ourselves. Now, I, fourteen years old, was leaving a madwoman who had already repeatedly and irrefutably proven her incapacity to take charge of an eleven-year-old and a nine-year-old. I didn't know how they would care for and protect themselves.

As it turned out, the answer came quickly, two nights later, just past midnight on my first Sunday night at my father's. I was still up, talking with BG in the living room, when the phone rang.

My father answered, listened briefly, forehead furrowed, said, "I'll be right over," and hung up.

He looked at BG, paling as he spoke. "She says she's killed Muff and Dixie."

Years later, Britt-Louise told me what happened that night. "I was sleeping. Then the doorbell started ringing. It wouldn't stop. On and on. No one was answering it, so I got up. I walked down the long hall, past Dixie's room, then to Mom's doorway. She was sitting up in bed, reading. 'Someone's at the door,' I said. She just waved me away. So I went and opened the front door and found two policemen standing there with Dad and BG. I let them in, we woke up Dixie, BG helped me pack some things, and they brought us over to you."

None of us ever lived with my mother again, but the days immediately following the midnight rescue tore my insides like tissue paper. I often stood by the living room window looking across the low roofs of the brownstones that separated my new home from my old one. I had a clear view through the back windows of the old penthouse apartment into Peggy's room, the gym, and the laundry room. I scoured the rooms for signs of my mother. I never saw her. But I didn't have to see her to know what was happening in that cavernous apartment. I couldn't stop thinking about her. She was all alone now. I worried about who would wake her up to start the day; she had little if any reason to get up. Without anyone to care for her, would she disappear?

7

All eights are crews, but a mighty eight can become a sisterhood. You learn each other's strengths and weaknesses. You coax out each other's self-confidence, confront and overcome obstacles together, challenge and compete with each other. It is often messy. Not everyone likes each other. You put each other down. You pull each other up. You gossip, argue and debate, needle and incite, protect and cover for each other. You develop trust and earn respect. Nine women combine in myriad ways to develop connections, consistent with their own styles and personalities. The result is a synergy composed of a pattern unique to you.

When you get in the boat and shove off from the dock, you know what matters: everyone is prepared to do whatever it takes to cross that finish line first.

Chris Ernst never raced with us again, but she sowed the seeds of the sisterhood that became the unstoppable Yale Women's Crew of 1979, three years after she lost her last college race. The day of her outburst, our crew's bond was thin, a handful of strands not yet wound together in a purposeful pattern. We had struggled individually through winter training, but we had not suffered together as a crew. We had not felt the sting of losing. We had not gagged on the stink of defeat. We'd not had to confront each other eye to eye and acknowledge we'd let each other down.

There is no way to learn how bad losing is, except by doing it. Unfortunately, you have to develop a personal and deeply familiar relationship with failure to become great at anything. Losing is the most effective way to inspire improvement and generate success. It paints the gap between dreams and reality in brilliant colors. It reminds you of what's important and why you care.

If you listen carefully, you can hear its whispered call, promising better fortunes if you recommit yourself, put your head down, and get to work. Or you can give up and go home. Your choice.

As I stood on the Gales Ferry dock while Chris berated our bedraggled and tremulous group of freshmen, I couldn't see the future; nor could she. Blinded by disappointment's glare, Chris blamed us for a trite truth: a crew is only as strong as its weakest link. Our eight was young and inexperienced. She was right.

Nine months of rowing was too short to learn to pull at full power for an entire race. It was not enough time for me to learn how to use my body optimally; to realize that I could pull for my teammates in front or behind me, even if I couldn't muster the belief to pull for myself; and, finally, to discover I deserved to win as much as the next person.

I had to learn that as much as losing sucked, it was as necessary to success as stairs and circuits. Without it, I would never discover the power of my own will.

By the time my class graduated, we had lost only two dual races over my four seasons, including that loss to Radcliffe freshman year. We won the Eastern Sprints twice and would have made it three times if gale force winds hadn't canceled the regatta my junior year. We won the Collegiate National Championships as seniors in the twilight of our shared competitive careers. We established the standard by which subsequent Yale women's crews would measure themselves for nearly thirty years. But that day, all I knew was that all the hard work, hours in the weight room, tank sessions, and stairwells hadn't paid off. Our season had ended shrouded in disappointment and sorrow.

What was to love about this?

The question followed me home from Gales Ferry and plagued me in the early weeks of summer, while Chris and Anne tried out for the Olympic team and ended up in Montreal as members of the first US women's Olympic rowing squad. Then I watched the US women's eight claim the bronze. I saw myself reflected in the late-night glare of the television set, standing tall on the victory platform, hands raised above my head, a medal around my neck.

I didn't take long to decide. Losing sucked, but rowing wasn't the problem. The problem lay elsewhere: lack of preparation. I knew from way back that the best defense was a good offense. Be strong, tough, unstoppable. Be prepared for anything, because disaster could strike from anywhere. Training was the answer.

Late August rolled around. I couldn't wait to return to the boathouse, greet my teammates, and step into a racing shell again. I yearned for the view from the water, the peaceful scenery balancing the energy within the boat. I ached to belong again. Captain Chris wouldn't lead our team anymore, but we'd learned so much from her. We'd figure it out.

But I had something else to figure out too: how to go about training for the Olympics.

I didn't know whom I could ask for advice or whom I could trust with my secret. My coach? Nat would pop my bubble as soon as I shared it. He'd say I was a young and inexperienced rower on a pretty fast crew. He'd warn me not to get my hopes up. He'd quietly doubt my potential, as he had from the moment he met me. He'd privately think I was nothing special.

Anne Warner? She'd listen all right, but I guessed what would follow: an incessant drive to show me how far out of her league I was.

Captain Chris? She had retired as captain upon graduation, but returned to the program as Yale's first women's novice rowing coach. I more than looked up to her; her confidence and forceful personality dazzled me. She had concentrated intensity that I had never experienced and a no-holds-barred willingness to kick anyone in the ass who tried to stand in her way, and was fearless in the face of authority and comfortable positioned out of the mainstream.

Heck, even being gay didn't make her hate or doubt herself. Chris didn't broadcast her sexuality, but her utter disinterest in guys, to the point of disdain, was obvious, although, in fairness I only saw her around the heavyweight guys, and they deserved disdain. She was the first out lesbian I had ever met, and her refusal to hide or apologize fascinated me.

I couldn't imagine being that bold or comfortable about an aspect of myself that much of the world, especially my world, with my father topping the list, condemned as deficient, if not depraved. I admired her matter-of-factness about who she was and her contempt for anyone who judged her harshly. I longed to be like her: that self-confident, that assertive, and that impervious to the opinions of others.

The mid-1970s were early times in the gay rights movement, with the Stonewall riots that served to catalyze the shift from a more conservative, less aggressive movement to one that was clearly out and proud less than a decade past. On campus, I didn't see any evidence of the movement, nor was there much discussion about homosexuality, although I wasn't looking or listening for any. In the small pond that comprised the Yale Women's Crew, everyone revered Chris, gay or not. If anything, her sexuality made her even more of a standout and more of a leader, as she modeled self-confidence and assertiveness in pursuing her goals without allowing the opinions of others, either individuals or society as a whole, to interfere with her dreams.

Maybe Chris would understand my impossible dream, my secret longing. Maybe she'd support my boldness, if nothing else. But memories of our last contact on the dock at Gales Ferry still stung and brought me back to earth.

Besides, no matter to whom I confessed my dream—Nat, Anne Warner, or Chris—they would all be right. I was crazy to want it. I knew that from the start. But the heart wants what the heart wants.

Sophomore year began. I sewed my first varsity letter, a big, dark navy Y made of felt, onto the traditional soft white letter sweater with its boat collar that had trademarked Yale varsity athletes for over one hundred years. Sewing and sports existed at near-opposite ends of the femininity spectrum, a span I didn't ponder as I wielded my needle. I was stitching myself into the role of pioneer, as I attached the flimsy felt to the chest of my sweater, my own personal story just one thin thread tugging at the fabric of American culture, helping to reconfigure the still-prevalent view that women's and girls' engagement in athletics posed a threat to their health and femininity.

I just wanted to wear my letter sweater proudly, but history had to play out in its own time to reverse the backslide in cultural norms. By the early twentieth century, most women's colleges and a smattering of co-ed schools offered instruction and competition in several sports, including archery, baseball, basketball, rowing, tennis, and track, but in the mid-1920s, a cultural rebellion against the concept of the "independent woman" slowed progress. Bearing in mind that this era birthed the Miss America pageant, the concerns that engagement in sports promoted "mannish" characteristics and produced women who would be too strong and unable to submit to their husbands' authority fit with the times. For the next four decades, educators and parents viewed female involvement in competitive sports as both a health and a moral hazard; women's colleges across the country downgraded their competitive intercollegiate offerings to intramural status, focusing on socializing and fun, not winning.

Few statistics documented women's involvement in sports; "ladylike" sports—badminton, golf, swimming, and tennis—were encouraged at the expense of more active team sports, like volleyball, basketball, and softball. Women's track events were limited to distances no greater than two hundred meters in competition. Avery Brundage, an American and the president of the International Olympic Committee, actually advocated reducing the number of women's track events in the Olympics to remove the less feminine ones, like shot put and distance running.

The arrival of coeducation to the Ivy League thankfully coincided with changing attitudes about women's involvement in sports, as the passage of Title IX demonstrated. Still, I didn't realize that official Ivy League competition in women's sports had started only a year before I ripped open my acceptance letter from Yale. In fact, the first championship awarded was in the sport of rowing. And with admissions departments debating whether to confer the same priority to women athletes granted to men, the death knell of the myth that sports harm women was beginning to sound.

I quickly settled back into campus life. No longer a freshman, my Old Campus days behind me, I moved into my residential college, Branford (where my father had lived, too). I shared a triple with Ruth and Sandy, two classmates I had lived across the hall from freshman year, who were acquaintances more than friends. We shared no interests, classes, or friends, and rarely gossiped, shared meals, or hung out. Our first week of school, we bought two-by-fours and plywood and constructed a third bedroom out of the living room so we could each enjoy the privacy of our own room.

Located at the top of the narrow tower situated on the west corner of Branford's dining hall, our suite took up the entire floor, as did the ones on the two floors below us. Only nine people lived in the tower, which meant our shared entry didn't see much action. That was fine by me. I loved the peace and quiet that came with being out of the fray, and the privacy, too. I could come and go as I pleased without having to satisfy anyone's curiosity and could choose what to share with whom without interference or prodding.

I allowed myself to fall hard for a guy, an upperclassman who seemed to like me, too. Don was a svelte New Yorker, an indifferent athlete, but nicely built, articulate, and funny. He was two years into an extended recovery from the loss of his first love, and I was glad to help ease his pain, not realizing that he had decided to keep his distance when it came to romance. Misinterpreting his casual interest for something more substantial, I spent my share of nights with Don at his off-campus apartment, enjoying our physical intimacy and loving the sense of emotional security with which I imbued our relationship.

I landed with a bad bump when he dumped me at the start of second semester, and although Don had introduced me to some fellow Branford students whom I liked, I withdrew from those budding friendships to save myself the humiliation of public mourning. Instead, I took most of the spring to recover and vowed that love was not for me.

But I did find one new friend in the process. David had also fallen for Don when they met their freshman year, but settled for friendship when Don defined the strict boundaries of their relationship. Don was not bisexual, so David had to settle for one-sided flirting and platonic dinners filled with banter about English literature and foreign movies. I appreciated David's biting, sarcastic sense of humor, and his self-deprecation about his situation with Don. We ate our share of meals together, trading tidbits about the guy we had in common, and when Don finally gave me the heave, David was there to comfort me.

Meanwhile, my father and I debated my major. I loved math and was drawn to computer science, but he suggested a novel approach:

"Do something that's hard for you, that you're not so good at." My memories of the red C minuses my freshman English professor had scrawled across the bottom of my papers, along with the oft-appearing directive "see me," floated at the periphery of my father's counterintuitive advice. A major in English would require lots of writing, but no senior essay. That seemed too easy, so I searched for another major with a heavy writing requirement and a senior essay. History fit the bill, so off I went.

But, really, I majored in rowing. I chose my courses according to its seasons and arranged my classes around practices. I worked out with my teammates and followed Anne Warner's lead without fessing up to any goals beyond gold for the Bulldogs. She'd returned from the Olympics with a bronze medal, but was bitter toward us, as her haughty attitude the previous year had resulted in the large group of irreverent freshmen (five of us who'd rowed with her in the varsity) electing as captain not her, but a top lightweight instead.

Bakehead, who had rowed the previous season in the six seat, was musing about trying out for the 1977 National Team. Anne Boucher (Bouche) had also joined us—our program's first-ever experienced freshman recruit. She came with an illustrious high-school-rowing pedigree and an open interest in climbing the highest rungs of the sport. I could stay safely under the radar and stealthily pursue my private fantasies without having to expose myself at all.

There was only one problem. Okay, maybe not only one, but this one blindsided me.

It shouldn't have, because my asthma had been a fact of life since sixth grade. Back then, a visit to the doctor diagnosed the condition, but in my hardheaded, defiant twelve-year-old way, I decided the guy was wrong.

After all, he claimed his specialty was ears, eyes, noses, and throats, and my problem lay south of my neck, by my estimation well below his geographic expertise. Plus, I couldn't understand how something could be wrong with me when everyone else in my family was A-OK. They all could breathe just fine. After all, we shared the same genes. To top it all off, he blamed my cats for making me sick. Those sleek, dark-brown companions with long, wavy tails—our pair of Burmese,

Chocolate and Vanilla, were my biggest fans. They showed up at the front door every afternoon when I returned from school and followed me everywhere until bedtime. I had slept with them nightly for eons, surrounded and protected. There was no way my cats were the problem.

The facts, however, were hard to dispute. My skin broke out in itchy blotches wherever Chocolate rubbed against me. Accidental scratches turned into jagged red lightning bolts and then swelled into angry welts. Sometimes when he slept snuggled up beside me on my pillow, I felt as if something was hugging me to death from the inside, squeezing all the air out of my lungs. I couldn't figure out how to grab hold of it, shake it loose, and throw it out of there.

In addition to cats, several other life essentials found their way onto the list of dangers: dogs, horses, hay, grass, chocolate, dust. Show me a place on earth without dust. I couldn't go anywhere without being threatened by my environment.

Part of my punishment required trekking to Midtown every Thursday in the middle of the school day for shots designed to desensitize me to the allergens that the experts insisted triggered my asthma. No one picked me up or accompanied me. My mom and her constant companions, Mr. and Mrs. Marlboro Lights (she had dumped Mr. Lucky Strikes for filtered cigarettes because they were supposedly safer), couldn't muster much sympathy. She kept the windows closed in my bedroom because the doctor insisted that cold air was tough on my breathing, and she sat me in the smoking section when we went to the movies. She insisted I take my medication, which zapped my pulse into the stratosphere like a jittery rocket and made me sick to my stomach, but her aversion to vomit meant I had to throw up alone, curled up on the bathroom floor, clutching the sides of the toilet as the waves of nausea gradually receded.

I'd been taught by experts to stuff my problems into silence. Maybe my body had taken the lessons to heart. Maybe this was payback: no more room down there, not even for oxygen.

My departure for boarding school in tenth grade had improved my health. Dana Hall was in Wellesley, Massachusetts, just outside Boston, where the air was cleaner, my bedroom was free of cat hair, and I was far away from my family drama. I had lived with my father, stepmother, and three siblings for less than a year when I fled to Dana Hall, desperate to escape the tension of living in a household dominated by a woman who continued to repeat that she never wanted children and didn't care for the ones under her roof. Constant arguing and putdowns by BG wore me down, especially because my father almost always took her side. No matter what I did, excelled or underperformed, BG was never satisfied. To counter BG's success in swaying my father's opinion, I welcomed solo time with him. Nonetheless, for a former star goody-goody, my change in status to bad-attitude girl felt crushing.

Maybe all my lungs had needed was a break from home. My entire first year I remained symptom-free. The next year, I quit my medical protocols cold turkey. Medication was for weenies, people who weren't strong enough to take care of themselves. And what happened as a result of going AWOL from my shots and medications? Nothing. I survived just fine. No wheezing, no asthma, no sudden attacks, no emergency room visits. I was cured.

Conned by the quieting of my asthma's symptoms in high school and their continued absence through my freshman year at Yale, I forgot about my breathing condition. The diagnosing doctor had warned my mother: when asthma develops at puberty, it will likely remain a lifelong condition, but I was determined to disprove that rule. Two years and counting without symptoms, and during that period I'd become a college varsity athlete. I'd rowed an entire year asthma-free.

Until now, October of sophomore year.

One night, I woke suddenly in my dorm room bed and grabbed for the pillow that seemed to be covering my face, but found nothing. It was pitch black and cold. I was breathing hard, as if I'd been running in my dreams, but the weight in my chest woke me up to confront a nightmare.

Breathing is supposed to come easy: an involuntary action, the most fundamental of survival skills. Conscious or not, awake or asleep, the human body keeps on inhaling, exhaling, doing its job.

Not mine, not now. I tried to inhale rapidly, hoping a quick intake would force the air to the bottom of my lungs. No such luck. I tried exhaling quickly, following that push with a second sharp intake. The air whistled inside me as it tried to squeeze through my narrowed bronchial tubes. I closed my eyes and strained. Muscles across my back and chest, ill designed for breathing, pitched in to move the oxygen down.

I wanted to yell, "I can't breathe! Help!" but I didn't have the lung power and I was all alone in my dorm room.

I found my alarm clock. It was 3:30 a.m. I wondered when I could call the Department of Undergraduate Health Services and reach Molly Meyer, the nurse in charge of the varsity athletes. "Wait until morning" argued with "This is pretty bad."

Suddenly I didn't even have the energy for the internal debate. I shut my eyes, forced my brain to shut up the panic chatter, and watched myself breathe. It was bad. Very bad.

The moments ticked by. The attack did not subside. Wishful thinking wasn't doing the trick. The snake had me by the throat; only medication would break its grip.

But, there was no way I would follow in my mother's footsteps and take pills to solve a problem I should be able to handle on my own. I had to tough out this attack. Giving in to my own demons would be the death of me, as my mother's had nearly been for her. Five years had passed since my mother's middle-of-the-night phone call to my father informing him she'd murdered their two youngest children, and she still had not recovered her equilibrium, continuing to drink heavily and pop mystery pills. She had spent much of her time living in Europe and maintained loose contact, writing aerograms and returning to New York for vacations and holidays bearing expensive gifts. But when it came to showing up as a reliable and sober parent, she struck out every time.

Training is simply a repetitive execution of a pattern of movement. Learning describes the brain rewiring that occurs when we practice anything. New neural connections develop and strengthen as skills improve. When our patterns become second nature, they've been committed to cellular memory. Cognitive thought processes are no longer necessary. And in difficult moments, when fear is in charge and unleashes adrenaline to course through your veins, mustering reasoning skills is enormously difficult. When the chips are down, your cerebral cortex is last in line to receive sensory information. It has no time to solve your problem, but your muscle memory can function on automatic pilot.

Now my fear, masquerading as intelligence, was warning me that if I took drugs, I could end up just like my mother. Weak. Dependent. Unable to cope. Mom had told me so herself one day when I was reciting all the ways she'd let me down. I swore I would be different. "Never say never," she responded. "You could end up just like me."

What unwritten lessons had I derived from Mom's breakdown? I'd never murmured a word of them to a sane adult. I didn't know that mental illness and addiction caused similar behaviors; no one had even told me that my mother was mentally ill. Dad knew—he had spoken to her doctors—but he kept it a secret and let us kids think she just had a drinking problem. He pretended she would be okay, just as he always wanted me to pretend I didn't have asthma.

But on this night I wasn't going to just lay there and let myself ruin my life. Betrayed by my deficient body with its ineffective lungs, I needed help. As much as the idea terrified me, I had to follow my mother's path. I needed medication to breathe, just as she had thought she needed alcohol and drugs to survive.

Slowly, I sat up and swung my legs over the side of my bed. I stood up, wheezing, and waited for the dizziness to subside. I shuffled to the phone, dialed the number for the campus health services. All I could think about was one deep breath reaching all the way down to my core, giving me a chance to live another day. Just give me that one hit of breathing.

"Ginny, you can't keep doing this to yourself," said Molly Meyer, who stood by my hospital bed, stethoscope hanging from her neck. Starting with that October asthma attack, my breathing had gone to hell: now it was winter and Molly could justly claim me as her most frequent visitor to Health Services. The presiding physician, Dr. Jokel, knew me on sight.

Night was ready to yield to dawn. Molly held my hand and stroked my forehead. My hair felt damp, my skin clammy. The aftereffects of the adrenaline were wearing off. My heart had stopped romping and slowed to a trot. I was breathing normally, gratefully.

"It's okay. I'll be fine." I was drowsy. Finally, I could relax and sleep. I was safe.

The next day I discovered how safe.

"Wait, what did you say?" I sat in a chair in Molly's cramped office. Disbelief made my voice squeak.

Molly shrugged, as if helpless and unhappy, but I could see the no-nonsense look in her eyes. "It's not safe for you to continue rowing without using daily medication to control your asthma."

"But I'm fine. Look at me, all better! Besides, I can't do that."

"You can't keep ending up in the emergency room in the middle of the night. Asthma is a serious condition. People die from it."

"Meds don't help. They make me feel horrible. I'll be okay."

"You're right. You will be." Molly handed me a sheet of paper. "This is for Nat. He needs to know you've been placed on athletic disability."

"What?"

"No more rowing until you deal with your asthma."

"You can't do this!"

"I can and I have. Dr. Jokel agrees. He approved the decision," Molly said calmly. "Ginny, you have a serious health problem. You need medication. Why is this so difficult for you?"

"I can take care of myself. I have to."

"You have to . . . what? There's nothing wrong with getting help when you need it. Your body can't handle what you're doing to it."

I heard the drumbeat start in my head and braced for the voice that would follow. Wimp, you can't do anything. What's wrong with you? That's right, take the easy way out.

Molly continued, "You are not responsible for being asthmatic. This isn't something you can fake or control. Your bronchial tubes are hypersensitive. They perceive danger where there isn't any and close up to protect you. You can't will them to be different. You have an overly vigilant defense mechanism with a hair-trigger response to many everyday allergens, and you can't ignore that anymore."

"Everyone else does just fine without meds. I'll be giving in if I take them."

"Giving in to what?"

"To my weakness."

"No, you'll be acting like a responsible adult. You'll be recognizing your limitations instead of denying them. You'll be taking care of yourself, instead of acting like a child and pretending that the problem will go away if you ignore it."

I wanted to row: Molly had me, and she knew it. Now I sighed, "Okay, what do I have to do?"

She smiled and held out her hand. "Give me back that paper. I'll get you on Dr. Jokel's schedule so he can get you started on daily medication. Ginny, I promise you will be all right."

Molly hugged me. She was not a small woman, and she didn't scrimp on the care or affection she bestowed on her charges. Her body felt soft, yet her words were strong. I didn't believe I could be okay, but I knew I had to trust her. For me, that was an unfamiliar feeling, confusing and unsettling.

Breathing is so basic. A normal person doesn't have to devote conscious thought to inhaling and exhaling. A normal person can rely on her lungs to do their job, allowing her to focus on the world beyond. But my body was an unreliable partner.

I had tried to bully my way through my asthma. That had always worked before, with everything: just keep going and no one will notice. But someone noticed this time. Someone stood up for me. Molly saw that I needed help, and she threw me a buoy. I grabbed it and hung on.

8

I took medication every day, twice a day, and still ended up in the emergency room a couple more times. I developed mononucleosis, too, and missed more training in the winter. Good old Anne Warner wasted no time in early February sharing her prediction with me: "You'll never make varsity this year."

There's a black-and-white photograph of the 1977 Sprints-winning Yale women's varsity eight, right after the end of the race. The stroke has left her seat and is standing with her back to the coxswain, facing her teammates who normally see only her back: Olympic stoic Anne Warner. Her feet precariously balanced on the boat's gunnels, she towers over me. I am sitting directly in front of her at her feet. To reach me, she has climbed over four rowers and now clasps me by the shoulders, caught forever in the careless glee of victory. I am returning the embrace, reaching for her with the same sense of unmitigated joy.

That photo likely captured the only time Anne and I smiled at each other that entire year. Anne was tough on me, no question. And no question, I deserved it.

Everyone knew I was abrasive, obnoxious, and brash. No one, not even I, knew I was timid, anxious, and afraid. I had never won anything big. Nothing. Suddenly, I was a champion, best in the Ivy League, a member of the fastest crew at a major regatta. I had helped something good happen.

We landed at the awards dock, proudly received our medals, and gave our coxswain the traditional victory toss into the lake, but the best moment was standing in a huddle with my teammates after the victory ceremony. The taste of closeness derived from shared success, not suffering. For once, caring enough to go the distance worked. I had learned how to pull, if not quite for myself, for my teammates. I was still unsure whether I deserved to win, but I knew for certain they did. I had become a team player, in spite of my external attitude and my internal disarray.

A month after our Sprints victory, in late June, thirty women rowers from all over the country converged on Madison, Wisconsin. Jay Mimier, the women's coach at the University of Wisconsin and the head National Team coach for the women, had invited us to participate in the selection camp. Four Yalies, including me, were vying for a seat on the US National Rowing Team. Nat also joined us; Jay asked him to serve as an assistant coach during the camp.

One coxswain and ten rowers—an eight and two spares—would be named to the National Team at the end of the monthlong process. That team would travel to Amsterdam, Holland, to compete in the 1977 World Rowing Championships in August.

I was finally taking the first step to realize my dream of Olympic stardom.

Madison summers were hot and humid. Thunderstorms frequently rolled in across the wide and often wild Lake Mendota in the late afternoons, chasing our boats off the water and shortening our afternoon practices. I welcomed the weather only because there were so few other opportunities to escape the heat. The lake water was so warm that swimming felt like bobbing in a bathtub, and the only place that offered sustained air conditioning was the movie theater. The lack of cooling doomed everyone to a near-constant state of sweating. Our rowing clothes, perpetually damp, disintegrated into moldy threads.

The entire point of a selection process, irrespective of the program's competitive level, is to determine the combination of rowers who together will best move a shell down the race course. Coaches consider rowing technique, power application, physical fitness, raw strength, and mental toughness in matching athletes and composing lineups.

They devise various challenges to identify individual strengths and weaknesses, both on and off the water.

Practices were scheduled twice a day: in early mornings before the wind kicked up and disrupted the sunrise gleam of perfectly flat water, and in late afternoons, which often took place on land or were cut short by the bad weather. Regardless, we rowed six days a week, with Sundays off, usually cramming in eleven or twelve practices.

I was eager to prove myself to Jay, but as the weeks ground on, my confidence diminished. The selection camp differed radically from the atmosphere of college, and I was not ready to rely solely on myself or to fight only for myself.

College athletics centers on a team experience. Of course, there are dog-eat-dog aspects of competition: my team certainly had our share. But those weren't the only moments or even the defining ones. We all knew we were stuck with each other as long as we rowed. We were part of each other's experience, and we came to rely on each other for inspiration, consolation, and honest appraisal. We were each other's cheerleaders, even if we didn't all like each other so much. Besides, our bond had extended beyond our on-water experiences to our lives beyond the boathouse. Many of us weren't merely rowing buddies anymore, but friends. And finally, we had endured difficult experiences together, character-forging moments that required us to stand together in order to move forward.

I was not prepared for the dearth of camaraderie that characterizes the National Team selection process, or for the psychological demands of that process. Emotionally, I wasn't equipped to stand on my own two feet, to cheer myself on, to quell my private doubts, to reinvigorate my resolve, to discern what to focus on, or decide what to ignore. I hadn't realized the powers of persuasion my Yale Women's Crew sisterhood wielded when it came to muting my private demons.

It wasn't that my fellow National Team aspirants were unpleasant. They just didn't care about me or the team. They weren't behaving callously or selfishly; they weren't rude or careless. They knew how to get along without going deep or getting weepy. They focused on the job they were there to tackle: competing against everyone else to win a seat. Pure and simple. They had to survive the selection process; then teamwork would matter.

Without sufficient emotional grounding, lacking a determined "I'm a top dog" belief in myself, the question of my physical prowess ended up moot. All the cardiovascular fitness and muscular strength in the world couldn't help me. Scaling the heights to greatness is impossible without a foundation of internal solidity. I needed mental toughness as much as I needed lung power and leg strength.

The Yale Women's Crew had supplied me with a ready-made structure of support, a community I could be part of, learn from, and lean on. I had not yet realized I was missing a piece of the competitive puzzle. My inner voice knew how to prepare me for the next disaster, but it wasn't used to cheerleading. Usually galvanized into action by fear of the future, I had no experience with positive thinking. My ignorance cost me.

A few days before making his final selection, Jay scheduled an afternoon run of several miles in lieu of going on the water. The course was an out-and-back romp along the lakeshore. The group set out and remained bunched together for the first half of the run. Once we turned around and headed for home, everyone knew the distance that remained. The pace picked up and the group stretched out into a long strand of individual runners. Jay loped along the course with the slower runners, lagging behind as the end approached. As we came into the last half mile or so, he pulled alongside me.

"Come on, let's see what you can do." He puffed the words out between short breaths. Of course, I picked up my pace to match his, determined to stay ahead. "You better beat him; otherwise it's all over," I thought.

I started to sprint the last bit, keeping up with him, pushing to make sure I would take him.

"I can't do it. My quads are burning. I'm running as fast as I can. I'm just too slow," I said to myself.

No other internal voice piped up to challenge me. The kick-ass, show-me voice that spoke so loudly and authoritatively during practices vanished in my moment of need, silenced by the pressure to prove myself to an outsider, one who didn't have a stake in my success and who just wanted to see what I could do. I translated that neutral stance into a negative, believing that Jay wanted me to fail, instead of hearing his challenge as an invitation to show him how great I could be. That mental lapse cost me. Just like that, my sprint died. Jay passed me and left me in his disgusted dust.

The end of my first National Team tryout came with no surprises. No one wants a quitter. Before Jay announced the final set of cuts, I already knew I wouldn't make the team.

A day or two after the lakeside run, he posted the list of athletes comprising the 1977 US Women's National Team eight. Of the four Yalies who'd spent the better part of the summer sweating through the selection process, just one earned a spot—Anne Boucher, who had been a mere freshman the previous year. Forget the fact that she had rowed in high school with a rowing résumé twice as long as my meager two years; she was a more seasoned athlete in nearly every dimension, calmer and more confident, stronger, better technically, and apparently unflappable. But, still, I wasn't prepared for the wallop of disappointment and the internal turbulence that began battering me immediately.

I stood at the boathouse door, staring at the list of ten names. Mine was absent. I felt a flush of heat rush to my face and my eyes flood with water. I swallowed hard and blinked my eyes rapidly to tamp down my reaction—"You got what you deserved."

I returned to the rowers' group house to pack up. I just wanted to slink away without a trace, evaporate from the scene like morning dew. Unfortunately, my exit was more like scared sweat drying on a dress shirt, marked by stained ovals of perspiration and animal stink.

Loser!

Bouche came in while I was packing. She stood in the doorway and hesitated before speaking. I glanced up at her and then away, studiously focused on my task. "I'm sorry you didn't make it," she said.

Yeah, sure. I hated her, yet I had to say something that would not alienate her forever. She was my college teammate. We had a life together beyond the confines of this dreadful National Team camp, and I had to do my part to preserve our relationship.

I could only speak gruffly, in short bursts, "Yeah. Well. That's how it goes." I sounded so angry, as if it were her fault. I knew it wasn't, that she shouldn't have done anything different. It was ridiculous to expect her not to be a better rower than I was or to give up her seat for me. Winning required someone to lose; that equation is a fundamental law of sports. This was my first up-close and oh-so-personal lesson, and there was no place to hide.

Bouche was only the first person I wished to avoid. News of my failure was not a private tidbit I could stuff in a drawer and unfold when and how it suited me. Anyone who cared about the composition of the US women's rowing team would learn I wasn't on the roster. The rest of my college team would hear. I would have to tell my family; they knew where I'd been all summer. I had no control over my image, no way to package myself as a success. Everyone in my world would know I wasn't good enough. My inferiority was now unavoidably public.

"You'll never be good enough," I said to myself. I shuffled around my small, humid bedroom, stuffing everything together willy-nilly into my suitcase. And I finally said to Bouche, "I hope you guys have a great time, and go really fast." I couldn't come up with a sentence that included "congratulations," so stingy was I in my rage with Bouche and with myself.

"Thanks," Bouche replied. She sounded like someone had died. We had never negotiated this unmapped territory. She had to figure out what to say to someone she'd just beaten out, who'd been summarily cut, essentially exposed as insufficiently qualified, not up to National Team snuff. "Tough shit, eat my dust" wasn't the right expression of compassion. Of course, she was happy to have come out on top. She'd accomplished what she'd set out to do. Possibly she'd have chosen me as a teammate if she'd been in charge, but maybe not. This was a true zero-sum game. Some folks won and got to go on; most lost and had to go home.

Years would pass before I appreciated the courage of any aspirant, regardless of endeavor, who is willing to put herself on the line and take a public, steeply down-sided risk. Without people willing to subject themselves to public measurement, no competition could ever take place. Many more of us lose than win. The grace of all these people is what makes sporting events possible. Losers create the conditions for winning. Yet the myth is that only winning holds value.

The silence between us grew from awkward to unbearable.

"Do you know how long you'll stay here before you head over to Amsterdam?" I asked as I glanced up at her quickly. As I kept packing, I saw her dark brows folding toward each other. There was no trace of a smirk, not even a smile, only concern and uncertainty from someone who by all rights could be dancing on the rooftops and singing that a dream of hers had just come true.

"No, not yet. I guess we'll hear all about that this afternoon at practice, or maybe tomorrow."

We had traversed the hardest part of the conversation. I didn't break down in humiliated tears, and Bouche didn't succumb to a glimmer of a gloat. Her decency was more magnanimous than my fury, which was sliding into despair. I kept my voice gruff to avoid tears and to stop my anger from wrestling free.

"Well, good luck. I'll see you when school starts again after Worlds."

"Yeah, sure. Have a safe drive back," Bouche said as she turned and left my doorway.

As I heard her step away, I called after her, half-heartedly. "Hey. Congratulations."

Bouche flew to Amsterdam with the US team and I flew to Stockholm for a reunion with Mom and her extended family. Peggy was turning twenty-one and my mother's baby brother, my uncle Bo, was newly forty, so aunts, uncles, cousins, and the four of us American kids congregated to celebrate on the island of Furusund, one of the many that make up the archipelago along Sweden's southeast coast. Bo and his family had a summer cottage there, remote and peaceful, on a slice of high bank waterfront that offered a stunning view of nearby islands and easy swimming access to the pristine and chilly waters of the Baltic Sea.

A week of midnight suns couldn't blind me to my mother's drinking, however, and my trip ended in embarrassment and rage. Just like the long summer days, Mom's drinking hours monopolized much of the twenty-four-hour cycle. No one could ignore her disheveled appearance, constant slurring, and unsteadiness. Nonetheless, she tolerated no discussion of her behavior, not from her siblings, and certainly not from her children.

On our last morning together, as I said good-bye, I couldn't contain myself. "I can't stand being around you when you drink," I said.

"What are you talking about?" Even in denial, she couldn't stop her words from running into each other as she tried to control her speech.

"I don't want to see you again until you stop drinking. I can't stand this."

"I'm fine. Just fine." She couldn't look into my eyes as her head wobbled on her neck. It was well before noon.

"I hate you! I don't ever want to see you again."

"Ginny." She reached out for my arm, but I stepped out of reach.

"I mean it. Leave me alone." I left the cottage and got in the car with my uncle to drive to the airport. Can't she just die? Get her out of my life. I'm sick of this. Yet beneath the rage, my fear rampaged. Could I end up like her? Could I end up hating myself like I hated her? I didn't know the answers, but I knew I had to keep my distance.

Meanwhile, the US crew that I had not qualified for finished DFL—dead fucking last—at the World Championships in Amsterdam. How embarrassing. I couldn't land a seat on a dead-slow crew. Double failure.

There was only one thing to do: keep training. Harder, better, more. I pressed the pause button on my classes for the fall semester, which allowed me the luxury of a singular focus, at least regarding juggling academics and rowing. My anger at my mom didn't dissipate, nor was it helped when I received a card from her with a single sentence scrawled in her illegible handwriting: "The door is open from this side."

I fumed at her card. She hadn't shut any door! Of course, she would ignore the one step she could take to open the door I had slammed: quit drinking. I bristled at her stance as a helpless victim suffering my unjust anger. As far as she was concerned, if only I could calm down, we could resume our relationship. As far as I was concerned, I couldn't risk allowing her back into my life. I ripped up the card and kept my distance.

My college years were flying by. I had already passed the halfway mark, yet felt far from ready for the real world. I decided to take the fall term off from school, but live off campus, get a job, and continue training with my crew.

My decision allowed me to focus solely on training for four months, which was good timing. The new academic year brought more challenge on the water, as now Anne Warner had graduated. We had no more Olympians, but we had Bouche, a newly crowned National Team member and only a sophomore. She was younger, stronger, more experienced, and more accomplished than I. She was fabulous. She wasn't cocky, didn't brag, was a model teammate, worked hard, and didn't rub anyone's nose in her superiority. I dreamed of crushing her.

Seven varsity rowers had returned from the Sprints-winning crew. We intended to repeat our previous year's performance and go undefeated and triumph at the Sprints again. Also, we would attend the National Women's Rowing Association (NWRA) National Championships for the first time. We planned to win those, too—a tougher challenge, as the elite eight race would include club crews, not just college programs. All the post-college National Team aspirants trained at those clubs. The prospect of pitting ourselves against the top competitors in the country gave me added training motivation.

Not that I needed more. This year I intended to transfer my crew's streak of success to my individual performance. I was determined my name would not be missing from a National Team list again.

The 1978 World Championships were scheduled for the late fall in New Zealand, instead of late summer in Northern Europe, so attending the selection camp would mean missing a semester of school without any guarantee of making the team. As many National Team aspirants were in college, the US Olympic Rowing Committee decided to fund a summer program for a select number of athletes. A European tour would provide international racing experience to a group of rowers viewed as Olympic potentials: the selection process for that tour would immediately follow the National Championships, scheduled for mid-June in Seattle.

The US Olympic Committee named Nat Case the sole selector and coach. His mandate was to choose athletes who possessed the potential to make the US Olympic team two years hence and then accompany the team to Europe and prepare them to race against many of the world's best.

Abbreviated and completely subjective, the selection process would involve no seat racing, an on-the-water tool that allows direct comparison of two individual rowers' boat-moving abilities. The invitation-only tryouts would last less than a week. The compressed timeline allowed Nat less than a dozen practices to sort out the top collegiate athletes who would most benefit from the European Tour experience, while optimizing the United States' chances to win medals at the Moscow Olympics in two years.

Despite the drawbacks of its selection process, I decided to compete for a spot on the European Tour. Trying out for the New Zealand team seemed too risky, as I would have to skip another semester of school, win or lose. The summer camp represented my best chance for breaking into the top tier of women rowers and establishing myself as an up-and-comer.

I kicked into a new gear and worked hard the entire collegiate season. I added in double workouts throughout the winter, lifting weights many mornings and packing in massive quantities of endurance-building workouts in the afternoons. I stayed healthy, took my meds, avoided the emergency room, grew stronger, and improved my fitness.

Not only that, life started looking up on dry land as well. After two years, thanks both to rowing and the natural process of growing up, I had not only learned to pull hard, but found my place on campus, too. My sense of belonging on the women's crew gave me sufficient confidence to explore life beyond the boathouse. Many of my friends were rowers, of course, but some weren't. I maintained my friendship with David, who lived off campus in the University Towers apartment building beyond Chapel Street, where Route 34 segued into Frontage Street. I often tramped to his place to enjoy homemade suppers, bringing a pair of pints of Häagen-Dazs ice cream for dessert and listening to his never-ending tales of woe. Either he was flunking one of his classes because the work was too boring to finish, or he didn't like the professor, or he was dying of loneliness because the boyfriend pickings were too sparse for his tastes, or he just had to tell me about the new guy he'd met in a bar and what had happened next.

Besides making me laugh, David's stories offered me glimpses of a life that traveled along a different dimension than mine, and I often felt thankful to be spared the struggles he contended with as a gay man. We didn't discuss his fears about the world's view of his homosexuality, but in his own way, he tried to maintain a low profile, dreading the embarrassment that could come as a result of people knowing too much about him. Of course, that proved a challenge for someone who prided himself on expressing his individuality, who sought attention and loved to worm his way into the center of a room, whose flamboyant behavior—raspy and loud voice, booming laugh, flirtatious charm that worked magic on both women and men—marked him as note-worthy. Besides, his consistently well-coifed appearance and elegant, slightly effeminate mannerisms branded him as gay to anyone who was at all astute in that regard. Still, David maintained his own boundaries, steering clear of the on-campus gay organizations and avoiding any public affiliation with the gay rights movement.

Nonetheless, privately, he was so calm about his gayness and never questioned or decried it. David didn't simply restrain from self-deni-gration; he accepted himself without question, without a shred of self-hatred. No denial, no guilt, he knew he was different, but special, too. I wondered how he could live in the world as such an obvious outlier and not absorb its assessment that there was something fundamentally, irretrievably wrong with him.

While David may have thought he was closeted in public, to me he was fully out, not just in private. His truth was impossible to hide, given his personality, and I admired him. Although he may have dis-puted that he was living out and proud, he was. Doing so demanded a level of courage and self-acceptance that, while I marveled at it from a distance, I knew I would never successfully muster. I had no problem associating with David; he was a good friend, loyal, affectionate, bit-ingly intelligent, and funny, but I thanked my lucky stars I didn't have to walk in his shoes.

As my social life developed, I even found a boyfriend. He was on the heavyweight men's team, but he wasn't a rower: he was the var-sity coxswain, a swarthy, scrawny guy who starved himself to drop his weight below a hundred twenty pounds and maintain an ideal phy-sique for the racing season. No crew wants to carry any excess weight above the minimum anchor that a coxswain represents. He was a sprite of a guy, but he seemed to like me and swaggered as if he'd hooked a hot girlfriend. For the first time, I had my very own cheerleader; he grew close enough to me to hear some of my witheringly negative self-talk and cared enough to challenge some of the claptrap he heard.

By university policy, I had to move off campus when I didn't en-roll for fall semester. I took a one-bedroom apartment on the ground floor of a two-story house on the corner of Dwight and Elm Streets, three blocks from the Yale gym. I decorated the two rooms to suit my preferences and learned to cook. I read *Diet for a Small Planet*, which entranced me with its thesis on the inherent inefficiencies of consuming animal protein. I swore off meat, became a vegetarian, and spent countless happy hours learning to cook and bake. Many loaves of bread proved more useful as doorstops than sandwich fodder, but I could whip up a mean carrot cake. Lisa, my best friend from Dana Hall and now at Yale, moved in upstairs with her boyfriend, giving me the equivalent of dorm life without the hassle of a roommate.

My mother, looking for a way to return to my good graces and nervous about my living off campus in a shaky neighborhood, insisted on buying a dog for me—despite my severe allergy to animal hair and my lack of enthusiasm for her solution to a problem I regarded as nonexistent. Nonetheless, when the German shepherd puppy arrived all the way from Washington State, I picked him up at the airport. He wriggled his soft, furry body against me when I put him in the car and lay beside me for the drive home, nosing my leg and panting quietly. By the time we got home, I was sold on him. I gave him my favorite name, Max, and he, in turn, with his spirited personality and relentless affection, set me on the path to reconciliation with my mother. Feeling angry and grateful simultaneously was impossible; I couldn't help but appreciate how Max had come into my life and the difference he had made.

At the end of the winter, as the ice broke up on the Housatonic and the end of our grueling indoor workouts beckoned, I steeled myself for my next leap of faith. I had kept my mouth shut long enough: now I had to come clean to my coach.

It was late afternoon at the gym. Most of my teammates had finished their workouts and headed for the showers. My tank workout had just ended.

"Nat, can I talk to you?" I asked. He was leaning against the railing, baseball cap pushed up high on his forehead, watching the day's final tank session. He turned in my direction without shifting his attention.

"Yeah, sure."

I swallowed hard. "Hey, I wanted to tell you. I'm going to try out for the European Tour."

Nat straightened up and looked at me directly. I felt the heat of his sudden stare and made myself keep going. "I've decided to train for the Olympics."

He looked down at the floor, rocked back on his heels, and plunged his hands into his pockets. Milliseconds stretched beyond their limits. My heart pounded in the silence and seemed to crawl up my throat.

"Ginny, you're a good college athlete on a strong crew. That doesn't mean you have what it takes to be an Olympian."

The punch in my stomach had come as predicted, but I was still unprepared for the pain. I flinched on the inside, but maintained my tough stance on the outside. My anger flamed to the surface, rescuing me. "Oh, come on. Look how much progress I've made this year."

"Yes, but this is just one program. There are strong programs all over the country. Rowers who have trained longer than you, who are taller and heavier than you . . ."

His voice trailed off, as if he knew he'd said enough. But he hadn't. I had hesitated to confess my dream because I'd feared exactly this scenario, but I was still shocked. "Are you kidding me? I've done every workout you posted, and more! My erg scores have been competitive with Bouche and Cathy. What do I have to do to show you I can be good enough?"

Nat shrugged. He looked at me steadily. I saw something like certainty flash across his face. He crossed his arms. "Ginny, you're not cut out for the Olympics."

I could feel my perspective already shifting to accept his version of reality, to concede the inevitable outcome of my falling short. He says I'm not good enough. I cut off the conversation and made my escape. I was embarrassed and crushed. My own coach thought so little of me. How foolish I had just looked, confessing to wanting something that was permanently out of reach. My dreams were too big for me.

I headed home in the late winter twilight, a hint of spring nudging the chill. My trudge turned into a stomp as I gained distance from Nat. What the hell does he know? He was another naysayer asserting his judgment and experience over my desire, confusing his opinion for fact, and invoking his view of the present to justify his version of the future. To Nat, I was an average rower on a terrific college crew. Certainly I was an above-average rower compared to the national pool of women rowers in the late 1970s, but Nat was spoiled by the talent that flooded his varsity. He could nod his head from the stern to the bow of his top eight at rowers who could reasonably contend for a National Team berth.

All things considered, he had responded predictably. He worried more about the size of his rowers' heads than the size of their hearts. He believed in tearing down to inspire and motivate. The concept of building confidence to bolster physical capacity never occurred to him.

One could think I would have understood that his world outlook mirrored my own. Minimize the positive. Overstress the negative, focus on the risks, and work like hell to keep them from manifesting. Focus on the downside; ignore the upside. Prepare for the unlikely disaster. A glass half empty didn't adequately capture his bleak outlook; it was more like glass badly cracked and leaking steadily.

Inside, I did understand, all too well. Nat's skepticism found a ready internal proponent. He could be right. He is the coach after all.

Here I was again, me against myself.

Not good enough: I'd heard it so many times before from Nat. From my father. Rowing for Nat and hoping for encouragement was like searching for an oasis in the desert, and it was just the same with my dad. Of course he meant to show his support; he attended his share of races, in fair weather and worse. But his incessant needling, intended as humor, landed flat and hurt. Every time he proclaimed, "Rowing isn't really a sport," I bristled, stung by the vote of no-confidence I heard in his tone.

I shook my head to shake out my coach's bullshit. I was going to have to do this myself.

But it's awfully lonely to nudge a dream forward by yourself. If only someone would bet on me instead of against me, I was sure it would all be different.

9

The winter ice finally cracked and flowed over the dam in Derby, and spring ushered in the best time of year: racing. The Yale Women's Crew had a great season, and ostensibly I did, too. Unaccompanied by any announcement or discussion, Nat seated me as the varsity's stroke. He had to re-rig the boat to do it, as port rowers more commonly stroke and I rowed starboard. Stroking was a huge honor, a sizable responsibility, and an acknowledgment of my progress. I had reached the pinnacle of the varsity, but Nat's expressed doubt about my Olympic dreams confused me and made me question the honor. What was he thinking? I'm not stroke material.

The stroke is the leader of the crew, on the water and off. Everyone follows her. She sets the cadence in the boat and the mood on shore. The coxswain strategizes with her, absorbs her staccato comments huffed out during pieces, and translates them into technical directions and tactical adjustments for the rest of the crew.

A good stroke hauls self-confidence to the brink of arrogance. She believes in herself. She drips assuredness like an oar sheds water. She speaks authoritatively and commands her crew's respect. Her assumption of leadership is critical if a crew is to excel. She needs to view herself as deserving of this distinguished role, as special, and maybe a tiny bit superior. Along with controlling her crew's cadence, she establishes the odds for success. A good stroke needs to exude strength. Her teammates count on her toughness if the chips are down, adopting her mental stance as they follow her stroke. They rely on her to do whatever it takes to win and will do their best to back her up.

A poor crew will outperform if they have a good stroke; an excellent crew will underperform without one. With a good stroke, a crew can move mountains; without her, they're dead in the water.

Technically, I was a passable stroke, but beyond that I believed I was abysmal. I lacked confidence. I was afraid of losing and of disappointing everyone. I was afraid of our coxswain, Joyce Frocks, whose great sense of humor was biting and precise. Instead of relaxing into her style and joining the fun, I bristled when she focused her pointed, disparaging humor at me. Her comments pierced my brusque exterior and wounded me, but I couldn't admit that and didn't know how to parry with humor of my own. I didn't know how to give and take, to allow people room to disagree without trying to win them over. I knew how to be tough, to work extremely hard, but I didn't know how to ignore or downplay my internal doubts; they had me by the throat. In short, I lacked the mental tenacity required of a good stroke.

Despite my private concerns, our crew went undefeated the entire regular season. I attributed our success to the freight train behind me, whose powerful engine compensated for my lack of leadership in dual races against poor competition. Meanwhile, my confidence ebbed to the point that I longed for relief from stroking.

We came into the Eastern Sprints seeded first and the clear favorites. We had raced and defeated every varsity crew entrant, except one: Wisconsin. We were poised to reclaim our varsity eight title.

Unfortunately, the weather intervened. The wide open waters of Lake Onondaga northeast of Syracuse, New York, the site of the Sprints regatta, turned into a churning sea late in the morning on race day, thanks to gale force winds. Rain drenched and froze competitors. Waves washed over riggers. Boats flooded and sank. The howling storm forced everyone ashore, leaving no option but to cancel the regatta.

Eager to dredge some victory from the cancellation, Nat and Jay Mimier agreed that Yale and the University of Wisconsin would meet early the next morning and race for the unofficial title of Eastern Sprints Champion. We spent an extra night in Syracuse in our dumpy motel and sullenly sat through our banquet—during which I received the first-ever Anne Warner award for leadership.

Early the next morning, under the cover of low gray clouds and greeted by perfectly flat water, we squared off against the Wisco women. I stroked my crew to its last victory of the season. No crowds cheered us on; no victory platform awaited us; no medals were draped around our necks; no trophies were awarded to our coach.

More disappointment followed. Our varsity eight headed west to compete in the NWRA Nationals, sited in Seattle. We stopped in Wisconsin to race the Wisco women one more time—and lost, breaking our two-year string of victories. It was only the varsity's second dual race loss in three seasons, and the proof I had long expected of my unsuitability as stroke. We continued to Seattle with our confidence shaken. We raced in the Championship Eight event on rotund Green Lake and made the finals, but struggled from there. In our last race, we finished an undistinguished fifth, hardly the glorious season-ending performance we had envisioned.

We had lost our Olympian stroke when Anne Warner graduated and I was her replacement. That was the only substantive change in the lineup from the previous year, when we had won everything. I knew the truth about the woman in Yale's stroke seat, even if no one else did. She may have been good enough to lead her crew to an undefeated regular season, but she was unreliable in the big moment. She wasn't up to the job of leading anyone to a national championship.

The internal battle raged on.

By the end of my junior year, I had learned to trust Molly Meyer with my health. I had taken a leap of faith and capitulated completely, no halfway compliance. For nearly two years, I'd stuck to her prescribed regimen of twice-daily pills and bronchodilators before exercise, ignoring the putdowns and warnings I heard screeching within every time I swallowed or puffed. My asthma had become manageable. I had completed winter training without succumbing to illness. I hadn't missed a race all season.

A month later in Seattle, I discovered exactly how little I could trust Nat Case with my dream. I had followed his instructions for nearly three years. I learned to push myself beyond reasonable. I didn't merely suffer through his punishing workouts, but attacked them. I was a fighter. I had become one of his top rowers, despite my internal doubts. And none of it mattered. Directly following the end of the Nationals, Nat convened the camp to select the European Tour squad. He ran the process as advertised, short and subjective. On the afternoon he posted the names of athletes who would represent the United States during the European Tour, I gathered around the list with the other hopefuls and waited for a clear view. My name was absent.

I went in search of Nat, forcing down my tears as my protest worked its way up. I found him fiddling with a rigger in the boathouse, hiding from the rowers.

"Why didn't you choose me? I was the best rower on our squad this year!"

His eyes were hooded under his baseball hat. "Ginny, you did a fine job for Yale. But that's not what this trip is about. It's my job to identify rowers who have Olympic potential."

"You starboard-stroked the boat so I could lead the crew, and now you're telling me I'm not good enough to become an Olympian?"

Nat shook his head. "Ginny, you're just too small. You'll never make an Olympic team."

"So you're taking Cathy Pew because she's bigger than I am?"

"I'm taking Cathy Pew because she has more potential." He paused. I wanted to kill him.

"Yeah, well, what's potential if it never delivers? How long are you gonna wait for that potential to become potent? You know I'm better than Cathy."

Nat said nothing, shaking his head.

He was the coach. The decision was his. He'd made it in character, betting on brawn, hedging against heart.

And he was right about Cathy's size. At six feet, she towered over me by five inches. Those extra inches translated into a longer stroke through the water, which meant more time to apply power to the oar and move the boat. With longer arms and legs came more opportunity to build muscle mass. She would be able to pack more muscle onto her body. She did have more physical potential.

For Nat, that potential would always be worth more than my actual performance.

"Wow," I said. "Some coach. Thanks a lot. I'm never rowing for you again. You can go to hell!" I turned around and walked out. No crying in front of him.

My own coach had thrown me aside. I got the message, loud and clear: give up your dream now, 'cause it's too big for you.

I left Seattle dejected and flew back across the country. I had sworn off ever rowing for Nat again, but I couldn't leave my sport. I ended up spending the summer in New Haven, driving to Derby early most mornings, taking out a single, and learning how to scull by myself. It was my first taste of rowing as a solitary endeavor.

I started running seriously too, working up to half-marathon distances. Visiting my mother in East Hampton, Long Island, I often woke early and launched my runs before sunrise to beat the heat. Loyal Max often accompanied me, but he also regularly cut his run short as the sun rose and the pavement heated up, and found his way along alien back roads to my mother's rental. Mom would grumble when I returned home later, sweat-soaked, red-faced, and exhausted. "That dog is smarter than you. At least he knows when to stop."

The European Tour ended in late summer and Nat returned to coach at Yale. And, of course, I rowed for him again. While the World Rowing Championships unfolded down under in New Zealand on Lake Karapiro, the Yale Women's Crew headed into its last full year with the class of '79 dominating the varsity boat. Six of us were seniors now, five rowers and the coxswain. We were collectively determined now. We had agreed among ourselves: no one—not another crew or our negative coach—would deter us from an undefeated season, first place at the Eastern Sprints, the Collegiate National Championship, and the Elite Eight National Championship trophy.

And I was going to earn a spot on the National Team, once and for all, this year before the Olympics. The third time had to be the charm. The 1979 Worlds would be held in Bled, Yugoslavia, again in August; team tryouts would therefore take place in the summer, requiring no juggling of academic schedules. This time, a new coach was in charge: Kris Korzeniowski, a Polish émigré with a long résumé detailing international successes, who had just landed the head women's coaching position at Princeton University. The US Olympic Rowing Committee named him to serve as the US women's Olympic rowing coach. He would be in charge of the women's National Team in 1979 and 1980.

I knew nothing more about him, nor did I care to. It didn't matter who the coach was. I just had to be strong enough, tough enough, fit enough, dedicated, and persistent enough to make the team, pure and simple. There was nothing complicated about the challenge. It was not easy, but straightforward.

Nat relegated me to the three seat, a major step down from my stroke role of the previous year. Mary O'Connor, who'd been my seven seat the previous year, took over as stroke. She dove with authority into her leadership duties. Brimming with confidence, Mary was a great choice. She was easy to follow. She was unafraid to stand up to a confrontation if one arose. She knew how to assert herself without worrying about whether she came across as arrogant.

The Yale women's varsity achieved nearly all its aspirations over the course of our last season together. Undefeated season, check. Eastern Sprints champions, check. Collegiate National Champions, check. Elite Eight National Champions . . . not quite check: the Canadian National Team beat us, and so did a club crew, Vesper Boat Club, comprising several Olympic aspirants. Nearly thirty years would elapse before Yale would win another National Championship in the women's varsity eight event.

At graduation, Cathy Pew, the Yale Women's Crew captain for two years and my fellow varsity rower for our four years together, was recognized as the university's female athlete of the year, which every graduating member of the women's varsity crew reveled in and claimed partly for herself. But I didn't spend much time savoring my role in my class's terrific success on the water. I could boast four varsity letters, only two dual-race losses, and a Collegiate National Championship, but I had more important things to do and no time to waste enjoying my accomplishments or reflecting on the past. After all, there was no better way to cap a tremendous senior year of rowing victories than with the fulfillment of my dream to make the National Team. I was ready to exchange my wannabe status for the real deal, but I had no inkling of how well south of success I remained, and the twisted path ahead.

I started out pretty well. I garnered an invitation to attend camp. So did Mary and Bouche. I'd been there before and felt ready. I was two years older, two years tougher, fitter, more determined, and emotionally prepared.

However, so was everyone else. The pool of candidates had grown, the rowers all seemed taller and tougher, and everyone was generally fitter and stronger than the cast of characters from the 1977 team. The first day I surveyed the competition for starboard seats and wondered how I stacked up; I didn't notice that my precious confidence had already begun to dwindle.

To a northerner, Princeton is practically the south, especially in the summer. Weather conditions often paralleled Madison's 1977 summer—oppressive humidity broken by explosive storms that whipped the water into a fury. We rowed in steam-room conditions, minus the fog.

Beyond the weather, however, nothing resembled Madison. The dainty and confined Lake Carnegie, a mere three miles from end to end, acted more like a river. Barely two hundred meters of water separated its opposing banks. Princeton University's boathouse occupied one end, and the race course took up the other, separated by some gentlemanlike bends and one ornately decorated footbridge.

The Princeton atmosphere seemed too refined and straight-laced to permit anything as chaotic as a raging thunderstorm to chase its rowers off the water. Stately homes lined the lakeshore. The setting seemed a fancy location for a National Team selection process, but its elegance disappeared soon enough in the camp's intensity.

I kept my hopes up through the entire camp. I rowed hard, maintained my focus, and tried to behave. I attempted to contain my emotions, not to show anger, seem desperate, or exude cockiness. I tried to keep my cool, retain an air of detached interest, suppress my eagerness, downplay my excitement; and treat people with friendly, if distant, respect. This was a tall order under the best of circumstances, but I was on my best behavior.

I don't recall how many athletes attended the selection camp, when it started, how long it lasted, or when cuts were made. In the waning days of camp, Kris Korzeniowski seat-raced me against a newcomer to the National Team selection process, a newly minted UCLA graduate named Carol Bower. Seat racing involves racing two crews, side by side, usually in four oared shells, then pulling the boats together on the water and switching one person from one boat with one from the other, and racing again. The difference in winning margins between the two races determines which person, of the two who were switched, is the more effective boat-mover.

Carol was a National Team wannabe novice; I was an expert. Surely I should've walloped her. We raced in fours. I lost, perhaps narrowly, perhaps by open water; all I remember is that I lost. He didn't race me against anybody else, so I kept my hopes up. After all, one lousy loss was merely a single, isolated instance, not a pattern or proof of anything.

A couple of days later, Kris announced the cuts. I hadn't made the team.

Walking down the path away from the boathouse, steaming in the hot sun, I heaved my empty water bottle into the bushes. Goddammit! How could he cut me on the basis of one simple race?

I sought Kris out and forced a conversation with him. He spoke with a thick Polish accent but had no trouble making himself crystal clear. "Carol Bower beat you," he said.

"Yes, but I didn't race Bouche. Why didn't you give me a chance against her?"

Kris stared at me, squinting slightly as if he didn't quite understand. "Bouche? She will just be a spare. You want to race her so you can be a spare?"

"Yeah, you should've raced me. It's not fair. I could've beaten her."

"You want now a chance to race her? You can race tomorrow if you want. We will do ergometer tests."

Now I was staring at Kris.

What do I do now? Do I take the chance? What if I blow it?

Silence.

Not one cheerleading voice spoke up to parry my sudden gutlessness.

No one said, "No guts, no glory."

No one said, "Finally, a fair chance, go for it! You can do it!"

No one piped up, reminding me, "Think how hard you've worked, how much you want this."

Not even me.

Kris was looking directly at me, his hands well apart and raised around his chest, palms upward in a slight shrug as if to say, "It doesn't matter to me who the spare is. She will not be racing."

I turned my hands over and looked at my palms, rampant with running sores and cracked blisters oozing watery serum. They hurt. Exhausted and worn down by the weeks-long selection camp, I'd not bargained for a chance or a choice. I'd sought Kris out to complain, to position myself as a wounded and cheated warrior. Instead, he'd turned the tables on me and given me an opportunity to claim a position on the team in a fair fight.

"Uh, I don't think I can do that," I responded slowly. "My hands are so ripped up, I don't think I could hold an oar long enough to finish an erg piece."

I heard my voice copping out. In disbelief, I saw myself turning away from a fight I'd longed for, one I'd actively sought out and worked for so long and so hard. I didn't recognize myself. I didn't know what was happening to me, that my fear of failure had overcome my desire to prove myself.

"Okay then," he said as he nodded at me. Our conversation was over. And so was my third consecutive attempt to make a National Team.

I O

My Yale racing career was over. My four years of eligibility had expired, even though I had one more term of college to complete. I no longer had the cover of college sports to obscure my training for the Olympics. I had no proof of progress with which to console or inspire myself. The real world of college graduation and employment beckoned. Time was running out on my dream of greatness.

Four years as a solidly successful varsity athlete on a superior college crew made no ripple in my thinking. Three years of rejection from three different National Team coaches, however, reverberated. Three hard-thrown, hard-to-ignore punches in the stomach: not good enough, not good enough, not good enough.

I couldn't get anyone to want me. I had convinced no one to take a risk on me. No one had discerned any flicker of something special to invest in and build on. I wasn't worth a leap of faith.

Yet, I couldn't stop myself. Last chance, last chance. The longing would not die quietly. The 1980 Olympics hovered on my horizon.

I started my final term in the autumn of 1979. All the varsity rowers from my senior class, now college graduates, chose to train in New Haven one last time for a shot at the Olympics. Sally Fisher, Elaine Mathies, and Cathy Pew rejoined Mary O'Connor, who had made Kris Korzeniowski's US team along with Bouche. Having successfully stroked our collegiate crew to a National Championship, Mary stroked the US eight and, sure enough, Bouche was sidelined as a spare. The eight won a bronze in Bled and returned home with visions of gold.

But Mary brought home more than her medal and a newfound confidence. "You really impressed Kris, Ginny," she told me one day at the Yale gym. "He thought you were really feisty. You should keep training."

"Really?"

"Yeah, you could make it. He loves spirited rowers."

What? I was shocked to learn that my bailing-out of the erg test he had offered hadn't torched my credibility. I didn't flunk that test of character after all.

My father thought it was ridiculous. Three strikes and you're out, as far as he was concerned. "It's time to grow up and enter the adult world," he said. "You'll be graduating in December. What about finding a job?"

"Dad, you don't understand! I want to make the National Team. I came so close last time."

"You've tried out three years in a row. The market's trying to tell you something. You're just not good enough." My father could read the writing on the wall, even if I wouldn't.

He'd been a good supporter for four years. Yes, he had jazzed me about rowing, applying his trademark teasing to test and toughen me, but he'd made his share of trips to Derby to stand on the dock and witness the last snippet of many victories. He'd taken my phone calls and listened to my reports of team victories and private failures. He had followed my story closely, but now he was ready to turn the page and move on.

To get him off my back, I told my father I would stop training. But I kept showing up at the boathouse and heading to the gym. The heart wants what the heart wants.

Morning lifting sessions joined afternoon rows, and soon double workouts framed my waking hours once again. As the semester wound down, I prepared for my final exams and completed my senior essay.

I broached the truth with my father shortly before coming home for the Christmas holidays: "Dad, I've decided to keep rowing. I have to try out for the Olympic team. It's just one more try. A few more months."

He sighed and said, "Well, as long as you can support yourself, I guess it's up to you." At least he knew enough not to waste his breath on a done deal.

I didn't relish the idea of staying in New Haven through one more winter, training in the steamy bowels of Payne Whitney. No matter. I organized every logistic to further my task of making the Olympic team. I tossed my newly minted BA certificate into a cardboard box, landed a menial job at Yale Medical School filling out grant application forms, and fed my training habit. I swallowed workouts like a whale gulps minnows. I welcomed the flow of physical challenges that defined my days, the twice-daily tide of workouts that washed away everything else.

In the four years since I had first learned to row and fallen hook, line, and sinker for my beloved sport, I had developed a prodigious appetite for the work involved. Instead of five to six weekly workouts, the number rose to ten, eleven, twelve, depending on the week. The quantity of total work multiplied, as each workout grew longer, with more exercises, more minutes, and more repetitions to complete.

I never had a chance to feel lonely as I submersed myself in the deep, narrow pursuit of rowing excellence. Every day I greeted Mary, Cathy, Bouche, Sally, and Elaine at the gym, just as I had for the past four years. Even though we were no longer training for the Yale team, we still regarded each other as teammates. Unspoken was the obvious truth that most of us wouldn't make the Olympic team. But that was for later, under the faraway cloud of the selection process, which would take place in Princeton again, starting in early May. We focused on the now: today's weight circuit, tank session, or stair run. The future would arrive soon enough. We had to be ready.

I had tried out three years in a row and ended up empty-seated every time. Any sane person would've acknowledged the obvious: it was time to give up and move on with life. But I never questioned the relevance or purpose of my goal. I just had to work harder, want it more, and prove myself tougher. Maybe I could make things happen. Maybe what I did would make a difference.

Just one more time, one more time. I know I can make it this time. I chanted encouragement to myself repeatedly, in spite of my exhaustion, my asthma attacks, and the writing on that damn wall.

Global geopolitics wreaked havoc on my dreams more fully than any coach. The Soviet Union invaded Afghanistan in the last week of 1979, ostensibly to support the country's prime minister, Hafizullah Amin, whose attempt to reduce the influence of Islam and introduce a more Western approach had triggered a civil war. Muslim leaders declared a jihad on him, joining the Mujahideen, a guerilla opposition group, to overthrow the Amin government.

The Soviets then proceeded to assassinate Prime Minister Amin, replacing him with Babrak Karmal, another local leader, but one who depended on the Russian military's support to maintain his position. Naturally, the Mujahideen weren't wildly enthusiastic about this arrangement either, but the Soviets claimed the Amin government had requested military aid to maintain its democratically elected hold on the country: they had simply selflessly responded to prevent the Afghan government's downfall at the hands of a terrorist group.

At any rate, the Mujahideen wanted their country back and generously extended their jihad to include the Soviet Union. Meanwhile, the United States, embroiled in the Cold War and dedicated to preventing the spread of communism, interpreted the Soviets' maneuvers as an invasion of Afghanistan with an end goal of transforming the country into another communist bulwark. Of course, the West could not allow another country to join the Communist Bloc.

American foreign policy was headed by a president ostensibly dedicated to peace, generally not a problematic concept, but Jimmy Carter was also struggling politically. Halting the spread of Communism was not the only issue his administration had on its plate. All was not copacetic on the country's domestic front. Going into an election year, Carter's presidency was marred by the US energy crisis and the long lines at gas stations, the Three Mile Island nuclear meltdown, rising unemployment, and inflation that exceeded 10 percent. The November 4 seizure of the US Embassy in Teheran added an international flavor to the pervasive scent of defeat wafting around the president. He could not risk further accusations of weakness.

Determined that no soldiers would die during his presidential tenure, when faced with out-and-out aggressive behavior by his number-one Cold War opponent, President Carter faced limited options to encourage the Soviets to do the right thing. What's a president to do when all military options are off the table?

Certainly, celebration was not the order of the day, so Carter chose the role of party pooper. He tried to cancel a world party, the one held every four years in the name of global peace. On January 20, 1980, he wrote a letter to the US Olympic Committee president, Robert Kane, advocating that if the Soviets did not withdraw from Afghanistan within a month, the USOC should petition the International Olympic Committee (IOC) to relocate the Olympic Games scheduled for late July in Moscow or cancel them.

The president publicized his position during his State of the Union Address on January 23: "And I have notified the Olympic Committee that with Soviet invading forces in Afghanistan, neither the American people nor I will support sending an Olympic team to Moscow." He set a deadline for the Soviets to withdraw: February 20.

Since the establishment of the modern Olympic movement in 1896, only World Wars I and II had succeeded in aborting the Games. Now the leader of the free world had determined that abrogating Olympic participation would somehow bolster the prospects for world peace.

That night, in one fell misguided swoop, Jimmy Carter single-handedly threatened the dreams of several thousand athletes around the globe. Over the next several months, he used the power of his office to destroy them. Not only did every American athlete lose a cherished opportunity to compete at the Games, but the US government successfully pressured allies and friends worldwide to join the boycott as well.

February 20 found me competing against Sally Fisher in the main stairwell of Payne Whitney, racing through our sets of chest-burning ascents.

"Why are we doing this?" I gasped at the end of one set. "The boycott is now official. The Soviets haven't withdrawn from Afghanistan."

"I know. But we have three more sets to finish." Sally turned to jog down the stairs. I followed her silently, saving my breath.

I didn't know about all the machinations occurring behind the scenes to try to save the Olympics. I knew the name Anita DeFrantz because she was a 1976 Olympic medalist, a member of the bronze-winning US women's eight; because she had earned a reputation in the women's rowing world as an unflinching and powerful competitor, and was a member of the National Team cadre of athletes who trained and raced out of Vesper Boat Club in Philadelphia; and because she rowed on the starboard side, like I did, and therefore was my direct competitor for one of the coveted eight starboard seats (four in the eight, two in the four, and two spares) that would be filled at the Olympic selection camp. In February, I knew nothing else about her, but by June, I would know much more.

A newly minted lawyer, Anita spearheaded an athletes' protest of President Carter's decision to boycott the Olympics. Obviously, the Soviet military would not be deterred from its geopolitical goals by an American president's facile sacrifice of a group of athletes. Not only that, the president's interference in the actions of private citizens represented a fundamental violation of democracy.

Finally, Carter's action threatened the Olympic movement, its role in promoting world peace, and its apolitical status, designed to operate independently of and beyond the control of world governments. The connections that occur when individual athletes meet and compete in harmony, and pursue a shared purpose on a world stage in full view of people from all over the globe who share in those moments and claim them for their own offer vivid examples of a world that, despite the vast differences and disagreements, can unite in a shared experience.

Politicizing the Games undermined their future, too, but the week after Carter's State of the Union announcement, the House and Senate passed resolutions to support the president's decision by overwhelming margins. On February 9, the IOC rejected the United States' request to change the venue for the Moscow Olympics or cancel the Games.

Even the improbable victory of the US men's hockey team over the Soviets in the medals round at the Winter Olympics in Lake Placid, New York, on February 22 couldn't shake the country's resolve to pursue the boycott of Moscow's Games. The "Miracle on Ice" provided all the evidence needed to showcase the Olympic spirit, as the men's team came from nowhere to challenge "The Big Red Machine," a team that had defeated the Americans 10–3 in their last pre-Olympic competition, and sent the entire country into a frenzy.

Five weeks later, on the first day of spring, Anita visited the White House in the company of approximately 150 Olympic aspirants, seeking to suggest an alternative that would serve the President's publicly stated goal to protest the Soviets' behavior without ruining the upcoming Games: send the US delegation to Moscow, let the athletes compete, but pull them from the opening ceremonies, which were broadcast worldwide. Designate a single representative, one lone athlete to carry the stars and stripes into the stadium, and deliver a visual message the Soviets and the worldwide television audience would understand. Our country's absence from Moscow would gain nothing, but lose much.

President Carter was not interested in reconsidering; he granted none of the Olympians an opportunity to speak, but hogged the podium for himself. "I understand how you feel," he asserted and then proceeded to defend his decision, stating, "What we are doing is preserving the principles and the quality of the Olympics, not destroying it." His assertion demonstrated profound ignorance of the purpose and promise of the Olympic movement.

On April 12, pressured by the country's leaders and threatened by its financial sponsors, the USOC delegates voted by nearly a two-to-one margin to boycott the Moscow Olympics. Joined by eighteen other athletes, one coach, and a lone USOC official, Anita took one final legal step to fight the boycott, filing a suit against the USOC to force the committee to field a team. The suit and its subsequent appeal lost.

Nonetheless, all over the country, American Olympic aspirants kept pursuing their dreams. The president had destroyed their opportunity to represent their country, but these athletes persisted in fulfilling the part of their dreams that they could still control. Every single National Team vowed to complete their selection process for the upcoming Olympics. They named 461 athletes to 22 teams, from archery to yachting—including athletics, basketball, boxing, canoe-kayak, cycling, diving, equestrian, fencing, field hockey, gymnastics, judo, modern pentathlon, rowing, shooting, soccer, swimming, volleyball, water polo, wrestling, and weightlifting. Playing matches throughout the month of March in San Jose, California, and Edwardsville, Illinois, the men's soccer team earned a spot in Olympic competition. Trials for the women's Olympic basketball team took place in Colorado Springs in late March. After the USOC's April 22 vote to boycott

Moscow, USA Swimming held its Olympic trials in Irvine, California. On May 24, the men's marathon trials took place in the humidity of Buffalo, New York, led for thirteen miles by a competitor who wore a T-shirt proclaiming "The Road to Moscow Ends Here." The US Track and Field trials ran in Eugene, Oregon, from June 21 to 29, ending less than three weeks before the Olympics' July 19 start date.

Because the Olympic Rowing team would still be named, I still had a job to do. But maintaining focus grew increasingly difficult. It was a confusing time. Training for the Olympics had traditionally been a point of pride. Suddenly I felt like a traitor, pursuing a dream in defiance of the president's orders. I lived in the greatest country in the world. I was forced to sacrifice my biggest aspiration for the cause of world freedom, and I was behaving like an ingrate. Citizens of every generation fought for our country and laid down their lives, and I, given an opportunity to do my part for the greater good, no loss of life required, was not stepping up gladly and generously. Even my own family berated me for opposing the president's policy. Coming home for a weekend visit, I couldn't avoid discussion about the boycott. "It's just sports, not that big a deal," my stepmother lectured me.

Outrage ballooned inside me. "What do you know?" I demanded. I couldn't articulate the rest of my retort, but rowing, competing, and challenging myself beyond the ordinary felt pretty big to me. Sport is one among many human endeavors, one possible path in the search for meaning, self-expression, and purpose. It is intimately personal and universally important, this business of striving beyond one's limits, of aspiring to perfection and inevitably falling short, failing, and risking again, reaching ever higher, damn the torpedoes, full speed ahead.

I couldn't say any of that sophisticated stuff. My stepmother's smugness made me feel small and wrong, as if I were still a child, especially because she was echoing the opinions of millions of Americans: "People are dying all over the world, and all you care about is yourself."

Everything felt like an outrage. No one would stand up for me, not even my own father, who knew how much I ached to make the team and was ordinarily an avid supporter of individual rights and small government.

All the knowledge I had accumulated from rowing seemed to vanish. Was BG right? Should I just buck up and shut up, take the medicine my own country has prescribed, and do my part?

Although I left the room and the argument with BG, my thoughts kept coming. I went to my bedroom and flung myself down on my bed. As I lay there, eyes closed, images of rowing flowed by and I regained my calm clarity. This is not bad or wrong. Nothing that can make me so alive and can teach so much could be pointless. Never before had loving something set me apart as a pariah, but I would not walk away.

Of course, I was in no position to sacrifice anything, yet. I wasn't an Olympian, merely a wannabe. As much as the pall of disgust and dismay over the president's dictum hung over the spring weather, I still had nothing concrete to whine about. All I could do was stay focused, keep training, and make that damn team. Until that happened, the boycott was irrelevant.

Somehow, I stayed on track. I garnered yet another invitation to a selection camp. I survived another training camp in placid Princeton. I kept my anger in check and poured my anxiety and eagerness into the strokes I took during the extended tryout sessions. I kept my distance from the coaches: Kris K, the National Team coach from the previous year, and Nat, who'd been named as the assistant Olympic coach. Just my luck. I was the same size as I had been nearly five years earlier when I approached him on the Old Campus at Yale as a curious freshman, when he turned away from me before I even had a chance to introduce myself. I was the same size as I had been two years earlier when he unceremoniously cut me from the European Tour squad. I was part of the juggernaut of one of the university's most successful athletic teams. I helped catapult him to the top of the women's collegiate coaching pile, yet I knew he'd cut me in a second, given half a chance. I didn't talk with him, except when necessity required interaction.

On the morning Kris announced he would post the final roster for the Olympic team after practice, I froze. I had waited for this moment, had done everything I could, had maintained my focus and confidence, had held my tongue, and given no coach any excuse to strike my name from the list. I had rowed hard and well in practice after practice. I'd pulled consistently, stroke after stroke, and prevailed in every test. And I dreaded the humiliation to come.

The entire flock of aspirants crowded around the flimsy sheet of paper Kris posted on the boathouse door. The mass of people was impossible to plow through. I waited, motionless, my gaze fixed on the floor.

Don't get your hopes up! Remember, remember, you're not good enough . . . The market, the market, it's telling you something, it's told you you're nothing. Walk away, walk away now! Your name is not on that list

Could it happen just this once? For once could I find a happy ending?

The crowd thinned quickly; the group of nearly three dozen women knew how to read their own names. I stepped up. Ready to greet the demons of disappointment. Ready to blame myself for dreaming too large and wanting too much, for thinking I could grasp what my heart desired.

Alphabetical. By last name. I forced myself to start at the top, scanned BARBER, BARNES, BOWER, BROWN, but I wasn't solidly in control. My eyes darted down to the middle of the page. I caught GRAVES. I was breathless with the effort of maintaining some modicum of control. Okay, too far. Back up.

Try to look cucumber cool on the outside. Don't let anyone think this is a make-or-break moment. You've been here before. You're ready, braced for another slug of disappointment, ready for another free fall. Taking a deep breath, I blinked, savoring my hope for one last moment. I looked.

GILDER.

I stood staring at the sheet. The news crashed into my heart, stunning me, and then took another beat to reach my brain. Zipping to make the connection, racing ahead and calling back to the rest of me, gleeful and triumphant, my emotions shouted back to my reason: Gilder, your name is on the list!

I forced my eyes back to the middle of the page. There it was, just above GRAVES, below DREWSON. GILDER. The headline at the top of the page, 1980 OLYMPIC ROWING TEAM, in Korzeniowski's scrawl made it real.

Standing there, my eyes stretched wide and my mouth curving upward, I felt the jumbling inside me sort into a new order. I watched myself toss off the weight of hopeful, fearful aspirant I had lugged around for eons, walk across this brand-new territory, step up to and dance through the door marked "Olympian," across an interior and private threshold between wannabe and made-it.

As I accepted the congratulations of the other athletes, I looked back across that threshold and saw the door to my past shove shut with a firm click.

It happened in an instant. It had taken years. It would last forever.

I I

I had prowled outside the National Team village for so long, shaking the locked gates, trying to force my way in. Now the doors had opened, granting me unfettered access.

As members of the Olympic team, we settled into our roles and bonded. In slogging through tough daily workouts, we compressed years of learning about each other into mere weeks: together we endured the ordeal of training for a competition we were banned from entering and dealt with the loss of what should have been our shining moment in the Olympic sun. Lifelong friendships emerged, bits of gold shining through the pressure cooker of intense preparation.

I hadn't made new friends in a long time. National Team tryouts were hardly conducive to the vulnerability required to forge new connections. During the previous selection processes, I put all my energy into maintaining my internal equilibrium. I had become an expert outsider, but I was inside now.

The top boat was the eight. I was named to the second boat—the four with coxswain—along with several other first-time Olympians who were also novice National Team members. Besides me, Val Mc-Clain (our coxswain), Sue Tuttle, Kathy Keeler, and Hope Barnes, who battled the experienced and famous Anita DeFrantz for the bow seat and ultimately lost, were newbies. I ended up liking them all, but two stood out.

First, there was Hope. Tall, lean, and serious, she rowed in the seven seat of the University of Pennsylvania crew that claimed the Eastern Sprints title right before the Olympic selection camp began. She was a confident multisport athlete, an excellent rock climber and skier, and an accomplished scholar, preparing to enter graduate school in medicinal chemistry. Focused, organized, and efficient, she managed to pack all her interests into her life and still had time for fun and games. We shared a broad swath of commonalities beyond rowing. We both hailed from complicated families riven by divorce and could recognize the subtext of sorrow in the descriptions we offered each other of our backgrounds. We also set our sights beyond rowing, albeit for different reasons: Hope was genuinely drawn to her academic career, while I knew I could not dally long in my sport without losing critical family support.

I learned firsthand about Hope's penchant for silly humor early in our friendship. Introducing me to her older sister, Faith, Hope proceeded to regale me with stories of her other siblings, sister Charity and brothers Patience and Earnest. Wide-eyed at the thought of such a pure family, I initially missed the twinkle in her eye and the grin beneath her serious expression. After that, she never let me live down my gullibility, teasing me whenever her sister's name came up.

Then there was Kathy Keeler. We had actually met the previous summer, at Kris K's Princeton selection camp. Because she rowed port to my starboard, we were not direct competitors, making the prospect for friendship more promising. At the last practice before the 1979 National Team was named, we were sent out alone to row in a pair while the rest of the crew went out with the coaches in eights. Kathy correctly intuited that we were both about to be cut. We spent our last practice paddling instead of doing the hard strokes Kris had assigned us, grousing about the likelihood of our fast-approaching date with failed destiny and plotting how to make the cut next year.

I'd never heard a fellow National Team aspirant voice some of the thoughts that ran through my head, questioning the fairness of the selection process and griping about having to accede to a system that stripped her of any control. Listening to Kathy, I felt some sense of connection. Now as Olympic teammates, spending concentrated time together, our friendship blossomed.

Kathy was a no-bullshit straight talker who didn't waste words: she either kept quiet or spoke her mind plainly. She didn't waste time posturing or manipulating. She wasn't shy about her aspirations, nor did she worry about measuring up. For her, only Olympic gold would suffice. I admired her forthrightness and her lack of concern about others' opinions of her. I was awed by how matter-of-factly she spoke of her dreams without hedging.

In late June, when the men's and women's Olympic teams joined up in Lucerne, Switzerland, to race, Kathy set her romantic sights on one of the men's coaches, Harry Parker, who was coaching the men's eight.

Harry was no average Olympic coach. He was the best of the best: the head of the venerable Harvard University rowing program and one of the country's premier rowing coaches. He had compiled one of the most impressive résumés in rowing, but he barely spoke enough to boast of anything. He was a classic demonstration of actions speaking louder than words, and his bellowed volumes.

Following his fifth place finish in the men's single sculls event at the Rome Olympics and a brief stint as the Harvard freshman heavy-weight coach, Harry assumed the varsity coach position in the spring of 1963 and compiled a tremendous record of coaching achievements. In his twenty-three years with the varsity, Harry coached his crews to a dozen Eastern Sprints Championships. They won the San Diego Crew Classic three times and were acknowledged as the National Champions half a dozen times. During his tenure, thirty-four Harvard varsity athletes competed for the United States on at least one Olympic team. And for eighteen consecutive years, his crews trounced the Yale men in the annual four-mile dual-boat race. Every true blue Yale rower and alumnus regarded Harry as evil incarnate.

Harry also coached his share of World Championship, Pan American, and Olympic team boats. He had coached an American crew in each of the past four Olympics, dating back to 1964, including the United States' first women's Olympic eight. In both 1975 and 1976, he served as the head women's coach, and his crews won back-to-back medals those years—silver in Nottingham, England, and our country's first women's Olympic sweep rowing medal, the bronze.

Kathy showed excellent taste. The guy was a stud. In American elite rowing circles, Harry was often cited, affectionately or derisively, as the God of Rowing.

Yet, for the life of me, I couldn't fathom Kathy's attraction. Harry was good-looking enough: ruggedly attractive with deep tan lines creasing his face, above-average tall, fit and strong, with ropy muscles and tousled, thinning blond hair. But he was much older than she, divorced, with two boys nearing college age. And the guy was just too damn quiet. His sparse use of words and his typically serious demeanor put me off. He was so remote.

Clearly the strong, silent type appealed to Kathy. In no time, she decided he was the man for her. She recounted the details of her late-night escapades, sneaking out of her room to meet Harry on the sly. By the end of the summer, the secret was out and they were an item, working their way into a long-term relationship.

That must've been why I liked Kathy. She wasted no time in going for what she wanted, ignored the outside world's odds-making regarding her prospects for success, and never got sidetracked by internal dithering or paltry self-confidence. Over the course of our brief summer racing schedule, we cemented our friendship, which would blossom over the next few years when she made the Boston area her home base, allowing her to date Harry and train hard with me.

In 1980, while athletes from eighty countries prepared for the Olympic Games, the US women's rowing team prepared to race together in two European regattas and then disband at the end of June. The full impact of the boycott finally landed on me, a meteor from outer space, destroying my world. Now that I had earned the right to represent my country, I couldn't.

Anita DeFrantz's final end-run attempt around the boycott—a petition to the International Olympic Committee to grant the US athletes permission to compete under the Olympic flag—failed. When the US State Department threatened to revoke our passports, our dream of competing at the Moscow Games finally died, leaving only bitterness and regret.

Joining us in our misery, athletes from sixty countries lined up behind the United States and boycotted the Moscow Games. The US government stilled the dreams of Olympians from all over the world, including Japan, China, West Germany, Argentina, the Philippines, and Canada. Many attending countries did not participate in Moscow's opening ceremonies, and sixteen countries did not allow their athletes to compete under their national flags. Instead, the Olympic anthem replaced their national anthems at medal ceremonies. Other countries, including the United Kingdom, France, and Australia, supported the boycott but sent smaller delegations, allowing their athletes to choose whether to participate.

As the countdown to Moscow's opening ceremonies neared its end, the women's Olympic rowing team traveled to Switzerland to race on Lake Lucerne, my first international regatta. Organized as a pre-Olympic regatta, Lucerne was intended to give crews experience for the real deal and meant nothing as a stand-alone performance, but for us Americans, it was freighted with extra meaning.

At the race course, various languages floated through the air. Crews from different countries intermingled. Rowers in colorful National Team uniforms carried oars and boats back and forth from the docks to the storage areas. Equipment vendors were everywhere, laden with wrenches, screwdrivers, and levels, ready to help coaches tweak the rigging in final preparation for racing. The race course was lined with seven lanes of perfectly straight, pristine white buoys. Giant orange lane markers hovered above each lane at the finish, providing every coxswain an easy target to point toward. Every five-hundred-meter mark was labeled by colored buoys. A huge scoreboard hung at the end of the course facing the grandstands. The scene said it all: rowing was a big deal, boycott or not.

Beyond the race course, the delights of a foreign country beckoned. I wandered through the streets with Hope, exploring bakeries, sitting in outdoor cafés drinking espresso, and devouring pastries. I sampled raclette and indulged in fondue. We deciphered the unfamiliar public transportation system to get ourselves from our hotel to the course, and walked the streets and canals in the evenings, surrounded by the commingling of French and German spoken by passersby. I loved the poufy comforters that replaced the standard US top sheet and blanket; it was like sleeping under a cloud.

When it came to racing in Lucerne, our four turned in a pair of nothing-special performances. Not surprising, as it was our crew's first race together, but disappointing nonetheless, as we had only two chances to race against the lucky, Olympics-bound crews and to measure ourselves against the eventual medal winners. After that, our team drove to Amsterdam, Holland, to race one last time in its pre-Olympic regatta. Our four came in third, a solid performance against the full complement of competitors who would travel within the month to Moscow. To me, that meant we would have been in contention for an Olympic medal.

But we were not. I got the team-issued gear, the Levi's and cowboy boots, the gaudy track suit, but I was not a full-fledged Olympian. I traveled under the aegis of USA Rowing, lugged red, white, and blue oars through airports, got my passport stamped with exotic symbols, but I would not be racing when it counted.

Opening ceremonies in Moscow came and went on July 19. Various adjustments to Olympic tradition had to be made. Because the boycott prevented Montreal mayor Jean Drapeau from traveling to Moscow, the final torchbearers from the previous Games participated at the opening ceremony in his stead, helping to usher in the start of the Games. At the closing ceremony the Los Angeles city flag—rather than the United States flag—was raised to signal that city as the next host of the Olympic Games. Nor could the mayor of Moscow transfer the Olympic flag to the mayor of Los Angeles to launch the start of the next quadrennium.

Along with the rest of the US Olympic team, I received an invitation to attend a recognition ceremony in Washington, DC, hosted by the USOC to honor us. Disgusted and disheartened by Carter's behavior, I decided to remain in Europe instead, along with Hope and Karla Drewson, the stroke of the women's Olympic eight. The idea of standing anywhere near the president made me gag. I also skipped the mammoth country and western party at Smokey Glen Farm thrown by Levi Strauss & Co., the team's outfitters; a "Washington After Dark" bus tour with stops at the Lincoln Memorial, Iwo Jima Monument, Jefferson Memorial, and Washington Monument; a fresh seafood dinner at a waterfront restaurant, where the entire staff lined up and feted the team with a ten-minute standing ovation; a special evening performance of *Joseph and the Amazing Technicolor Dreamcoat* at Ford's Theatre, followed by a cast party; a gala at what was then called the Museum of History and Technology of the Smithsonian Institution;

a two-hour parade and concert at the US Marine Barracks, including a performance by the US Marine Band; and, of course, the medals ceremony on the steps of the Capitol, where each athlete stepped up to receive a gold-plated medal from the USOC officers; and the White House reception at the South Lawn, attended by the Carters, including a receiving line and a team picture. All the recognition could not salve the loss I felt at my exclusion from the Games. When the weighty congressional medal that commemorated my sacrifice arrived in the mail, I wrapped it in a cheap plastic bag and stuffed it deep into a basement closet.

But before I left Amsterdam, I sought out Kris K. He'd made me earn my place on the Olympic team, challenging me to fight. And he'd been fair. He had judged my output, not my size. He'd recognized potential in me that no one else had ever sniffed.

"Hey Kris, I'm leaving now. Just wanted to say bye and thanks for everything."

He was squatting next to a boat, unscrewing the riggers. He looked up at me, squinting slightly, as if trying to figure out who I was. Then he stood and grasped my hand. "Ginny, Ginny, where are you going? What are you doing?"

"I'm going home. It's time to move on."

"What? Are you giving up rowing? You are so young. You have so much potential." Kris swept open his arms.

Me? Little Miss Too Small To Make An Olympic Team? I have potential? Really?

I gave him a big hug, thanking him for the unexpected gift—the news that, finally, now that I was retiring, I had potential. I looked in his tanned, deeply lined face and smiled. He smiled back.

I packed up my gear and bid adieu to my beloved sport.

By late summer, no one cared about my Olympian status. The country wanted to forget the reluctant soldiers wounded by the boycott. In my own family, patience with my decisions had worn out.

I followed my Yale boyfriend's footsteps to Boston. In the process, I dislodged my dog, Max, from his old haunts and his long stay with my friend, David, who had cared for him all summer, depositing him unceremoniously in a new life, without his old routines and familiar friends. I didn't know what else to do. Or perhaps I was compelled to return to the city on the Charles River, by whose banks the course of my life had changed six years earlier.

I needed a job, almost any job, but it had to be an office job, something with substance, not menial. I had already traveled far off course from my father's wishes, and it was time to return to the life I was meant for, the life he meant for me. A million questions hounded me: What was I good at? What did I like? What could I do? How could I be useful? What did I want? I lacked answers to all of them. I simply had no idea. I knew nothing at all, except how to remain on task until I achieved my goal.

Two months into my job search, my boyfriend convinced me to give up Max, who had grown increasingly unhappy being cooped up all day in the small house we rented and was becoming progressively more vicious. He snapped at children during walks and knocked down an elderly woman, luckily not hurting her. My boyfriend located the shelter that promised to find Max a home, put the dog in the car, drove us the distance to its door, and waited in the car while I went in with my faithful companion, who did not deserve the abandonment I was about to inflict on him.

The person in charge of intake took one look and guaranteed that Max would be claimed: "He is gorgeous, strong, and sleek. He will land in a good place." I said my good-byes, hugged him hard, and looked deeply into his eyes. I couldn't verbalize how guilty I felt for leaving him, despite his protecting and loving me for the two years he was mine, and how much I hated that my life had changed in a way that made him so miserable.

I cried the whole way home. I couldn't even take care of a dog.

Slowly I recovered from losing Max. The shelter called and told me it had found a home for him on a farm, where he was free to roam. The news made me feel marginally better.

Job hunting was miles from Olympic glamour. For six months, miserable perseverance and blind determination kept me company. Unable to stop myself, I made my way to the Boston rowing community, as if the waters of the Charles could reassure me I belonged somewhere. I dredged up my sculling skills so I could row on my own schedule and keep myself available for that one perfect employment opportunity lurking just ahead. The daily routine of showing up at the boathouse, getting into a boat, and working hard kept me grounded as I tried to forge my way in a brand-new world.

The Charles replaced the Housatonic. Radcliffe College's mammoth Weld Boathouse superseded Yale's remodeled Robert Cooke corollary. Early morning practices took over from the 3:45 p.m. bus to Derby. I left the anonymity of sweep rowing, with its focus on team, and joined the ranks of two-fisted rowers. I became a single sculler. I was a grown-up now, twenty-two whole years old, doing the right thing. Take care of myself, put aside childish toys, earn a living, and stand on my own two feet. Easy. Make a plan and do it.

Plan to leave the sparkling river behind; the smooth, varnished hulls with their fragile bottoms; the intensity of the "all for one and one for all" mission to excel; the unity inspired by shared purpose; and the eternal opportunity to defy my flawed humanity in pursuit of that perfect stroke. Ignore the ache of my empty hands, whose useless calluses stubbornly refused to disappear. Blink away the hole in my day, the loss of focus.

I ended up in an office with a boss who seemed to think that my Ivy League degree and athletic accomplishments suggested some ability to work with her customers, listen to their complaints about her software product, identify their underlying problems, and help concoct solutions. I worked standard full-time hours, eight hour days, five days per week, with limited vacation and no summer break.

I thought I could do it: leave my love behind in the name of growing up. My future was calling, that was what I told myself, but something else was browbeating me into compliance: that familiar pressure to please, the fear of losing big if I went my own way. I wanted to be a grown-up, show my freedom to set my own course, but I remained ensnared in my father's expectations. I didn't want to be on the receiving end of any more conversations filled with his pained sighs and pointed remarks, or to discover how life would feel without any parental support.

Intentions head one way, led by the intellect. Life goes another, yanked by the heart. Once I adjusted to the scheduling requirements of my new professional life, I found myself not giving up rowing, as I had promised, but training again. The heart wants what the heart wants.

Don't ask me how I grew so quickly restless with the idea of settling for recreational rowing for the rest of my life, how I yielded again to the nagging drive to set my sights too high. Don't ask me how during my first postretirement spring racing season, I found myself backing into a starting platform again, this time in a flimsy one-person shell. It was the river, calling gently. I belonged there. Rowing made sense. It made the day matter; it made me matter, if only to myself.

My non-rowing coworkers came to their jobs every day without having savored the sweetness of the sunrise, the softness of the rain pattering on the water, the roughness of the winter wind blowing icicles through the air; without having luxuriated in the hours when time stretched out like the sea's infinite reach to the horizon; without reviewing the daily lesson that no matter what havoc humanity wreaks, life will sweep on through.

As for me, the river and my dreams swept out my best intentions to be a good girl. The river returned me to myself.

I finagled a week of vacation from my boss in advance of having earned it. Perhaps my request for time off to attend the Olympic Development Camp sounded sufficiently official and important to convince her to defy company rules and spring me from my full-time jail barely six months into my life sentence. Or maybe she got bored with my whining.

Either way, in early July I flew to Los Angeles and caught a ride to Newport Beach, missing only the first day of a sculling camp dedicated to learning, not competing. How I got an invitation to join this select group, taught by the masterful Tom McKibbon (who'd coached the first American woman to an international medal in the single sculls, the legendary Joan Lind of 1976 Olympic fame) was beyond me, but I wasn't going to ask questions.

I joined several other scullers from around the United States to spend a week learning the finer points of rowing with two oars, equally applicable to singles, doubles, and quads. The camp had nothing to do with selection, as no team was intended to emerge from the process. There were no seat races, ergometer tests, or cuts. There was no humiliation, just encouragement.

Sculling technique certainly overlaps that of its sweep brethren, but success in a single requires additional skills. It's possible to bury flawed technique in the middle of an eight, especially with vigorous power application and indefatigable endurance. Power can trump style in a bigger boat. Technique is power in a smaller one.

Developing a feel for rowing a single takes time, even for an Olympic sweep rower. Maneuvering such a slip of a shell requires a sensitive touch, but there's no such thing as a delicate stroke. Pulling is pulling, regardless of the number of oars, but the margin of error for getting those oars in and out of the water declines with the decrease in seats. Initially, merely staying upright poses a challenge; flipping comes more naturally than pulling hard. No companion is present to counter a bad stroke or to smooth the rough edges of choppy technique. It's all you, babe, for better or worse. There's no one to blame or hide behind, no one to defer to or direct.

The first morning of development camp, Tom organized the accumulated rowers into pairs, as doubles provide a more stable base for practicing sculling technique than singles. He sized me up and matched me with Ann Strayer, who was my height, give or take an inch, another shrimp in a salmon's world. We were roughly the same build, too, although her arms were bigger and my legs were stronger. Perhaps Tom thought our physical similarities would translate into symmetry on the water.

"Oh goody, fresh blood. I get to row with the latecomer," she said.

I rolled my eyes.

"Seriously," Strayer said as she held out her hand to shake, smiling. "You come with a reputation. I'm looking forward to this."

She hailed from the Ivy League, too, a senior at Princeton University, land of the exclusive eating club scene, but Ann Strayer couldn't even pretend to be snooty. Cheerful and energetic, she reminded me of a playful puppy, eager for attention and adept at getting it.

Synergy kicked into action that morning when we stepped into a double together. Our bodies clicked into sync right away. We were about the same length through the water, which helped our blades exit the water simultaneously. Our body angles at the catch and the lengths of our reach—the angles created as we extended our hands to drop our oars into the water—also matched. These details set up optimum conditions for an effective drive.

Tom was right. We were a good match. After that first morning practice, he kept us together the entire week instead of rotating us among other partners. Strayer stroked and I followed: a good thing, because otherwise she'd have talked nonstop. Only the wind could catch her words from the stroke seat, unless she turned around, which was too disruptive to her rowing motion and the boat's balance. She had no choice but to concentrate.

She was easy to follow. No jerk in her stroke, a smooth body motion without any hitches, clean blade work, and consistent pacing. And she was sufficiently sure of her competence to qualify for the stroke seat. I was content to follow and steer, to match her technique and punch it up with my aggressiveness.

Our personalities meshed well, too, but not because they matched. She was happy-go-lucky, fun loving, and ready to joke, but sometimes had to be reminded to buckle down and get to work. She shoved worry on the back burner and spent no time considering potential obstacles.

It wasn't that she couldn't be serious. Of course she could be. But she approached life almost wide eyed, ready to be entertained and amused. Self-protection was not her concern. The future would sort itself out. Her job was to find the fun in the present.

Following Strayer brought me into the moment, dragged me away from my apprehensions; feeling me behind her, muscling the boat with intense purpose, in turn inspired her to bring her focus in and concentrate on the goings-on within our boat. I lured her in, and she tempted me out. Together we created a present with room enough for us both.

By the end of the week, we knew that our double had world-class potential written in bold ink. We were destined for greatness. Actually, Strayer said that; she could make those kinds of assertions without swaggering, but with genuine amazement at us and our promise as a fast boat.

I knew something different. Yes, we could be fast, and I could be in trouble. I was enjoying myself far too much.

Our camp coach was a master of the finer points of sculling technique. Tom described minute details of body position and rowing motion as a painter might describe hand position and brush strokes. We were artists in training, pursuing the perfection of rowing, steeping in the finest technical points, imprinting our learning with deliberate accuracy on the cellular level.

He sat patiently on the end of the dock beside Strayer, who balanced in a single beside him. He talked to her quietly, almost reverently, painting a picture of the perfect stroke. She sat with an oar loose in her hand, listening to the sound of the blade meeting the water as she dropped it in. Close your eyes. Feel the motion of the oar backing in, a little bit of backsplash, but not enough to disrupt the water too much. That will slow the entry. You want to feel the instant where the blade backs in and starts going forward. Hear what that sounds like. Try again.

The Southern California summer sun beat down. The water lapped gently against the dock. Her hand moved a few inches toward the stern, up into the catch. She noticed where her hand traveled, how it changed direction and affected the blade at the other end of the oar. Do it again. She sensed the linkup traverse her arm and connect with her upper back muscles. Again. She felt the relaxed grip of her fingers contrast with the contraction of those muscles as they engaged to start the stroke.

I watched her at the dock with Tom. I sat beside her on the grass outside the dorms of UC Irvine. I listened to her voice, the lilt of her questions, the laugh that gurgled beneath her words, suppressed sometimes in serious conversation, flashing to the surface again when she returned to sunny subjects. Her disarming honesty coaxed down my barriers. We traded our stories of growing up and filled in the details of our family histories as we sketched the start of our relationship.

Close your eyes. Feel the motion of the conversation, heading into unguarded waters. You don't want to disrupt the course of this budding friendship. That will derail it. You have already missed the instant when your casual interest shifted into desire. You want to feel this transition as you keep moving forward, as the intensity ramps up. Hear what falling in love sounds like; the sunshine in her laugh, the catch in her breath during power tens, her voice reaching for me, a heat-seeking missile, dead-on accurate.

My thoughts lapped up against my heart's wants. Strayer brushed her hair out of her eyes, and my hand wanted to follow hers, smooth the hair, and brush the down on her cheek. Try to focus again. My entire body on alert, heart beating, thoughts fluttering, blood rushing. Again. I imagined taking her hand in mine, feeling the taper of her fingers, the contrast of her calluses with the softness of her inside wrist.

Strayer captivated me. I could listen to her talk about almost anything. And I was on fire around her. It became progressively harder to restrain myself from touching her, to stop myself from inventing excuses to rub up against her warmth or accidentally stroke her skin. Her biceps looked juicy, a standing invitation to fondle and squeeze. Whenever she touched me—her hand on my foot when she turned to talk to me in the boat, her fingers grasping my shoulder to get my attention, the friendly hug she enveloped me in to say hello—I felt her energy zap through me. I had to steel myself to keep from grabbing her.

"Hey, I bought some gifts for everyone," Strayer said on our last afternoon practice of the camp. We'd have one more the next morning. Then good-bye.

She held the bag out toward me. "I thought I'd hand them out at practice."

I peered inside at an assortment of pastel-colored, handgun-sized water pistols made of cheap hard plastic with little rubber stoppers.

"Are you kidding? What makes you think Tom's going to go with this?"

"Really? I think he'll enjoy a break from our routine." She grabbed the bag back, dug her hand inside, and pulled one out. "This one's for you. You can fill it up before we launch."

Tom grinned when Strayer presented him with his very own water gun. He tucked it into his waistband. "No shooting the coach," he instructed.

We launched with the standing shove Strayer had taught me earlier in the week, a move that requires more dexterity than I would dare attempt solo. With her instruction and encouragement, I'd taken the plunge. Standing with one foot on the boat's floorboard, right between the seat tracks, I placed my other foot on the dock, avoiding the riggers. Holding the handles of both oars in one hand, and using my landlubber foot, I pushed the boat off from the dock in time with Strayer's foot shove. Now waterborne, we both slowly brought our free feet into the boat and sat down on our seats without jarring the boat or falling into the water.

"Hey, Gilder," Tom called as he motored up in his launch.

I said, "Strayer, get your gun!" We grabbed our loaded water pistols and cocked them toward our coach, but he was too quick for us. His camera was loaded and he had already started clicking pictures, admonishing, "Don't shoot the coach."

By then we had spent nine days together, attending double practices that, although technically demanding, were not physically challenging. We had had lots of time to break down the discrete parts of a rowing stroke and study their details. We'd had ample opportunity to tell our life stories and learn the ins and outs of each other's personalities. Our canvas had the broad strokes of our future outlined.

That moment in the boat, cocking our water pistols, silly grins on our faces, summed up how Strayer changed my experience of rowing. When I was in a boat with her, the pleasure trumped the pain.

I was an Olympian, well trained in the subjugation of desire. I knew how to ignore the plea to stop the pain. I didn't even wonder if I could ignore the parallel plea for pleasure. Suppression was a tool I reached for naturally in managing my life.

We said our good-byes at the end of the camp. Strayer had the US National Team camp to attend, the World Championships in Munich to compete in, and senior year in Princeton to finish. I had my full-time job and live-in boyfriend in Boston. It was a relief. Distance would protect me.

I 2

But it did not. The letters began flowing immediately, like the start of a race. A state change: from dead stop to all out in an instant. Sitting motionless, poised to explode, watch for the tremor of the red flag signaling the starter's intention to swish it down as he utters the commands: "Are you ready? Ready All? ROW!" or, in French, the language of FISA, the international rowing federation, "*Êtes vous prêts? PARTEZ!*"

Your oars are not to move until the last part of the command, on the "row" or the "*partez*." Of course, you go on the "r" or the "p," but it's better to go on the flag's motion. Light travels faster than sound. You will see the flag move before you hear the commands. Go with what you see. The best start is the jumped one that's not called back.

Strayer's first letter to me was actually a postcard. It started with "Dear Jerk-face" and ended with "love." It got me going right away, smiling at the memory of the private jokes we had shared. That first note covered so much distance, inviting, inciting, and establishing our inevitable direction. So much for calming the waters. Her words churned me up, like those first strokes off the line: a couple of short, light ones to launch the boat out of its dead-in-the-water torpor. The oars dig into the swirling puddles left by the first stroke. The next few strokes grow progressively longer to propel the boat to maximum speed. Don't waste any time gearing up.

Not that this was a one-sided affair. There she was, nearly halfway across the world, a perfect excuse for a measured response, one which I devised accordingly: a dozen long-stemmed dark red roses sent overseas as a good luck gesture. Exactly the bouquet anyone would send a new friend. Good luck, my ass.

A starting race cadence typically exceeds forty strokes per minute— a kind of controlled hell breaking loose—until about a minute into the race, when the coxswain calls a settle to lower the stroke rate (number of strokes rowed per minute) to somewhere in the mid-thirties. By then all major muscle groups are starting to burn, lungs are heaving, and the body's oxygen debt is building rapidly. The level of initial exertion will prove impossible to maintain somewhere between two and two-and-a-half minutes into the race, depending on the rower's fitness. Once that anaerobic threshold is reached, the battle for superiority among crews is joined by the internal battle to keep pulling.

By mid-November, Strayer and I were ramping up to maximum intensity. In three months, we wrote and mailed over forty letters to each other, whose closings started with "see ya," progressed to "love," and blew through "I love you dearly" to "All My Love." We explored our feelings within the boundaries of stilted sentences and oblique references, acknowledged the indefinable yet precious quality of our friendship, and even admitted that our closest friends characterized our relationship as obsessive. Yet we would not go further. We couldn't confess our wild and mutual attraction on paper and couldn't admit the rawness of the desire that was clawing at both of us.

After such an intense beginning, there was no knowing where our relationship would settle. We saw each other in late October at the Head of the Charles regatta for the first time in nearly three months, but we were both busy with training and racing. Strayer rowed in the seven seat of Princeton's varsity eight in her last autumn as a college rower. As for me, my dedication to sculling paid its first significant dividend. During my first year of rowing in Cambridge, my memory had imprinted the contours of the Charles River in its stores as my muscle memory consolidated my hours of training into substantially improved sculling technique. In my first major single's race, starting eighteenth in the pack of forty elite women's scullers, all of whom proceeded to cross the starting line one by one and then raced to pass the competitors ahead of them, I rowed superbly. Maneuvering around more than half a dozen scullers, cutting every corner expertly, exiting from under the Anderson Bridge and skimming my blades inches above the Belmont Hill dock as I hugged the shore at the start of the course's last big turn, I nearly pulled off an upset. Despite rowing through the choppy wakes caused by my seventeen preceding competitors and rowing a slightly longer course, the result of passing frequently, I finished second. Only Judy Geer, who'd rowed to fifth place in the US women's double with her younger sister, Carlie, at the World Championships two months earlier beat my time. I beat not only my former Yale teammate, Anne Warner, but Anne Marden, another Ivy Leaguer, a recent Princeton graduate, who'd also just raced at the Worlds as the US single and finished eighth. In one showing, I catapulted myself into the ranks of US sculling contenders.

That was enough excitement for the moment, which was extremely gratifying, but the following weekend brought a completely different wave of challenge and opportunity. Strayer and I met in New Haven to row the double together, far from the hullabaloo of a crowded racecourse. We rowed out of the Yale boathouse in Derby on borrowed equipment, courtesy of Chris Ernst, who was still coaching the novice women.

On that quiet river, as we worked on drills and did some longer pieces together, I came face-to-face with the facts of my physical longing. Every time I slid into the stern for the next catch, I was tempted to drop my blades and grab the woman who sat mere inches in front of me. Every time I released my blades from the water before starting my recovery, I had to quell my impulse to let them go completely and pull her into my lap instead.

We rowed up to the top of the navigable stretch of the Housatonic River, four-and-a-half miles from the boathouse, where the shores veered close together and the water grew shallow, with rocks poking up in the middle of the river. I concentrated on our motion, listening for the sounds of synchronicity, and ignored my inner voices pleading for a different kind of unity.

We stopped and sat quietly for a moment before turning the boat downriver. Strayer turned around and put her hand on my lower leg, just above the ankle. She was saying something, I heard her voice, but the feel of her hand on my skin disabled my hearing. I was melting, turning to liquid inside, wishing I could return the touch, stroke her hand, or take it in mine, pull her toward me, something, anything. I closed my eyes for a long moment, drinking in the feel of longing as my wishing thrummed its message throughout my body.

"I love it when you touch me like that," was all I could say as we sat there together in our private craft. And still, we did nothing but row back to the boathouse.

The next weekend ended the wondering and waiting. Under the guise of attending the Yale-Princeton football game with my father, I visited Strayer. I drove down from Boston on the Friday of November's first weekend, arriving on the Princeton campus late in the evening. I spent the night on the floor of Strayer's dorm room and the next day with my father and his classmates, drinking heavily and cheering Yale on as its football team played to a dispiriting loss. Then I kissed my father goodbye and turned all my attention to the real purpose of my visit.

Clarity came in darkness. In the hallowed deep-night silence meant for peaceful sleep, I ended up snuggled next to Strayer in her dorm bed, our bodies wedged against each other in the narrow space. I don't know if I left my spot in the sleeping bag on the cold concrete floor to seek out Strayer's irresistible warmth or if she fished for and found my hand and tugged me up. Certainly, no words passed between us. Speaking and writing had taken us as far as they could. Intellect had brought us to the brink of rationality and could go no further. Emotion was now our reason to row, to yearn, to dream, to push on despite the risk.

Strayer and I could not voice the truth that burned between us, but thankfully we shut up and allowed our lips to take over and speak for us. Her mouth opened ever so slightly. A pure invitation, devoid of aggression, wanting without insisting. I closed my eyes, and everything beyond her touch disappeared. Her tongue welcomed mine, no power struggle in the exploratory hello that ensued. The heat of her first liquid touch ignited me, setting my entire body on alert. Just a kiss, but I was already all in.

I didn't pull away, she didn't stop, as we descended together into our own world. I sank into our embrace, which now extended down the full length of our bodies. I stretched my legs alongside hers and caressed her feet with mine, my hands stroking her round cheeks, my fingers twirling the wayward strands of hair that curled by her ears, as our kiss lingered. I had never felt desire incited by such a light touch as that of her fingers circling the base of my skull below my hairline.

We found ourselves in a hot and steamy affair that defied us to deny that we were madly in love with each other. We oozed all the hallmarks of passion—holding hands and looking starry-eyed, the rush of blood at the sound of each other's voice, the weakness in the knees when we regained each other's presence, the incessant urgency to stand together, row together, talk together, sleep together, be together however, whenever, wherever we could manipulate the circumstances to force that outcome.

But I knew better, that those things did not belong between us: two girls, upstanding citizens, models of potential and promise, on the straight track to success.

I had dated my coxswain boyfriend since halfway through college, over three years ago. We were close. I'd gotten pregnant and had an abortion with him. Well, not exactly with him: he was too embarrassed to confess the circumstances to his rowing coach and refused to ask for a lousy practice off to accompany me to the clinic. So I went without him. So maybe we weren't that close.

But we were living more or less amicably together. Our conversations about the future started to veer in the direction of "either break up or get married": not the dialogue of compelling romance, but at least someone wanted me, and he was a nice guy. He offered a safe harbor, and, given my family history, I could justify the choice of security over romance. But Strayer jerked my world upside down.

And there was the problem, right there . . . the world. I dreaded what the world would see or say. Forget the world, what about me? What would I say? Sex with a girl? Me, gay? How had I arrived at this juncture? I had always liked guys and, now, out of the blue, this . . . mess. What was happening to me?

Sex had never been a big thing with me. Take it or leave it. I knew it was supposed to be important, but it had never been all that. Now, all bets were off. Deep-seated desire hijacked my body and left my brain in the dust. It wasn't just the sex, but the experience of being wanted and treasured, adored. I didn't want to think about meaning and implications, truth and consequences.

All I wanted was Strayer. Simplicity, not complexity. Give me the girl. I blotted out the big questions about sexuality and identity. I didn't know what was happening, who I was becoming, but I loved being with her.

I didn't want to think about the path I was heading down, but I knew I couldn't stop others from observing, wondering, judging. That was a problem, a big one. I couldn't bear to think about what the world would do to me, about me. The hell with the world: my father would disown me.

I needed my father. Yes, he left my mother and left us kids to take care of her. Yes, he taught me to buck up and shut up. And he introduced me to baseball, taught me how to throw, played box ball and running bases. He wrote me countless notes and letters when I left home for boarding school, filled with the Yankees' box scores, news of his business trips, and musings about the companies he'd visited and whose stock he'd purchased or sold. He came to my races, paid my college tuition, got drunk with me at Yale football games, gave me reams of unsolicited advice, and mostly cheered me on.

Falling in love with rowing had never fit his picture of what I should do. Falling in love with a girl would destroy his picture of me. He would toss me from his life, I was sure.

But none of that could stop me.

Seven months later, I broke up with my boyfriend, under the guise of supporting him in a move to New York for his career. He knew without asking that I would not accompany him there, or anywhere else. He asked me directly about my relationship with Strayer. "Nope, there's nothing between us, just friends," I assured him. Strayer was dating a guy in Princeton, but following graduation, she moved to Boston to train. She left her boyfriend behind, but maintained the pretense of their relationship.

Ten months of a honeymoon existence ensued, starting with the selection process for the 1982 World Championship team. We both raced in the singles trials, held at Camden, New Jersey, in early summer. I came in second, losing to Judy Geer, who earned the right to compete as the US single sculler at the Worlds. I was only mildly disappointed, as the prospect of rowing in the quad with Strayer consoled me.

We ended up as the bow pair in the quad and traveled to Lucerne, our daytime status as teammates and roommates obscuring our secret life as lovers at night. Our crew came in fourth, just out of the medals, and yet I returned home happy, blissful, my life filled with all that I loved.

In September, we became housemates, continuing our charade with separate bedrooms to show the world. Strayer not only took over my heart, but moved into my life. We spent the next seven months training together for the 1983 National Team by day, sleeping together by night. We cooked together and shared expenses. She struggled through the transition from college student to gainfully employed adult, while I kept on working at my day job and focused on my training. I kept improving in my single, even as we trained together in the double. No matter the rigors of the daylight hours, nighttime would find us lying side by side, safe and secure with our secret, bolstering each other in the special way that only lovers can, smoothing over the rough spots of the just-completed day, and paving the way for the one to follow. We learned all there was to know about each other, keeping no secrets— except the giant one we both sheltered from the rest of the world.

Strayer expanded my established training repertoire. On the water, we regularly alternated between rowing our singles or together in our double. I even purchased a sleek, wooden racing double, specially made for women our size, from Stämpfli, the Swiss boat builders in Zurich. My father named the shell *Mobile Bay*, recalling the famous Louisiana Civil War battle when Colonel Farragut had decreed, "Damn the torpedoes, full speed ahead." Dad had no idea how appropriate I found that name.

Somehow Strayer coaxed Harry Parker into coaching us. It wasn't my idea, that's for sure. We already had Lisa Hansen, who had begun coaching me in the single the previous autumn when I decided to train seriously again and then agreed to include Strayer in the bargain. Lisa possessed her own impressive résumé, having raced and medaled internationally as the stroke of the famous Hansen and Hills double in the late 1970s. But in the early summer of 1982, just as Strayer arrived in Boston to live and train, Lisa left town for an extended break. She would be gone until the fall. We needed a replacement.

Strayer sought Harry out and put him on the spot. "We need a coach, Harry. Come on, how about it?" She teased him into submission. "Please? It'll be fun. You can try to teach a Yalie how to row." She prodded him gently, offered home-baked cookies, promised good behavior, and swore we would be fast and make it worth his while.

As for me, I was too proud to ask for help from a god. I wouldn't risk the humiliation of rejection. Besides, I didn't have the greatest track record with coaches. I doubted their utility, so kept my expectations low.

Harry had ample excuses to refuse—his varsity program with about thirty men, National Team coaching obligations, and a passel of heavyweight men's scullers, Olympic aspirants who'd flocked to Boston to train under his near-silent direction. But he said yes.

And he meant it, allowing us to slowly worm our way into his daily life. We started out by joining some of the male single scullers on the water so Harry could check our technique. Then Strayer cajoled him into taking us out separately so he could watch us row more closely. In the early fall, after we returned from the Worlds in Lucerne, Strayer and I stalked Harry at Newell Boathouse, across the Charles from Weld, and begged him to design our training schedules. Strayer's sense of humor must have been a deciding factor. Her joking and easy banter often made Harry tip his head back and laugh, which was good, because I was always challenging him. I couldn't help my Yalie self; Harvard and Harry Parker were my alma mater's nemeses, and I could not traipse to the dark side without some semblance of a fight. Nonetheless, Harry was generous with his time; for the first several months, I repaid him with smart-ass comments.

Harry's influence started to show up quickly, starting with the Head of the Charles. Strayer and I raced twice in that regatta, a flagrant violation of the rules, which my former college coach, good ol' Nat, pointed out to the race officials when he lodged an official protest. We joined our other quadmates from the Worlds to enter the elite women's four event, which we won, although our entry, and victory, was disqualified, and then we all raced our singles. This time, starting in the second position instead of back in the pack, I not only kicked butt and won, but set a new course record, beating Judy Geer, who'd raced at the Worlds as the US single. Luckily, the race officials allowed me to keep that medal and the course record.

Strayer and I lifted weights; ran stadiums, which involved racing up the steps of every section in Harvard's football stadium; rowed ergs; slogged through long, slow runs; and spent hours talking technique and racing strategy. We flexed our biceps and compared measurements, tussling for bragging rights over the strongest arms. We discussed the future, speculated about our speed, and dreamed of standing on the victory platform, medals around our necks, hands clutched tightly in victory.

We talked about each other incessantly when we weren't together, which raised some eyebrows. Our parents heard about our friendship and thought nothing of it: both our families had met their share of female rowers over the years and understood the close bonds that formed in training and racing. Strayer's best friend, Barb, however, wasn't so easily conned.

Their friendship went all the way back to their high school years at Exeter. They attended Princeton together, too, and Barb stroked their varsity eight with Strayer right behind her. Barb noticed her friend's near-total preoccupation with our friendship at the start of their senior year. Strayer attempted to describe our closeness as a "special" friendship, but her explanations left Barb suspicious and unsatisfied.

Barb also moved to Boston in pursuit of her lightweight National Team aspirations and continued to push Strayer to define our relationship. Strayer described countless conversations peppered with Barb's oblique but probing questions. But Barb never asked the one question that would force her best friend to lie outright.

Strayer had Barb to manage, and I had my friend, boss, and mentor, Paul. I first started working at my company in customer support, identifying problems with our mainframe software product and reporting the bugs to the programmers. Paul worked in the programming group, where I transferred after a couple of years. By then, we were friends outside of work.

"Ginny, how far does your friendship with Strayer go?" he asked me one day at lunch. We were eating pizza, one of his favorite foods.

Strands of mozzarella cheese dangled from his mouth for a few seconds as he chomped them free from his pizza slice.

A hand reached into my gut and started squeezing. Suddenly, I wasn't hungry anymore. I kept my eyes on his slice of pizza. "What do you mean?" I said.

"You've been talking about her for eons. You broke up with your boyfriend and moved in with her . . ."

I took the last bite of my slice, chewed precisely and swallowed. "I needed to live with someone. Besides, I like her. We're good friends. We have a lot in common."

"Well, is there more to it?"

I reached into the box for another slice. "Like what?"

"It just sounds like you're really close."

I dropped the slice back in the box and got up. "Yeah, I guess. I gotta get back to work. I'm leaving early for practice this afternoon."

We kept our hands off each other in public, but we couldn't hide our closeness from our friends in the rowing community. Everyone knew we adored each other, but no one pushed for details. Certainly we weren't the only gays training for the US rowing team, but sexuality was not exactly an open topic of conversation, even among friends. Besides, many of the men training for the US team blithely assumed that most, if not all, their female counterparts were dykes. It was hard enough fighting the assumption that "athlete" and "femininity" were oxymora without providing any evidence that could be construed as proof of that. If lesbians populated the top echelons of women's sports, that state of affairs would pretty much kill any mainstream embrace of female athletes as healthy and normal. Thus, even in our own small, aquatic world, we lived our own agonized version of "don't ask, don't tell."

Of course, our epic arguments about rowing may have diffused questions. Demanding and picky, I was often dissatisfied with our rows in the double. We developed a reputation for our on-water yelling bouts and earned a platonic nickname, the Heater Sisters, which, in its own way, helped us hide in full view.

Living in secret proved tough: showcasing the acceptable me and shoving away the part that charcoaled my insides with the burn of shame. Held hands in private; scoffed at the idea of our relationship being more than "just friends" in public. Smooched in the dark; wrestled playfully in broad daylight. Melted by the secret caress of her hand between pieces during our workouts in the double; frozen on the steps of Harvard's football stadium in icy weather, trying to kick her ass like she was just another training partner. Crept into her bedroom at night to fight off the loneliness of despising myself; yelled the girl in the mirror into silence during the day to distance the swell of self-hatred choking up my throat.

In rowing, we say fly and die. Start the race at an impossibly high cadence and don't settle. Hang on for dear life, fight the oxygen debt, and row as if you can maintain that anaerobic intensity beyond the human body's limit, even though it's not possible.

Starting high and not settling is a recipe for disaster. You can't fight your body's limits. You will cave, against your will, perhaps, but your technique and your power will fail if you attempt to race above your capacities. And it will hurt. Ignore your limits and you will pay.

And I paid. The ecstasy of loving Strayer blurred with the agony of my shame. I had swallowed the world's party line: being gay was sinful, criminal, and in my father's eyes, unthinkable. My identity should have been mine to define and declare, but I didn't dare. I traded my independence for social safety and my father's love, a transaction that positioned me to live at odds with myself. A master of deception in training, I followed in my parents' footsteps, living one way in private and acting another in public.

I couldn't stay my own course. Try as I might, I could not step away from the familiar and the sure. Eighteen months of wildness was all I could take. The ups of being with Strayer in private couldn't balance the downs of facing myself everywhere else. To make matters worse, we progressed in our on-water training into a competitive double. Our goals ran in parallel: National Teams, the Olympics, medals.

I fed myself many lines, many lies, to create some separation, misapplying logic in my clumsy attempts to regain the control I had lost. I don't want to be the only egg in her basket. I don't want to be responsible for her. I want to race the single and she wants me to race the double. I want to have kids. I want a normal life.

I was starting to hate myself. When I looked in the mirror, even my bulging biceps couldn't distract me from the lies I saw staring back at me.

I had buried myself before. Swallow hard and it will all disappear. Ignore the suffocating effects of the world's judgment; no one cares. I'm comfortable with struggling to breathe.

The conversations took place over a series of weeks in April, always under cover of darkness, as we lay next to each other, entwined. They proceeded along the same course, as if we were practicing for the real thing, always starting with me.

"I can't keep doing this."

"Don't you love me?"

"Yes, but this is too hard."

No words in response, just passion. Whether to grab every last chance or to remind me of what I would lose, Strayer kept us going as long as she could.

If only I could have shaken out the desperation that bounced in my brain, like needless salt rubbing into my private wound. My shrill fear, mouthing the value of integrity, demanded I return to a life where I could walk with my head held high. My desperate heart begged just for once to be heard and considered, not stuffed down and forgotten. Just like old times, getting pulled between my parents, trying to determine right from wrong with limited information and my judgment skewed by fear.

Love does not thrive in hiding, or in bed with lying. It will turn on itself, devour its best facets, and leave a gaping hole to mark its absence.

We were in Strayer's bed, in her room. The lights were off. I lay stiffly beside her, self-hatred poisoning me, spilling over into disgust with her. I sat up and hugged my knees, too itchy to remain lying down. Sleep was far away.

"I'm not doing this anymore."

The moment had been approaching for a while, but Strayer said nothing. I heard her sniffling and steeled myself. There was no going back. This was tough enough as it was.

I got up, walked across the hall to my room, closed the door, and crept under the cold sheets.

I dumped my true love like she was a sack of nothing. Kicked her to the curb like she was an empty can. Walked away without looking back. Ignored her tears, her begging, her protracted attempts to understand why I didn't love her anymore, her long letters pleading for reconsideration that over many months petered out to a stream of Hallmark cards scrawled with a couple of lines wistfully hoping to remain friends, and ended with her bitter glances when we found ourselves together over the course of the next year as we both continued to pursue our Olympic dreams.

I stole back all the letters I'd written her over nearly two years, from the innocuous notes to the embarrassingly detailed declarations of love and lust, to the curt, clipped explanations of why we couldn't continue as a secret couple. I lifted them out of the trunk of her car one afternoon, tucked them under my arm, and walked away. I found a covered garbage can on a faraway street corner in the middle of downtown Boston, tossed them in, and left them behind.

No more rocking the boat.

Through the emotional upheaval, I kept moving down my competitive life's stream. Thank god for rowing. I needed something solid to rely on, something I knew how to do. Just because everything was going to hell inside didn't mean I had to crumble. At least I didn't feel shame when I stepped in my single.

No wonder I was so smitten by my sport. The surface calm distracts from the chaos of the deep. The beauty of what you see belies the pain quivering underneath. Repetition and the pursuit of consistency lie at its heart. Whatever happens, don't stop. Keep on going. You can control the chaos within, if you train hard enough.

In rowing, dealing with the inevitable pain is a means to an end. Glory comes to those who not only deny it, but crush it. Focusing on it is deadly; the trick is not to acknowledge it or think about it. Learn to keep going no matter what.

Focus elsewhere. Ignore the signals. Keep your eyes on the prize. No matter if the ache was in my heart instead of my quads. Muscles are muscles. Pain is a matter of interpretation. It hurts if you say so. It's a challenge if you think so. It's a lesson if you see it that way.

13

Within weeks of spitting Strayer out of my bed, I rebounded into the arms of my future husband, the brother of my best friend Kathy Keeler. He was an out-of-towner, from Seattle, yet connected to my world; a warm body to help keep me from being alone with my truths and to show off to the world that I was fine.

I met him at Harry's one afternoon when I came over to do my laundry. A red-flecked, bearded, brown-haired guy with broad shoulders, Kathy's blue eyes, and a light sprinkling of freckles dancing from his wrists to his upper arms, he was sitting on the couch. "Hi," he said. "I'm Josh."

We got to know each other quickly because I spent a lot of time avoiding my own home base where Strayer moped and wept. He was gentle and unassuming, listened when I wanted to talk, and seemed content not to pry or prod. Maybe impressed by my accomplishments and aspirations, but not cowed. As we spent time together, I saw he was comfortable to stand in the background, not force himself to the front, and ready to be proud of me, not disappointed. A male who did not believe his opinion was the most important. That was novel, and welcome.

Josh offered me a return to normalcy, a path to secret redemption. He was just what I needed: a guy. A big, strapping, silent one, with long, sinewy muscles, a wing span that spread wider than his 6′4″ height, a rower's build minus the heavyweight's superiority complex. He was strong and physical, the perfect choice when it came to hoisting a couch and wedging it through a narrow doorway, digging a new garden from rock-hard, weed-infested soil, or tackling a construction project that involved both ungainly building materials and heavy equipment, even though he couldn't stop his pale English skin from burning poison ivy red in the sun.

In those first few weeks with Josh, I mistook his devil-may-care approach for self-confidence: I only saw a man who didn't care what the world thought of him. The hippie Birkenstocks, shaggy brown hair, full backwoods beard, torn jeans, and wrinkled polyester button-down shirt convinced me. I missed his lack of confidence because I was looking for something else. I looked into his blue eyes and thought I saw dreamy; only later did I discover I'd been staring into distance.

The first time Josh called to ask me on a date, less than a month after I had stopped sleeping with Strayer, he paused so long after "Hi, this is Josh," that I thought the phone had gone dead. His breathing echoed across the line and stopped me from hanging up. I had to take over and ask him out, set up the logistics of our meeting, and direct him where to meet me. I had a zillion things to do; I had neither time for him to sort out what he wanted to say nor patience for him to muster his courage and get the hell going.

Our first date was fine, a meal at a nameless Mexican dive in Cambridge followed by a lovely walk around the Charles River between the Anderson and Eliot bridges. I could smell his strong animal scent as he nestled me under his arm. Tucked away for safekeeping, I walked with him along the dirt path that followed the river.

That evening I started convincing myself that this could be the man for me. Of course, I stepped over the divide from gay to straight without a thought or a word, just as I had slammed the door on the issue of my sexuality when I shoved Strayer away. Fear had forced out sound judgment weeks earlier, playing for survival, not success. Poor Josh was clueless as I rewrote my identity with stoic determination and forced my heart into compliance with the new status quo.

I deluded Josh about me, and I deluded myself about him. I mistook his physical size for the capacity to protect me, his silence for attentiveness and proof of good listening skills, his lack of traditional education as evidence of entrepreneurship. Okay, he was not a college graduate . . . yet. Okay, his prospects for high-level employment seemed shaky . . . remediable. He was a guy who would accept me fully without judging me or badgering me to be someone different than I was. He was kind, not full of himself, neither aggressive nor pushy, but patient and accepting.

And he wanted children; family was important to him. Me too! That one commonly held desire supplied me with enough substance on which to base an entire future. I had always dreamed of having a family. I was determined to prove that raising children didn't have to end in a burned-out marriage and an abandoned family. I had left my girlfriend to search for happily-ever-after normal, and marriage and kids defined normal.

I wouldn't let myself think about Strayer anymore. I wouldn't think about how good she smelled even when she was sweaty, the fresh scent of hard work commingled with the salty taste of her skin. But the first time I drove in a car with Josh, when I breathed in the stink of his bare feet, a pungent mix of unwashed, musty sweat and the sweet acrid scent of onions, I should have noticed the difference. Instead, I pretended I was hot and rolled down the window.

I wouldn't think about how in sync Strayer and I were, on the water or ashore. We could finish each other's sentences, read each other's moods. We spent so much time trading secrets that we knew each other's fears, insecurities, and weaknesses. We knew when to pipe up with advice, when to offer comfort, and when to shut the fuck up. We knew how to help each other be strong when the going got tough. And when one of us caved into our respective sorrows about family matters that we could do nothing about, we knew how to stand by and respect the confused commingling of grief and fury without judging.

I didn't think about the price tag on a relationship with Josh. I had already prepaid the biggest chunk when I left Strayer. I didn't pause to consider whether I had enough emotional savings to see me through a lifelong dry spell of love. I sure as hell wasn't going to admit I was in breakup mode, much less allow myself to ponder whether it was possible to fall for a guy when I'd just been head over heels for a woman. I knew something about love, but too little about life. I was barely twenty-five. I didn't know how lucky I'd been to find Strayer. I didn't know the havoc I could wreak on Josh, much less myself.

Meeting Josh was all just fine, an unexpected benefit, but no one and nothing would deter me from my goals: two months after I shredded my relationship with Strayer, and four weeks after I met the guy I christened as the man of my dreams, I raced in the National Championships in Indianapolis. I won the women's elite single. No one had trained harder, with more determination or spirit over the past year. No one could match my hunger for success, or my capacity to inflict and tolerate pain.

Then I teamed up with my ostensible best friend, my secretly shattered-hearted ex-girlfriend, to win the women's elite double, in spite of the fact that we could barely talk to each other. I could not even look her in the eye. Strayer's spunk had withered. Her sagging shoulders and downcast face made her look like a widow in active mourning. I didn't recognize her murmured half-sentence replies to my determinedly lighthearted banter. But I felt her eyes on my back when I walked away, burning with longing for a return to our old times.

At least on the water, sitting behind her, I could freely give her what she wanted: a chance to click together and power into a gravity-defying dimension where mundane matters of identity and sexuality, or what our parents would think, or who we wanted to be were left behind. In the double, our still-mutual attraction worked its magic: a pair of well-synchronized butterflies winged down the course, skimming the water as we beat together in a perfect rhythm and crossed the finish line in first place.

The US Singles Trials a month later to select the sculler for the World Championships were easier, at least with regard to Strayer. Racing solo, I could reconstitute her as an enemy, one of the many who positioned themselves on the starting line. I was justified to ignore her, to keep her at a distance as I girded myself to go it alone.

But driving down to the trials in Princeton, I knew I wasn't really alone. As physically prepared as I was, as hungry and determined, fear still haunted me. It would not let me sleep in on race day. It would not let me eat: a few bites of rye bread, minus the caraway seeds, and a swipe at a banana had to suffice for breakfast. My fear would not shut up, could not leave me in peace, shoved confidence into the corner and took center stage in my head, turned my legs into jelly and my belly into butterflies. I'm so tired; I won't be able to pull. What if I stop rowing a hundred meters into the race?

But as I took my first strokes away from the shore and began my warm-up, every stroke reminded me: you know how to do this. My breathing quickened, trickles of sweat dripped, and the boat started swinging easily.

I lined up at the start, and with the red flag's downward swish, I dug in and began my race. Within ten strokes, I was worry-free again. Forget about the stakes waiting at the finish line, the press of the uncertainty, the omnipresent drumbeat of failure. The future vanishes in the heat of the moment. Life telescopes tightly on right now: this stroke. Propel those legs down, pry your back open, oar handles reach your midriff, gently relax your grip, feel the water release the blades, and now start the recovery, breathe, gather yourself for the next explosion of methodical, excruciating effort. Notice the translation of energy into boat speed, a mysterious alchemy of physics, power, and desire. Winning and losing settle into the background where they belong. Now there is only the battle.

Suddenly, it's over. I've crossed the line. My competitors trail behind, multicolored beads scattered across the water. Fear recedes into distant memory, like the pain of childbirth, blotted out by the glory of the moment. I've done it, earned the right to represent the United States at the World Rowing Championships. Row to shore, accept congratulations, and let the feeling sink in. Satisfaction commingled with relief. A tiny voice caws triumphantly inside: I did it!

A dream rushes in from the distant horizon and arrives in the present, alive. It's rumpled, not quite ready for prime time, a dress that's traveled cross-country in a suitcase. Give me a chance to put it on, adjust its fit, and smooth its wrinkles. I'll make it mine. Just give me a chance to get used to it.

I was a hotshot now; if only I could feel like one. I had just claimed the top rung of the US women's sculling ladder. My life had merged onto the path of my dreams, good within shouting distance of great. Now I could justify allowing everything beyond race preparation to recede into the deep background. Yes, I was still balancing my full-time job and twice-daily workouts, squeezing in long-distance phone calls with Josh, who had returned to Seattle. I trained in Boston during the weeks and escaped to Hanover, New Hampshire, on the weekends, skipping the Charles River's pleasure-boat traffic and the city's stifling heat. I was one fast woman. All I had to do was keep getting faster and maintain my confidence. I was number one, heading to the Worlds as the single for the US of A.

Yet nearly every journal entry in my training log following the trials chronicled only exhaustion. Here I was on top of the only heap that mattered, and all I longed for was sleep. I didn't know what the hell was happening, why my attitude didn't match my accomplishments. My confidence was ebbing instead of overflowing, as if I'd failed at the trials instead of winning.

The US Olympic Committee offered me the chance to test a new single that offered cutting-edge technology. I accepted, thinking a new boat might give me added speed. Manufactured in nearby Watertown by the same company that had built my personal shell, this Van Dusen was also extremely light. However, in a complete reversal of my history with rowing equipment, its riggers moved and the seat remained stationary.

My problems with the boat began immediately. Nothing felt right. The catch was completely different. My power application was wrong. I kept missing the precise moment of transition to the drive and jerked my limbs into action without smoothly linking the various muscles in their usual sequence. My body fought the stationary seat, which chafed my lower back and etched a strip of raw meat into both sides of my tailbone.

The equipment did nothing to help me mentally either. I ricocheted between confidence and terror. I wanted to believe in myself; for long moments, threaded together by my tally of the work I'd done and the victories I'd won, I could. Unfortunately, the smallest error derailed me, and there were many of those as I tested the new equipment.

It was big news, an honor, that the US Olympic Committee had offered me cutting-edge equipment. I recoiled at the prospect of establishing a reputation as a half-ass who couldn't meet the challenge of adjusting to new technology, who insisted on staying with the dog-meat-slow outdated stuff and didn't know how lucky she was. My self-talk flashbacked four years, dredging up an ancient status quo: it was me against the world, no one believed in me, and I had to prove myself all over again, as if I'd never made an Olympic team and never won the trials. I had laboriously crawled from underdog to top dog over the past couple of years, leaving the shadows of "wish I were good enough" and arriving in the fully exposed sunshine of "damn, I am good." I was alone in the limelight, without any teammates. I wanted it this way: no one to blame, no one to hide behind, and the ultimate opportunity to test myself and prove my toughness. Coming from the dark recesses of the land of underdog, I never contemplated the pressure that would greet the top dog at the pinnacle.

I couldn't stop the storm of negativity that washed over me and threw me overboard. I dreaded every workout. The effort required to maintain my training overwhelmed me. My speed diminished. My five-hundred-meter times leaped upward. Everything slowed to a slog, as if I were rowing through marshlands instead of clear water. I cried on the water after practices, barely able to retain enough self-control to stop myself from combusting into full-blown tantrums.

Thank god for Harry. He saved me from myself.

"It's fine to use your own equipment. Do what's right for you," Harry instructed, shutting down further second-guessing. Problem solved. Then, we moved on to focus on training.

I don't know why he continued to coach me solo. Strayer charmed him into coaching our double, but I was a pain in the ass from the moment we met. I needled him constantly. I downplayed his stature, poked fun at his accomplishments, and playfully resisted acceding to his superior knowledge and considerable experience. He responded in kind with his own teasing banter, utterly unoffended by my lack of visible respect and apparently amused by my behavior.

His coaching plate already groaned under its load. Add to that his own maniacal commitment to his continued fitness (he still trained in his own single, raced annually in the Head of the Charles, and routinely ran stadiums with his rowers during winter training, beating many of them), not to mention a hot, high-performance girlfriend to keep him extra busy, and a pair of sons he saw at least occasionally. The last thing he needed was a moody, mistrustful prima-donna single sculler.

I had been easy on my first coach: I came to Nat as a college freshman in full ignorance and with no expectations. Seven years later, however, I was a head case masquerading as a know-it-all, my hopes and dreams routinely colliding with apprehension and doubt.

Harry couldn't design a training regimen without back talk from me. No matter what he wrote in the twelve to fourteen boxes scattered throughout the weekly calendar that comprised my training schedule, my inevitable questions followed: "Don't I need to do more work than this? Is this really enough? Why only four five-hundreds? Why not six to eight?" I maintained a ravenous appetite for demanding workouts, regardless of how tired I felt, physically or mentally. I was a master of overtraining, hurting myself physically to shore up my mental state.

During these repetitive conversations, Harry remained implacable and imperturbable. No matter how I behaved, Harry persisted. He sketched out training plans, accompanied Lisa Hansen on launch rides, watched me row, and occasionally offered terse technical tidbits. He clearly enjoyed himself.

One morning, out in the basin, on the Boston side of the river between the MIT and BU boathouses, he and Lisa puttered in their launch behind my shell. Eyes ahead, I concentrated on pulling hard while maintaining the technical adjustments they suggested.

All of a sudden, my port oar whacked something big. My boat careened to starboard and I jammed my body to port to stay afloat. Instantly flooded by my standard terror of drowning, I looked over to see what I had run into. Bobbing gently in its usual place, a giant buoy that I always managed to avoid when rowing solo seemed to wave hello.

I glared at Harry and Lisa. "Why didn't you warn me?"

They were laughing too hard to answer immediately. "We just wanted to see what you'd do," Lisa replied when she finally caught her breath.

As my adrenaline level returned to normal and I calmed down, I couldn't exactly laugh, but I did realize they would rescue me if I fell in.

Prepare, prepare, prepare. To me, more was always better, despite monthly bouts with colds that wormed their way into my chest and exploded into full-blown asthma attacks, each time derailing my training for several days. Despite having suffered with this health condition since age twelve, I wasn't much better at handling the symptoms or the aftermath at age twenty-five. My asthma presented a trifecta of symptoms whenever it broke ranks into a massive attack that kept me up nearly all night and required increased medication to bring it back under control, three to four times each winter: the inability to breathe, an uncontrollable fear of dying, and an instinctive self-blaming mechanism. Every time my exhaustion from overtraining slid me over the edge into a cold, and my airways narrowed with viscous yellowish-green mucus, I lost at least a night of sleep. I had to sit up to breathe because lying down made forcing air in and out harder, and sleep did not come easy in that position. Worse, I was afraid that I would die if I wasn't awake to make myself keep breathing.

Somehow, my attacks always seemed to come at night, or maybe my busy schedule helped distract me from the symptoms during the day. At any rate, the middle of the night was the worst time for an attack, as the minutes seemingly ticked by at half speed in the dark silence and the rest of the world slumbered peacefully, breathing offensively carefree. As I sat propped against the pillows, I tried to focus on my breathing, to ignore the scratchy whistling and muffled wheezing that sounded inside my chest and to repeat the mantra that would, with any luck, break the attack: slow, deep, relaxed. I had to resist the temptation to breathe out hard, to force out air and free up more space for incoming oxygen. Inevitably, such energetic expirations inflamed the situation and exhausted me more quickly. I also had to stop myself from reaching for my inhaler, which could help prevent an attack, but lacked sufficient power to calm already-inflamed tissue.

In the moments when I forgot to remind myself to remain calm, I rewarded myself with a multiversed chorus of self-denigration and blame. Weak. Inadequate. Damaged. A problem and a disappointment. The litany of criticism stuck in my brain, skipping through the same tired phrases, like an old, scratched, forty-five-speed record, drumming my failure into the silence of the night, adding to my desperation and frustration. I had been singled out by the universe for a reason, and this illness was my fault. I knew that, even though saying as much out loud sounded like crazy talk. I couldn't explain why, but I felt that I deserved what I was getting.

Somehow, in the morning, I woke up, weak and groggy, but breathing easier, relieved that I was still alive, back and chest aching. Miraculously, as daylight peeked in the window, my resolve to combat this bodily failure of mine, this supreme indignity of being undermined so profoundly by my physical self, rose with the sun. The memory of the night's struggles faded quickly, a victim of my determined denial; regardless of my health, I would soldier on. There was work to do.

Harry knew I struggled with asthma, but I kept the frightening details from him—the emergency room visits, the increased doses of medication required, the doctor's advice that I back off from training. I did not view the prospect of arming Harry with more data that could keep me off the water as helpful. Harry stayed the course. He listened to my tirades when I was injured and couldn't train, when I got sick and couldn't breathe. He was helpless to stop me jabbing at myself, but not when it came to repairing the damage. Accessible and available, immune to my anxious gibberish and my belligerent attitude, Harry gave me what I needed most: an unsinkable buoy.

I knew how debilitating my fear was, and how much more powerfully it gripped me when I was racing alone, but I always swallowed the experience. It was just the way of my world. In my years of rowing, no teammate or training partner ever talked about how they felt before a race.

Lisa broke that silence by raising the topic of race preparation. "What do you eat before your races?"

"What makes you think I can eat? Besides, more food would just mean more bathroom trips."

"Ah, the good old PRTs. I remember those." The pre-race trots. Apparently I wasn't the only one whose intestines liquefied on race day.

"I feel awful before races," I said hesitantly. "I'm so afraid I won't be able to pull hard. Warm-up is nearly impossible. All I can think about is how badly I might do."

"Of course it's difficult," Lisa replied. "But if you love racing, you have to love all of it, and you have to be ready for all that it involves. That includes the fear: that sick feeling you have when you wake up in the morning on race day, the heavy sensation as if your leg drive leaked out overnight. The questions about whether you'll be able to make your body respond to the starter's commands or pull hard enough the entire race in spite of the pain."

"What are you telling me? Everyone is afraid?" Really? They feel shaky and exhausted on race day? Too many toilet paper swipes rub their butts raw too?

"Fear is a matter of interpretation. Physiologically, what's the difference between excitement and fear? Your heart rate rises, pulse quickens, respiration increases. You decide it's fear. You're the one labeling your emotion. You could just as easily describe your bodily sensation as excitement," Lisa continued. "But whatever you call it, you have to embrace it all as part of the sport you love. And you have to be ready for it on race day."

That interaction was startling enough, but Harry topped it with a conversation of his own prior to the start of the World Championships. We sat together talking at the end of dinner one night in Duisburg, Germany, a few days before the racing started. I twirled my fork on my empty plate as I listened to him describe the racecourse and its normal weather patterns.

Then he caught me completely off guard. "I think you can win a medal here," he said.

You think I can what? Of course, that was the obvious goal. Go to the Worlds and go for gold. But honestly, I had discounted the likelihood of winning a medal before I boarded the plane to Germany. So many more competitors lose than win and go home with nothing to show but their name in a program. Yet I knew by now that Harry didn't bluster, rarely spoke effusively, and didn't exaggerate.

"Ginny," he said. I saw the weather-beaten lines of his face creased in his most serious expression. "You're prepared. You know how to race. You'll do well."

He thinks I can medal.

I nodded, shocked. I came to the Worlds happy to have made the team, yearning to be a standout, afraid of making a fool of myself, and unsure how I would measure up. Here was my coach, setting the bar and raising the stakes all at once.

I left our conversation in a trance, awed by the extent of Harry's confidence in me. Over the next few days, I found some new confidence in myself. Well, if he thinks I can do it, I guess I can. All these months of second-guessing the guy and, finally, I believed him.

Five hundred meters gone. The two-fifty-to-go marker was coming up pretty damn quick. My semifinal race in the women's elite single at Duisburg was blowing by. I was out of it, far back in fifth place, barely ahead of the lone rower trailing me. To progress to the finals, I had to finish in the top three. I craned my neck to gauge how far behind I was.

Wow, what happened?

It's okay. Top twelve your first time at the Worlds in a single is pretty good. Maybe you can win the petites.

What? I felt a surge jolt through me. What do you mean it's okay not to make the finals? What is that shit? You come this whole way to race in the petites? What the fuck are you talking about? Get going!

I stepped into overdrive. I jerked my head on straight, dug in my oars, and raised my cadence. I stopped listening to my raging inner debate. I stopped negotiating and arguing. I lost track of my competitors' positions; I stopped tracking my own. I heard oars splashing in and out of the water. I felt the ache in my muscles accelerate into a full-body burn, flames rushing down my throat to set my lungs on fire, but the pain seemed blurry and far away. I paid no attention to the conversation my body tried to restart, something about needing to stop or ease off just a tiny bit. I shut all that down.

In the roaring silence, well-honed instinct took over. Countless strokes had imprinted their instructions on my muscles, which now needed no further direction. My conscious self—all those thoughts and emotions cascading in their own endless loop under my flesh and blood, muscle and sinew, bone and ligament—vanished. I forgot myself and my goal. The joy of the pursuit took me, and I embraced it; my passion and love for rowing coursed through me like its own river. This was what I lived for, what I loved: the water splashing up refracted diamonds as my muscles strained against the oars and a wildfire raged inside me. I was vividly and wildly alive. I was not to be denied.

I no longer thought about winning a shiny medal. I reached for the ultimate: I merged into the surroundings and became an extension of the shell, connected to the water. Time fell away. I rowed, focused wholly on each stroke, caught in a rush of connection so powerful that the memory is still etched into my heart.

Nothing could stop me.

The cheers from the grandstand grew louder as I approached the finish line. I jacked my stroke rating up for the last part of my sprint. The lane buoys changed colors. Fifty meters to go. Every muscle screamed. I was listening for something else, the beep that sounded as each crew crossed the finish line. One, two, three, four . . . The buoys changed colors again. The race was over.

My trance broken, I sat in my shell, oars finally at rest with their blades flat on the water, breathing ragged, trailing my hands in the water as I waited for the results of the photo finish to flash on the scoreboard. A cheer went up. I took another deep breath in, as I drew courage to look at the posted results. I glanced up quickly. My name was in third.

No guts, no glory. I shut down the naysayer in myself, if only for a few seconds and a few hundred meters, and in those moments someone else emerged. I went head to head with my doubt and fear. Some part of me shoved away the doubting for an instant and gave me breathing room to remember what I was supposed to do: just row. And in that instant, my love for all of it came pouring out and changed the course of everything.

Love conquered all; love, showing my heart instead of protecting or hiding it, that's what won the day. I had never known that yielding to the truth would make such a difference.

By the end of 1983, I was the top female sculler in the United States. My summer racing season started with a matched pair of National Championship gold medals and flowed from there. In late August, I returned home from the World Championships with a bronze medal swinging from my neck, raced in the pre-Olympic regatta at Lake Casitas in Southern California in early September, and won the Head of the Charles regatta again in late October.

During my year of working intermittently with Harry, I had started to change. I had spent years proving people wrong, and now Harry gave me the luxury of proving them right. With his quiet words and imperturbable calm, he coaxed a nascent self-confidence in me, grounded not in the nightmare of my past, but in a dream of my future. From there, without knowing what was going on underneath my surface, I'd ventured out and tried something new: racing for the joy of it, not to escape or ward off disaster.

My sense of possibility and awareness that I was capable flowed naturally from the results of that hidden shift. I was now able to rely on hard evidence: competitors I bested, medals I won, records I established. This new part of me found its voice and showed its strength during the Worlds. I began to believe.

I 4

Intuition. Trusted and left to its own devices to hover in the unseen, to pick up signals, to interpret meaning from subtle shifts in the environment, and to transmit its conclusions to an open mind, it can be a powerful ally, despite the difficulty of tracing its process or justifying its judgments. This type of knowledge comes from deep within and, as such, contributes to the strengthening of one's self-confidence. When its wisdom is borne out, the self gets credit for success, and confidence grows.

I didn't believe in myself enough to respect my vague apprehensions that something was off. Instead I trotted down a path of pretense with Josh, convincing myself I was attracted to him and wanted him in my life going forward. When he announced his decision to move to Boston while I trained for 1984, I told myself I was thrilled. When he proposed to me the week before Thanksgiving, I accepted with alacrity, ignoring my internal jangling and the uneasiness that settled in my gut. I didn't want to say no, because I didn't want to think about what that answer might mean.

We set the date for a year later, after the Olympics, and began the usual preparations for the usual sort of wedding. Josh asked whether an engagement ring was necessary. He was poor, and I put on a pragmatic face. I told him that of course I didn't want one. I didn't need an ostentatious show of love. Why make the guy feel bad? I couldn't wear a ring anyway; it would convert the callous at the base of my ring finger into a blister overnight.

I was secretly sorry that Josh took me at my word and disappointed that he never questioned whether I was lying. Strayer would have ferreted out the truth and would have insisted on knowing the real story. And I would have told her. She and I had created a safe haven where we could show ourselves to each other.

But I traded that safe haven for a different kind of refuge, where my real identity could hide from the light of day and I could escape exposure. In that place, getting what I wanted would not be possible, for being fully known was out of the question.

I happily anticipated the next cycle of National Team selection and all that it would bring: one final bout of winter training with my competitor friends to prepare for the Olympic Games; rowing on the river I loved through one more round of late winter, early spring, and incipient summer; plotting my training regimen under Harry's tutelage; endlessly discussing the finer points of my technical flaws with Lisa; the constant back-and-forth of pushing harder, demanding more, hearing my weaker self's plea for mercy and glorying in my increasing capacity to ignore its call. I looked forward to testing, testing, testing. I relished every opportunity to flash my untouchable brilliance when I lined up for a practice with Carlie Geer, Anne Marden, Strayer, Judy Geer, whomever—it didn't matter: I was going to make sure they all knew they didn't have a chance, a hope, or a prayer to beat me. Period.

On January 1, 1984, I leaped at the chance to go for a row on the magically open waters of the Charles. The first day of the Olympic year! No ice on the water, a miracle given the season. Clouds skimming across the gray backdrop, the temperature below forty degrees, but not freezing. No one else was out in the blustery weather. I seized my chance to gain an edge, however slim—an extra water workout while the others consigned themselves to the drear of an indoor practice or allowed themselves the luxury of a day off in honor of the New Year.

I gloried in having the entire river to myself. I rowed the four miles down to the Museum of Science, digging into the strong head wind that buffeted my oars as I reached back for each stroke. Bring it on; I welcomed the chance to develop more of the toughness required to row into a blustery head wind.

I turned around to head upstream back to the boathouse. The now-strong tail wind caught my oars. I had forgotten the corollary to a strong head wind—the destabilizing effect of a tail wind. Whitecaps broke over my hull as I struggled to maintain my balance. If I flipped, my odds of self-rescue in these hypothermic conditions were slimmer than my single.

I was in trouble.

My arms started to quiver and then shake uncontrollably. I looked around. I was rowing near the Cambridge side of the river, where a thirty-foot-high stone wall ran for over half a mile from my current position through the two bridges that lay ahead of me—Longfellow with its salt-and-pepper-shaker buttresses and the plain Massachusetts Avenue span. No shore met the water until past the MIT boathouse, beyond the second bridge. I had a long way to go before I would reach the safety net of nearby dry land.

Just shut up and row. It'll be okay.

I had rowed into a potential disaster, ignoring the weather and obvious signs of danger. I had overlooked the warnings. Now I had to put my oars into the water carefully and pull steadily, but not gingerly, to return to safety.

I made my mind go blank, refusing to entertain the hovering what-if questions, and concentrated on the job at hand. Every time a wave caught one of my blades, I relaxed my grip on the oar to prevent its motion from disturbing the boat's balance: tension would stiffen the blade and reduce the oar's give, setting me up for a flip. I wanted to hang on for dear life, to clutch those oars like they were my babies, but I fought to keep my hands loose.

The seconds passed like minutes. Wave after wave crashed into my hull; I could neither regain nor maintain my balance. I wondered for a second if I'd switched sports; the boat behaved more like a surfboard or sailboat, despite its unsuitable design for either.

Finally I reached the MIT boathouse and cut close to the shore, where the water was shallow and slightly sheltered from the wind. I could stagger to dry land if I flipped along that stretch. As my adrenaline ebbed, the tension in my arms released. I felt as if I had rowed a grueling race, against the weather and against myself.

That was the beginning of a long winter of injuries and illness. Strep throat and asthma kicked up like winter storms, shredding my meticulously designed workout plans. Myriad minor but irritating muscle pulls also blew me off course. I fought against these head winds to maintain my position, taking downtime to rest and recover, staving off the despair I felt beginning to build.

The cycle of nagging injuries, persistent exhaustion, and illness suggested that something was off, yet I missed the shift in my internal weather pattern. Focused on external yardsticks, I tracked my progress with conventional metrics: my stadium-running times improved, my bench-pull reps increased, and my coaches' comments regarding my technique turned more positive. Despite my periodic setbacks, I grew physically stronger and my rowing improved.

Yet my confidence dwindled.

"I'm tired of rest. I need to train," I ranted again at Harry. It was late March, and we were squeezed into his cramped office at Newell, at the top of the stairs on the second floor, wedged among chairs with wool vests, sweaters, hats, gloves, and rain gear stacked everywhere. Harry's desk was drowning in piles of paper, weighted down by stroke watches. He was dressed for the water, wrapped in foul-weather gear from the waist down, his jacket off, while he tried to console me.

"You have to remember the goal. If you take care of yourself now and are healthy by the trials, you'll be fine." Harry repeated the sermon he'd been preaching for over a month.

I nodded, as if to agree. "But Harry, if I'm not strong enough or fit enough, who cares if I'm healthy by then? It won't matter anymore."

"You can maintain your fitness doing other activities, you know that. There's no point to risk additional damage by rowing. Does your chest still hurt?"

"Yes, a little." I had pulled several intercostal muscles located in the center of my chest. "But we're getting so close to the trials."

"Stay off the water until you're better. You can get race-ready quickly as long as you're healthy." His serious expression matched his tone. He would brook no debate about training through injury.

"Okay, okay." I sighed deeply. As I left, Harry smiled at me, gave me a giant hug, and ruffled my hair. "You'll be all right." I wondered if he knew I was going crazy inside.

I tried to be good. I went out on the water, but rowed lightly for one, maybe two practices. Even so, I felt waves of pain cascade from my chest. I knew I shouldn't be rowing at all. Even normal breathing hurt after I got off the water.

In early April, I interrupted my recovery and flew to Los Angeles to accept an "Up and Coming Athlete" award from the Women's Sports Foundation. I participated in a pair of workouts run by the women's Olympic sculling coach, John Van Blom: he would be selecting the women's quad following the singles trials, not that I cared about that, given my laser focus on winning the single trials and going for gold alone. But I welcomed a chance to gauge the speed of the Long Beach scullers, a group of competitive and confident women who included the queen of women's sculling, Joan Lind, of 1976 Olympic fame. However, jet-lagged and distracted, rowing in a borrowed boat, I did not comport myself well. In fact, I rowed horribly against that passel of women. It was one more reason to feel disheartened and afraid.

I returned to spring: calm waters and sunshine. It was hard enough to stay off the water in crummy weather, but nearly impossible in dead-flat conditions. I was short on patience and long on worry: time was running out. My flight to the Olympic trials in Long Beach, California, would depart on May 7, and the first round of elimination heats was scheduled for May 10.

Ten days before my departure, I caved. I was gradually increasing the intensity of my workouts, and my intercostals were slowly recovering. The tide of pain was slowly receding. I took a chance and went out for a row, just to be on the water. I barely rowed, just easy paddling strokes, babying my waning injury. Partway through the workout, I felt some muscles jam under my right armpit, a knot of spasms settle between my ribs and a localized swirl of pain. A new problem at a new location. Damn.

I showed up at my physical therapist's office early the next morning and got four trigger-point injections directly into the spasm, two of Novocain to relax the contorted muscles and two of cortisone to decrease the swelling and speed recovery. Along with reducing inflammation and promoting healing, cortisone masks pain and weakens scar tissue—problematic side effects for someone who can't listen, who ignores her body's warning signals, and who won't follow directions.

"No rowing today. Give the injections a chance to do their work. You can do a light work out tomorrow," my therapist said.

"Yup, no problem. I can do that." One day off and I'll be all better. Surely I could restrain myself that long. I'd dodged a bullet; a single day off in exchange for a full recovery was a bargain. I drove out to my Waltham office and spent the day working, tending to customers' software problems, happy to distract myself.

Yet, somehow, five o'clock found me waltzing down the Weld Boathouse dock with my single balanced on my head, oars on the dock ready for duty. Sunshine reflected off every shiny surface. The river mirrored the sky's perfect blue with an extra dash of diamond sparkle. The brilliant late spring weather had lured me down to the river and onto the water, but I sternly promised myself no hard work, as if my words carried any more weight than the air they floated on.

It was twelve days before my first Olympic heat.

I launched, headed upstream, and warmed up to the top of the Head of the Charles course. The pain was gone. I felt loose. My skin heated up in the sunshine. Perspiration trickled down my arms and the back of my legs, and my tank top darkened as the sweat soaked in.

Lulled by the ease of my warm-up and the lazy afternoon sunshine, I didn't devise a workout plan. I followed my desperate, misguided intuition. First I rowed a pair of three-minute pieces at a moderate thirty beats per minute. Maintaining the rating was difficult, but I concentrated and stuck with it. I had to power through the discomfort with the rating to refamiliarize myself with higher cadences. Then I rowed a pair of pyramids: sequential sets of ten, twenty, thirty, forty, thirty, twenty, and ten hard strokes, with even rest between each. Then I pushed the rating back up to my normal race cadence, low mid-thirties.

And kept pushing. If I could just regain that familiar feeling of certainty that I could move a boat on a whim, that I was unbeatable, I'd be ready. I could tell I was close. I was approaching that sense of supremacy, reaching, ready to pluck it like a ripe, juicy apple hanging off a high branch. I could almost taste my returning speed. I was eager to reenter the flow of joy and reclaim the satisfaction that I could count on myself to deliver once again.

As I headed downstream back to Weld, passing under Anderson Bridge in the middle of my final power twenty, I felt a pop under my right arm, like a tiny balloon bursting. A hot stab of pain followed.

What the hell? I stopped rowing immediately, sat breathing hard for a minute, waited for the throbbing to abate, and then started again.

I lasted one stroke. The pain sliced so hard and deep that I couldn't make myself pull.

Oh, fuck, what have I done?

Wait a minute, try again. Maybe something got temporarily tweaked or twisted up. Deep breath. Pause. Another stroke, more gingerly attempted.

Same result. Shit!

I tried to make myself take another stroke. Linking up at the catch and putting pressure on my port oar felt as if I were thrusting a dagger into my side.

Come on, one more power ten. I girded for the pain. But advance knowledge didn't help; my will collapsed at the first jolt of pain as intense as an electric shock. It felt lethal. "Do what I say" lost its power: I couldn't make myself row.

If ever a person could rewind time, this would have been a fine time to locate the reverse button. I longed to return to the moment when I had conned myself into thinking a brief row would be okay and inject an instant of good judgment. Give me one last chance to go back and remind myself to withstand the pressure of shortsighted desperation, to stop my fear from dictating the terms of my game just for once.

But I knew I had just killed my dream.

I finally made it back to the dock, wincing with every stroke, flinching as my arm muscles accepted the load of pulling. My eyes stung with angry, bitter tears. This injury was not going to be shot away with cortisone or coaxed to a manageable level by pills. All the training in the world was no contest when it came to the kind of damage I sensed in my body. Beguiled by my own sirens, I had pushed myself beyond my physical capacity. Lifting my boat out of the water, I felt my pulse throbbing under my arm right where the bubble had exploded.

I couldn't listen to myself anymore, but the words wouldn't stop. They poured through my head and heart in a rush of hopeless anguish. You blew it, it's over, you fucking idiot, how could you have done this, whatever you just did, this injury—whatever is wrong—is not going away overnight. It's all over.

But I tried to keep going. I struggled through the next few days, trying to row my workouts in spite of the pain. Impossible. I couldn't take a single stroke without crying. The dagger in my side twisted deeper with every pull of the oar. Poison seeped into my thoughts. I was a goner and had no one to thank but myself.

I floundered even deeper. I reverted to old habits. I didn't return to my physical therapist. A diagnosis would do no good. I avoided Harry as long as I could. Dealing with my situation alone was unbearable, but at least I could stave off the demise of our relationship.

But I couldn't avoid him forever. After all, he was accustomed to my regular, impromptu visits. On the afternoon of May 1, I finally showed up at Newell and confessed.

"Why are you doing this to yourself?" Harry asked, sounding more incredulous than angry.

I had let him down, the guy who stood up for me when I couldn't stand up for myself, who taught me self-confidence by modeling confidence in me first, who loved me not out of obligation but because he couldn't help himself. I flouted his instructions, discarding his irrefutable logic. I flung myself beyond the reach of his training and experience, and landed in a desolate sinkhole.

Still, he stayed in my corner. He made me talk to him about what had happened, and he made me listen to his reaction, both his fury and grief. He forced me to reflect on what I had done: my reluctance to seek support when I was floundering, my insistence on going my way alone, and the resulting disaster and disappointment. How my fear directed me. How it was in charge, not me.

A lot of people would have given up on me. But Harry didn't disappear; he rallied: "You can win these trials if you decide to. It's up to you." He took me out on the water, watched me row, and corrected my technique. He listened to my outpourings of despair and reminded me that I could decide how this story was going to turn out. I didn't tell him that I could see no happy ending: every stroke was painful, even on the paddle.

We kept working. On my last day in Boston before flying out to the trials, I took my final row. I told myself how much better my side felt. No soreness. I fantasized that my healing had started. By the time I landed in Long Beach the next day, maybe I'd be able to take some hard strokes.

Long Beach was a disaster. It couldn't have been otherwise. I went in the favorite and exited an abject failure. I looked good on the outside, but was a total mess on the inside. Harry and Lisa were three thousand miles away. No one in Long Beach rooted for me; I expected nothing more. No one knew I was injured until the trials were over. I would give no one the chance to gain a psychological edge, nor would I allow myself a smidgeon of a justification for poor performance.

The entire Olympic sculling team would be chosen from the two dozen entries. The winner would represent the United States in the single. The coach of the quad would choose the next four through a selection camp process. The remaining athletes would pair up to race in another set of trials for the double. But I only had eyes for racing solo and claiming gold. Settling for a seat in a team boat smacked of failure. So I refused to contemplate plan B, as I couldn't think about losing the singles trials without panicking.

Racing was miserable. I got slaughtered in my first heat, losing to Lisa Rhode by more than three seconds—an eternity in rowing. I'd known I was in trouble before the race, but now everyone else knew, too. To earn a spot in the finals, I would have to win a repechage heat—a second-chance race for all the entrants who had lost the first round—and finish in the top three in the semifinals. I would go to the line three more times, if I were lucky.

After my first race, I half wished the ground would split open and swallow me, free me from the torture that lay ahead. I couldn't bear to contemplate losing the single and not making the Olympic team. Life as I had dreamed would vanish. The fast-approaching public humiliation already smarted, and my desperation ate me like acid.

I called my father from a phone booth at a noisy intersection, sobbing, "Dad, I blew it. I lost my heat."

"Ginny, I can't understand you. What did you say? Slow down."

I spoke more clearly. His response? "The question is, how much do you want it? How tough are you?" He was concerned, but he didn't realize what I was worried about. If he had known I was afraid of losing so much more than the race, maybe he would have known how to reassure me. But we had no history of talking about the hidden doubts that drove me.

"I do want it," I said. "But I don't know if I'm tough enough."

We hung up. My dream was teetering. I had set myself up for impossibility and even I was not a superwoman.

Although Dad couldn't provide any verbal reassurance, he flew out for the semifinals and finals over the weekend. He watched me struggle without comment or judgment. He didn't run away, but offered support.

The next race, my repechage, was better. I eked out a victory against weak competition. The semifinals were next; the top three would progress to the final.

As I contemplated the semifinals and the increasing possibility that I might not win, I finally started thinking about the selection process for the quad. Even if I couldn't win the trials, I had to perform well. Even if I couldn't be the single, I wanted to make the Olympic team. I needed to position myself for the selection camp. I had to make the finals.

Harry coached me over the phone: "You have to maintain contact during the first four hundred meters. Don't lose your head or your control." Racing had taught me well to ignore pain, but this time it was so jarring and so deep that I expended huge resources of energy to override its compulsion to stop. I had to force myself to pull the first few strokes off the line of every race, knowing that every catch would stab me. Ten strokes in, the normal pain of racing took over and I forgot my injury in my competitive frenzy. Every time I crossed the finish line and stopped rowing, the intensity of the reemerging pain made me dizzy. Still, Harry intuited correctly that if I could survive the start, I could live through the aftermath.

But my start in the semifinals was horrendous. I was solidly in fifth place, unsuccessfully challenging Joan Lind for fourth, admonishing myself, "Don't stop!" The pain made it hard to steer; I veered off center toward the starboard buoys of my lane. As I dropped my oars into the water for the next catch, my starboard oar tangled in the buoy line and caught under the water. My port blade reared up like a flagpole and propelled me over my submerging starboard rigger.

I landed in the water beneath my upside-down boat. This race was over. That was it. My feet released from their foot-stretchers, and I swam to the surface and grabbed my hull to stay afloat. The referee's boat pulled up seconds later and I climbed aboard, dripping wet, embarrassed, and disappointed. I had lost my chance to make the finals.

Still breathing hard and a bit stunned, I reached over to right my single so the launch could tow it back to the dock. The head referee, Pat Ferguson, announced, "You were in contention. We're going to rerun this race."

What? The race was nearly half over! Contention? What contention? What was she talking about?

Surely she wasn't talking about me. I had passed the four-hundred-meter mark before I flipped, far beyond the one-hundred-meter breakage allowance. I wasn't anywhere near the competitors who'd been vying for the top-three finishing positions.

But I had forgotten that Pat witnessed my come-from-behind finals qualification at the Worlds eight months earlier from the bird's-eye view of the referee's launch. She saw me come out of nowhere and plow through the field to nab third place and a position in the finals, and row to a bronze medal the following day. She wasn't going to let the favorite sink so quickly out of contention, not after what she'd seen at the Worlds.

Having stopped the race and informed the other competitors of her decision, Pat directed the launch driver to head for shore. As we puttered by another rower in one of the adjacent lanes, I glanced at her. One of the Long Beach sculling crowd, another tall, well-proportioned Olympic aspirant, Beth Holacek, glared back at me.

"Hey, Beth, I didn't do this on purpose."

"Sure looks like you did."

I marveled at her conclusion. She unduly credited me with enough guts and quick thinking under pressure to flip myself and rely on a referee to stretch the meaning of "in contention." Maybe it was easier for Beth to think I'd bailed on purpose than to believe I had simply rowed badly.

At the dock, the referees explained their logic. The Olympic trials were designed to select the fastest boat possible. Eliminating someone because of onetime bad steering could hurt US prospects at the Olympic Games. Of course, steering is part of racing, and poor steering slows boats down: I was pretty sure if a different somebody had flipped at the same point in the race and in the same relative position to her competitors, the race wouldn't have been recalled.

But we re-rowed. And Pat Ferguson was right. At the halfway mark of that race, I was in sixth place. Then the pain receded, and once again, I managed to pull off a mighty sprint, sneak into third place, and earn a spot in the singles finals.

My luck and determination took me far. But winning the trials required perfect preparation, and mine was anything but.

So the following morning, my dream of singles gold officially died in the finals of the Olympic trials. I lacked power and intensity. I ended in fifth place.

In the time it took to row from the finish line to the dock, I had to decide whether I could put aside my crushed dream of stardom in the women's single and accept an alternate vision: reform myself into a team rower and compete for a position in the quad. If so, I had ten minutes to transform from a prima donna into an affable, easy-enough-going contributor who wouldn't insist on being the center of the universe, who could respond to direction from an unfamiliar coach and a take-charge coxswain, act like racing in the quad was her hands-down first choice, give up her solo dreams, and smile through her grit-toothed disappointment.

I hated losing. But I hadn't lost it all yet: the single was gone, but the Olympics remained within reach.

My earliest training in buck up and shut up served me well once again. When I landed at the dock, I was all smiles. I congratulated Carlie Geer, the winner. I mingled with the rest of the finalists, comparing notes about our racing. At Harry's insistence, I finally disclosed to John Van Blom the injury that had derailed my racing. At least the pressure was off. I had landed with a bump back in the familiar land of underdog. I knew the rules of engagement in this territory.

But I still didn't know what the damage was, because I'd refused a diagnosis before the trials. Now, however, I needed to know the score. Selection camp started in less than forty-eight hours. The Olympic Games were less than three months away. John would not choose an athlete whose injury had no chance of healing well in time.

The day after the trials, I visited a sports medicine doctor in Los Angeles. He took X-rays and, showing me the little white line, said, "You have a broken rib under your right arm."

"What? How long will it take to heal?"

"Oh, probably a couple of months."

"Can I row on it anyway?"

"Broken bones need inactivity to heal."

"No way. The selection camp starts tomorrow!"

"Well, you're not the only elite athlete who's injured. Many of our best athletes won't be competing in Los Angeles this summer."

The hell with that. I am going to LA. Forgetting my manners, I stomped out of his office and called Harry. After consultations with his local medical team, he called me back with their prognosis: the rib would heal with rest. I needed some time, but I would be ready by August. I just had to convince John Van Blom.

Harry helped there too. He talked with John. Given what I had put him through, I couldn't believe Harry would sing my praises, but he made a sufficiently convincing case for putting me in the boat. I was one of two American women currently competing who had won a medal as a sculler. I'd proven myself, despite my showing at the trials.

I must have done something right during the camp to bolster Harry's argument, because I made the team. By a squeak. John took the women who had come in second, third, fourth, and fifth in the trials: Lisa Rhode, Anne Marden, Joan Lind, and me.

For the next month, I rowed in the bow seat, rehabbed my broken rib, and made the necessary mental adjustment to team-boat dynamics. We traveled to Lucerne to race in the pre-Olympic regatta with Marden stroking. When we returned in late June, John switched us and put me in the stroke seat. My physical rehabilitation was complete. But my short-lived confidence had abandoned me.

"What if" governed me. What if I got injured? What if my asthma kicked up again? What if I wasn't strong enough, fit enough, tough enough? What if I didn't want it enough? No matter how hard I trained, how many personal bests I recorded on my weight charts, my timed runs, my stadium reps, my ergometer tests, I felt the hot breath of my fear on my neck and heard its disbelieving voice rumble at me. Enough was never enough.

I 5

On July 28, standing in the tunnel at the Los Angeles Memorial Coli-seum, about to step onstage and join the opening ceremonies of the XXIII Olympiad, I heard the roar of ninety-one thousand voices. So much had happened since I started dreaming of joining the ranks of Olympic competitors in 1976, and it wasn't all about me. A mere twelve years since the passage of Title IX in the United States, female par-ticipation in athletic events was gathering steam worldwide. Women's rowing had become an Olympic sport in 1976, but now, fifty-six years after doctors had asserted that women who ran the eight-hundred-meter event in track would "become old too soon," the International Olympic Committee had added the women's marathon and the wom-en's individual road race (cycling) to the LA event roster.

The times were changing even faster now. In 1900, a total of 22 women worldwide competed for the first time in the Olympics. In 1928, the year before my mother was born, 290 female athletes com-peted in Amsterdam. In 1956, two years before she gave birth to me, 376 women participated in Melbourne, an increase of less than 30 percent since my mother's birth. Now, another 28 years later, over 1,500 women would be competing under their nation's colors in LA, a growth of over 400 percent. Women would comprise 23 percent of the athletes in LA, despite the absence of nearly the entire Soviet Bloc, as compared to less than 15 percent twelve years earlier, and about 2 percent in 1900.

More than 6,800 athletes from 140 countries (an Olympic record), including 1,566 women (of course, another Olympic record), ready to compete in 23 sports comprised the main attraction of these opening ceremonies. The vast majority had preceded the American contingent of 500-plus and now filled the track. As the host country, the US team would enter the stadium last, which meant that our athletes waited three-and-a-half hours for the privilege and missed most of the occasion. At our nearby offsite location, we overheard strains of the theme from *Chariots of Fire* that opened the ceremony. We were missing the biggest audience participation event ever attempted in Olympic history, when all attendees turned over the placards placed on their seats and held them over their heads at the same moment to produce a tableau weaving together the national flags of every country attending the Games.

But I didn't mind. I was here. After four years, three more hours was no problem.

The energy was palpable; we were about to march into a love fest, and I couldn't wait. Wearing our Levi Strauss opening ceremonies uniforms—trim, close-fitting, red, white, and blue athletic jackets with matching blue pants edged with white piping—US team members buzzed with excitement, practically pawing at the ground to get going. Sporting baseball caps, wearing funny sunglasses, and waving tiny American flags, we entered the stadium cheering wildly, laughing, and absorbing the audience's adulation. No one thought of the fourteen Eastern Bloc countries that had absented themselves in a copycat boycott, or of Iran and Libya, which didn't attend for their own political reasons. It was a moment for happiness and celebration, to luxuriate in connection and joy engendered by a communal gathering focused on a pure purpose. It was time to revel in the excitement for all that awaited observers in the coming days: the inspiration and awe of witnessing otherwise ordinary people attempt extraordinary physical feats that would stretch them to their limits with grace, grit, and humility.

As I walked beside Kathy Keeler and Hope Barnes, well in the middle of the American pack behind the United States banner, I cried and laughed. All the hard work fell away: the memories of sitting alone in my single at dawn on late fall mornings, kneading warmth back into icy hands so I could grasp my oars properly; waking up in the dark to run stadiums on frozen winter mornings; skipping showers after evening workouts to squeeze in extra sleep; devouring muffins and yogurt on the run as I rushed to work; the disappointment of falling short, losing races, getting cut, being injured; the joy of my successes. All those pieces to my puzzle had come together and landed me here. Any residual bitterness from the 1980 boycott evaporated as I felt the love and excitement that permeated the Coliseum. We were here. I had finally made it to the Olympic Games as a participant.

I watched Rafer Johnson, dressed in pristine white track shorts and a matching racing singlet, take the torch that over thirty-five hundred runners had transported across the United States from the Moscow Olympics. He carried it up a steep staircase into the upper reaches of the Coliseum. It took a moment for the flame to travel from the torch to the giant urn. Then it lit. The Olympic Games were officially open. My wait was over.

The following two weeks flashed by in an instant, packed with peak life experiences that clambered over each other like a pack of puppies. The status and glory conferred on Olympians gave me a brief stardom: athlete credentials identifying me as autograph bait and granting me entry to every Olympic venue; housing in the Santa Barbara Olympic Village during the rowing competition, with access to a revolutionary messaging service that any world citizen could use to send best wishes to any Olympic athlete; surrounded by an international cast of characters and feted with an impressive range of domestic and foreign food choices; daily jaunts to the beach across the street from the Olympic complex for a quick dip in the gentle surf of the Pacific; the beauty of Lake Casitas, the Olympic rowing venue, deep blue water surrounded by the stark brown desert hills of Ojai, far from the California coast; and, of course, finally the opportunity to race in the premier event of my beloved sport.

The field for the women's quadruple sculls with coxswain event was narrow, with only seven teams: Canada, Denmark, France, Italy, Romania, West Germany, and the United States. The heats consisted of two races, one with three crews and the other with four. The winner of each heat progressed directly to the final. The remaining five boats would race in one repechage, with the top-four crews proceeding to the final. Ideally, we would win our heat on Monday and earn our slot in the finals without having to race on Wednesday, when the five losing crews would compete for the four remaining final spots. At the same time, I couldn't help but ponder the pros and cons of racing three times instead of twice. If we didn't win our heat and had to race in the reps, we would gain experience for the final and adjust both to the course and to the pressure that came with competing at the highest level. The trade-off for valuable experience, however, could prove costly. An extra race meant risking the chance of something bizarre occurring at the wrong time and knocking us out of the final. It meant expending additional precious energy to reach the final. No way would John Van Blom consider a strategy that sent our crew through the repechage to win a medal.

After perusing the entries for the women's quad, I indulged myself with a peek at the entries for the women's single. Carlie Geer was one of a field of sixteen. There would be heats, repechages, and semifinals to determine the top six scullers who would compete for the medals. Carlie would race at least three times. The East German and Soviet women who had finished ahead of me and taken gold and silver the previous year at Duisburg were no-shows, victims of the boycott. Carlie had a great shot at gold. My gold.

It still stung.

I liked and respected my boatmates. Racing with them was much easier psychologically than going to the line alone. The presence of a competent coxswain also reduced the pressure. I didn't have to steer or manage the race plan, nor problem solve alone if the ratio felt off or the cadence was wrong. I simply had to follow directions and execute our race plan with authority and confidence.

But I had learned to manage my pre-race jitters on my own, to back into a stake boat by myself, to call my own race strategy, and to impel my top performance at my own behest. Every time I raced in my single, I proved again my resilience to my toughest critic—myself. And I loved rowing alone, feeling my shell glide through the water under my own power.

Rowing in the quad didn't bring the same level of challenge or satisfaction. I didn't say those words out loud, but I knew. Of course I was thrilled to have made the Olympic team, to have landed in the stroke seat, and to compete. The fact remained: I was not rowing in the premier sculling event. I had no one to blame but myself, but that didn't change a thing. I was jealous.

Several of my family flew out for the Games. My mother chose the Olympics as her first race to attend, Peggy represented my siblings, and my father came without BG to divert his attention, accompanied instead by a film crew to commemorate the event. He'd engaged the crew earlier in the summer to film the trials in Long Beach, capturing that travesty on tape, so the guys knew me well by now. Josh was there, too, along with his parents, who were celebrating their daughter's success.

Races were held early in Ojai to beat the late-morning winds that ruffled the pristine reservoir waters of Lake Casitas. Thirty-six hours after opening ceremonies, we launched to race in the qualifying round. Our Monday morning heat ended in a nail-biter with a photo finish: after our crew crossed the line pretty much simultaneously with the Danes, long moments ticked by before the results flashed on the screen. The finish-line photo showed that our bow ball (the rubber attachment affixed to the pointy front end of every rowing shell to prevent injury in the event of a crash) had crossed the line a whopping one one-hundredth of a second ahead. We qualified for the finals without needing a trip to the reps.

After the first race, my mother erupted in uncharacteristic joy. I accompanied her to a restaurant that afternoon for lunch. Televisions were positioned in the room's corners, all sporting ABC's Olympic coverage. Our heat from hours earlier came on the screen, and my mother started shouting, "That's my daughter!" I shrank in my seat as other diners turned to look. Several people stopped by and offered their congratulations, all of which my mother accepted with pride. She had never held an oar, but now she acted like she'd been in the boat the entire race.

On Saturday morning, finals day, the sun rose into a cloudless desert sky. I woke to the usual race-day anxiety gnawing at my confidence. The forty-minute drive from the Olympic Village to the course in the quiet company of my teammates gave me time to force down some bites of banana and drink some water. We arrived early enough to allow my PRTs to work their way through my system and cleanse me of any extra baggage. Then I took a jog along the lakeshore to shake out some of my nerves.

The pressure of the upcoming moment made me nearly numb. The inevitable, unanswerable questions started. Would I pull hard off the line? Would I give up after twenty strokes? What if I let my teammates down?

Our crew had raced together only a handful of times, but we had established a pre-race protocol that accommodated our individual proclivities. We stretched in silence and brought our oars down to the dock. We had done all the needed talking the night before when we met with John, reviewed our race plan, and discussed any last-minute concerns. There was only one thing left to do: execute.

It happened so fast. Our start left us damn close to last off the line, in fifth place, nothing new there. West Germany jumped out fast and far. We were in lane six next to the Danes, however, and the Westies were across the field in lane one, so they didn't distract us too much. There's nothing like racing from behind to kick you into survival mode. Not that my adrenal glands needed any more motivation to ramp up production; I was already in the race of my life.

I'm not sure we ever really settled from our high strokes off the line: maybe for about twenty strokes. And a quad races one thousand meters a good thirty seconds faster than a single. No wonder the race flew by.

After we passed the five-hundred-meter mark, we started catching up to crews, but we couldn't ditch the Danes. They stayed with us, like pesky little sisters, the entire race, reminiscent of the heat. Maybe they thought they could beat us this time, given how close our heat times were, but we knew differently.

The West Germans began to flag; they had gone out way too fast, the classic faux pas of "fly and die." By 750 meters gone, the Romanians claimed the lead.

Our coxswain, Kelly Rickon, egged us on: "We're in third, you guys. We're in the medals! Let's go for silver. Come on, get me even with the Germans. I've got their stern. Give me their coxswain!"

Every cell in my body burned. Kelly called our sprint, and I brought the rating up over a forty. We shortened our strokes and pulled for home. The crowd roared as we approached the grandstand, a mighty swell that reminded me I was not rowing for myself alone. All the people who had supported my dream rose up: the strangers who scrawled good-luck messages at the kiosk outside the Olympic Village during the week; my cadre of work cohorts who sent me reams of printer paper with "GO FOR IT" typed down the pages, inscribed with dozens of personal well-wishes; Harry, who believed in me without reason and gave me reason to believe in myself; my father, who challenged my dream every step of the way and yet emerged as one of my most valiant supporters; the rest of my family, who did not understand much about my sport, but came anyway because they loved me; the many other friends who had seen me through the years' rough spots and high notes. Their energy alchemized inside me and poured out through my oars.

Kelly urged us on. Only a few strokes left in the race of our lives. She looked across the field. "I've got their coxswain! Get me that silver!"

We passed the West Germans with less than fifty meters to the finish line.

Standing on the podium with a silver medal swaying from my neck, listening to the Romanian national anthem—wishing we were hearing "The Star Spangled Banner" instead—a resigned satisfaction crept over me. It was over. No going back. My pursuit of an impossible goal, nearly a decade long, had transformed into an instant of accomplishment and was now morphing into a memory.

Later that afternoon, after the barbecue celebration with the entire crew, coaches, families, and friends, my father offered to drive me down to the main Olympic Village at UCLA where the bulk of the athletes were staying. Done with competing, all the rowers were moving there to attend the second week of the Games as spectators and then participate in the closing ceremonies.

He lowered himself into the driver's seat, slammed the car door, and grinned at me. "Well, kiddo, you're a has-been now."

I sat silently for a minute, digesting the compliment masquerading as a barb. "Better a has-been than a never-was, Dad," I responded.

He laughed.

For the longest time all I had left of that day was my medal and a photograph tucked in a cardboard box in a basement closet. For the longest time, the memories were gone. Why, I'm not sure. Yet when I look at that photograph, I see a hint. Four muscular women stand side by side with their beanpole-thin coxswain, hands clasped, arms raised straight above our heads like paper-doll cutouts. All identically dressed in snug navy blue rowing shorts and white tank tops with the USA Rowing emblem. All barefoot. Our medals hang from our necks, beribboned in green, pink, and yellow.

Look at me in that photograph, with my head down. The other four are looking straight ahead, faces brimming with smiles. A study in contrasts. It's easy to surmise what those four are feeling: happy, proud, satisfied. But not me. I'm not looking up, soaking in the moment with my compatriots, part of the happily-ever-after story going down in history right then.

The hole deep inside me that I kept hidden so long is right there for all the world to see. In that moment, I should have embraced the fleeting, happy present, savoring its texture and flavor. I should have gloried in all I accomplished, all I overcame. I should have appreciated all that happened and how it unfolded. But I was already turning elsewhere, toward the next approaching danger, pondering the risks in the territory ahead.

It took a long time, more long stretches of my life's stream, before I started to hear those take-charge voices of doom clearly. It took even longer before I recognized the havoc they wreaked, and longer still before I stripped them of their authority and started making decisions based on love and joy.

PART III

Release

1 6

There comes a moment in every stroke when it's time to stop pulling. That moment when your oar wants to come out of the water, that's the release. Let it go. After exerting all that effort to propel the boat forward, you arrive at the end of the stroke. Nothing is left. Depleted of oxygen, out of water, you need time to breathe. Your oar needs to find new water.

The stroke is over, but not the practice or the race. Many more will follow, more chances to perfect your technique, concentrate on power, improve your timing, and meet the struggle and joy that constitute every pull of the oar. Without this finish, there are no more beginnings.

Progress is impossible until you know when to yield. Loosen your grip. Free the oar to exit the water. Breathe. Move on.

My Olympic medal, elusive for eons, was mine to savor permanently. My decade-long journey to Lake Casitas had presented so much to confront and conquer. Surely I was well armed for life beyond the water. After all, I was resilient, persistent, never-say-die tough. I had pushed myself to tackle challenges most wouldn't contemplate, much less attempt. Surely I had learned all the lessons needed for a happily-ever-after life.

But I had never allowed myself to ponder what constituted happy. Doesn't success? Satisfying your family? I never dreamed the road ahead could offer obstacles steep enough to challenge an Olympian.

I'd been away from my job for over three months. My company

had retained me on the payroll for the entire duration of my leave; I had to get back to work. I skipped the Olympic medalists' tour around the country and trip to the White House, eschewing for the second time an opportunity to meet a US president and accept his congratulations.

I went home.

Of course, I couldn't stop my affair with rowing dead in the water. I raced in the Head of the Charles again and won the women's single for the third year in a row. But other than that fling, I tried to focus on real life, my job, my fiancé, and my upcoming November wedding, and to shove away nascent dreams of the 1988 Games.

But concentrating on the near future was tough. Another secret gnawed at me: I wasn't sure I wanted to marry Josh anymore. Gentle, unassuming, a genuinely good guy: I knew all that. But I also knew that he was no match for me. While I set my sights on reaching the stars, he kept his feet solidly planted on the ground. He happily cheered me on from the sidelines, safely sequestered from the competitive fray. Maybe I had enough fire in my belly for two, but could I thrive with a partner whose approach to life ran completely counter to mine? And, of course, I wouldn't allow myself to contemplate the most obvious mismatch, the one I hid from the world.

I secretly longed for Josh to break up with me; I knew I'd survive. But I couldn't bring myself to break up with him; I couldn't bear to hurt him that way. Crushing Strayer was bad enough. Over a year after our breakup, I couldn't look her in the eye anymore. I had devastated her as my father did my mother. I couldn't risk doing that to Josh, too, and shouldering the blame for having derailed one more person's life.

And I couldn't afford to blow my cover.

So instead I married the wrong person. I ignored my internal warning and catered to the preferences of the outside world. I submerged my private self to keep my public self above reproach. I fell back on habits learned in high school, when my father coached me in the first months after I moved in with him: pretend you don't have asthma and breathe normally. Act like everything is fine.

Swallow hard.

I didn't think about the consequences I was unleashing on Josh. I didn't know about pay now versus pay later with interest, that the price for lying would mount with every passing day. We would both pay for my deception. The truth would out. But I didn't know that at the time.

We married. We moved to Seattle, where Josh had lived before and I was glad to go, hopeful that if I left the type A East Coast, I would leave the type A, never-satisfied part of my personality behind, too. Josh didn't believe in a material life, and I hastened to agree with him that money couldn't buy happiness—me with my boarding school and Ivy League education and Upper East Side background, deeply immersed in one of the more equipment-intensive and expensive sports around. I didn't let myself think about the implications or difficulties of buying into Josh's Birkenstocks-and-jeans, minimalist view of life. I had no idea our list of differences would include money, career, lifestyle, success.

Maybe I could delude myself in my marriage, but I couldn't trick myself when it came to rowing. For the first time in my ten years on the water, although I'd already set my sights on Seoul in 1988, the prospect of training made me grimace. An infinite loop of work, work, and—oh yeah—more work. A grind. I couldn't put my finger on what was missing—maybe because I'd turned my back on my need for it elsewhere—but it should have been obvious: joy.

Nothing felt good or right. Waking up early felt like a chore; watching the sunrise glitter on the water lost its appeal. My workouts felt sluggish and uninspired; I couldn't dredge up any motivation to go the extra mile. The prospect of notching new personal bests in practices lost its allure. I told myself I still cared about training, but I felt like a fake.

I didn't allow myself to think about why I was struggling. Instead, I signed up to compete in the US singles trials for the 1985 Worlds. Who cared if things didn't feel quite right? Surely I could force myself into shining when the time came to put myself on the line.

But it didn't work out that way. My performance proved unremarkable, underlining my newly lost connection to my on-water purpose. I didn't even come in second! I felt like a fraud. How could I ever have been an Olympian? I was dead-ass slow. Once again, I was a mere wannabe who couldn't measure up. It was tough to hold my head up and look anyone in the eye.

After the trials, I loaded my boat and packed up my oars, say-

ing good-bye to the competitors who walked by. I overheard one of
them, Beth Holacek, of Olympics trial fame, who had accused me of
deliberately flipping two years earlier, mutter derisively, "Oh, just go
get pregnant and have a baby." It was bad enough I had performed so
poorly, but did that mean I was now only fit for motherhood? And was
motherhood a lowly pursuit compared to the high-falutin' aspirations
of top-level athletes, something that, because it was pretty much accessible to all females, was simply nothing special? Since when did motherhood and peak athletic performance represent mutually exclusive
endeavors, positioned at opposite ends of the opportunity spectrum?

Nonetheless, the comment bolstered some of my own private
thinking, although quitting didn't fit into my calculations. I wanted
a family; Josh wanted kids. If I timed things right, I could take one
year off. I would have a built-in reason for taking a break. The time
off would rekindle my love for rowing and rejuvenate my competitive
drive. I could return to competition the year before the Olympics, fitter, stronger, and hungry for a medal, with a more balanced life and a
refreshed approach to racing. Perfect!

I'd dumped my girlfriend out of shame and guilt. I'd married my
boyfriend out of fear. Maybe a baby would solve everything.

By the Head of the Charles in October, I was ten weeks pregnant
and already railing against the restrictions of my state. Slotted to start
first in the women's elite single event, which I had won the past three
years running, I was suddenly struggling with my asthma again, courtesy of the trip from Seattle and the temperature discrepancy between
the two coastal cities. Insisting on not sharing the pregnancy for a few
more weeks and not wanting to tip off my competitors, I swore Josh
to secrecy, asked his doctor father for an asthma inhaler prescription
without warning him of my new condition, and raced despite my chest
cold and wheezing lungs.

The outcome was horrible; Judy Geer passed me in the first half-
mile of the race, and matters deteriorated from there. My official finish
was a decidedly mediocre ninth. When I landed at the dock to greet
my father and Josh's parents, I could only muster one explanation:
"Not bad for a pregnant woman." They were mostly thrilled, but Josh's
father lectured me about allowing him to prescribe without knowing
the full details of my condition.

By New Year's, I felt the first faint flutter of my baby's movements, as gentle as a butterfly's kiss; I kept training. I biked down to the University of Washington shell house to lift weights throughout the winter months, huffing and puffing up and over the hill that separated the university district from our house in Fremont, in rain or less rain. I jogged increasingly slowly, stopped running stairs and hills, and reverted to walking them, as my doctor instructed me not to run my heart rate up into anaerobic territory. No excuses, no missed workouts for me.

I kept track of my appearance with regular mirror checks; my upper arms retained their muscular curves with no incipient sign of sagging, my quads still bulged, and now, so did my stomach, my own private hill, challenging me to respect its power. And that baby was powerful; I was growing more tired and seemingly less fit, no matter what regimen I maintained. Halfway through, nine months of sharing my body already seemed too long, and I was ready for freedom, freedom to drive myself hard again and focus on my own needs and wants. Resentment pricked me whenever I confronted the fact that I had to downscale my training to accommodate my baby.

By Mother's Day, Josh and I were settled into our new home in the northwest, and the baby's room was ready. We whittled down our list of names to one boy's and a handful of girl's. I was positive I was having a girl. If only she would get here already; pregnancy was clearly not for me.

The last weeks brought me to the brink of my self-control. I started walking stairs in my neighborhood to urge my baby into labor sooner, despite my doctor's concern about my increased blood pressure and caution to minimize my activity. I ignored her instructions to spend as much time as possible lying down. I ranted internally, unhappy with having allowed an alien being to occupy and reshape my body to suit its own needs. Here I was, a trained athlete at the peak of her competitive career, enduring the bodily occupation of pregnancy: the weight gain, loss of muscle tone, the attendant decrease in mobility, increased exhaustion, and the necessity to modify training and put another's needs before my compulsions.

I was less than wholly successful in accepting those restrictions. I was the same girl who overtrained for the Olympic trials, who ignored her coach's guidance and her physical therapist's instructions; now I could not comply with my doctor's orders. I couldn't imagine the worst that could happen. Until it did.

"Way enough. Hold water!" When a coxswain calls out that pair of commands, a crew responds instantly. All rowing stops and every squared oar digs deeply into the water, killing all forward momentum.

The commands are a survival call, designed to halt a shell moving at maximum speed. A sudden crisis looms ahead: the coxswain has detected some object in the boat's path, perhaps some flotsam in the water, or a sculler in a blind boat rowing against the established traffic pattern, or a pleasure boat gone overboard on fun. The coxswain has to avert disaster. Maybe she'll be successful; maybe it's too late. Perhaps she should have noticed the obstacle sooner, but was distracted by the goings-on inside the boat or absorbed by her own anxieties. Maybe the sunshine of the moment blinded her to whatever lay straight ahead. Perhaps she did notice, but misjudged its proximity and discounted the risk. Perhaps she assumed the problem would disappear before her crew reached its spot on the water.

Regardless, at the last moment, she recognizes there's a problem. She alerts her crew. And the shell stops, dead in the water.

The day started with so much hope. I woke to the gentle contractions of early labor. I dialed my doctor's office.

"Dr. Lardy, I think contractions have started. I already had an appointment scheduled for this morning. Do you want me to come in?"

"It's up to you. You can skip it and just come to the birthing center later, when the contractions get stronger."

"I think I want to come in. She was pretty quiet last night at the movies." During *Three Men and a Baby* at the Seattle Film Festival, what I hoped would be my last big night out before becoming a full-fledged mom, I had shifted my tummy to see if I could wake her up. I was rewarded with a poke in the ribs as something bony—her elbow—nudged me, and I sat back, reassured. Yet this morning, that faint concern had fluttered back up to the surface.

"No problem. I'll see you in a little while."

Sitting in a drab examining room, on the corner of Madison and

Broadway, Josh and I waited for Dr. Lardy. She bustled in and smiled. "Okay, looks like today's the big day. How are the contractions going?"

"They haven't really changed. About five minutes apart. Not too bad yet. I can take it." I grinned.

"Well, let me just take a listen and make sure all is well."

I pulled up the hospital gown covering my stomach, now stretched taut, and Dr. Lardy donned her stethoscope, bent over, and placed the chest piece below my protruding belly button. She listened intently for several seconds, moving the cold stainless steel circle around my vast belly. Standing up, she frowned slightly.

"I'm going to use the ultrasound to locate the heartbeat. For some reason I'm not picking it up with this. That happens sometimes." She pulled the stand that held the machine over to the examining table, squirted clear connective gel on my abdomen, and smeared it around.

The quiet room grew more still, as she sat down and moved the wand across the gel. She bent over me more closely and focused all her attention on listening. My heartbeat ratcheted up as she kept shifting the wand's position and my tiny flutter of concern ballooned into anxiety. I looked at Josh and shivered slightly. He was watching the doctor's movements and didn't catch my glance.

Dr. Lardy sat up straight and turned away to switch off the machine. When she turned back to me, her look of concern propelled my anxiety skyward. "I'm going to send you over to the hospital to get an ultrasound on one of the larger machines."

I asked "Why?" knowing the answer.

"They're more sensitive and should have no trouble picking up the sound. There must be something wrong with this machine. It shouldn't be hard to find the heartbeat of a full-term baby." Nonetheless, Dr. Lardy looked grim as she told me to get dressed and left the room to call the radiology department.

The floor had disappeared. How could I stop the sensation of falling? Who had shoved me over the edge?

We crossed the street and walked over to Swedish Hospital for our emergency appointment. We sat in the radiologist's waiting room among a group of placid patients, betraying no emotion or strain. I sensed the hand of doom hovering, ready to snatch away our happiness. I was helpless to stop it, as if a nightmare had replaced my real life, relegating me to observer status.

In the examining room, I watched the radiologist move the ultrasound wand over my protruding belly, searching for my baby's heartbeat. I saw his concern deflate into defeat. He would not meet our eyes as he put away the scanner and wiped the gel off my stomach.

I knew he wasn't qualified to read the test result, but I couldn't stop myself. "She's dead, isn't she?"

His head barely nodded up and down. "Yes, I'm very sorry," he mumbled.

He left quickly. I couldn't blame him—no one would want to be the bearer of bad tidings to an expectant couple, to kick them in the stomach, knock the hope out of them—but I did.

Fury gripped me. "He wasn't going to tell us? Make us go back to the doctor's office to hear the official news? What kind of crap is that?"

Josh took my hand and looked into my eyes. I saw bleak despair in his face, his features sagging. He started to cry.

I stopped talking. All the anger in the world was no match for the truth. She was gone.

Not fair, not fair. Such an inane protest, as if a judge or jury could magically appear and reverse reality. How could this be happening? Disconnected and dazed, I didn't cry.

The everyday sounds of our surroundings dropped away. We walked to the elevator and waited, clutching each other by the hand. We stumbled back to the doctor's office, across the street from the hospital, no longer a hop, skip, and a jump.

What happens when an expectant mother has a dead baby inside her?

Dr. Lardy was gone. Her office didn't know where she was. I had lost my baby and my doctor. The receptionist paged her and pointed me to a phone a minute later.

"I've been looking all over for you," my ob-gyn said frantically.

"We came back to your office," I stammered. "No one gave us instructions. We've been waiting for you here."

"Get over to the hospital right away. We have to deliver the baby."

But it no longer mattered whether we hurried or not. I knew what waited at the end of my labor, and I could barely move, as if the numbness I felt had leaked into all my muscles.

Way enough. Way too much for me. I didn't stop in time. I crashed into my future and crumpled on impact. I didn't see it coming. For once in my life, I hadn't been braced for disaster. I had not prepared for this.

Hold water. Mine broke, filthy brown with the evidence of my baby's distressed last minutes, her fecal matter expelled in her death throes.

When Josh and I finally reconnected with Dr. Lardy at the hospital, she settled me into a labor room. "I want a C-section," I told her.

"Absolutely not. There's no medical justification for that." She sounded so businesslike, chilly and distant. I hated her. I couldn't think of any better rationale for surgery than to avoid the horror of enduring a labor without any payoff. Her horizon was broader than mine: she was thinking about the added difficulty of recovery from a major medical procedure. But I simply hoped to survive giving birth to a dead baby.

"I'm going to give you some Pitocin to stimulate your contractions. Your labor will need some help to get started now that . . ." She paused, took a deep breath, and kept up her poker face, ". . . your baby can't help. I can give you some painkillers if you like."

If ever there was a moment to buck up and shut up, this was it.

"No thanks," I said. "She might be dead, but I can use this delivery to practice for the real thing. Train for the next one." Maybe a brave face would get me through this nightmare.

Dr. Lardy respected my decision and set up an IV drip for the Pitocin. As I lay on the gurney, my tears finally came.

The contractions strengthened. The facts raced around and around, unchanging. My sobbing increased in intensity and volume. Even the concentration demanded by childbirth could not overwhelm my outpouring, which must have echoed beyond my hospital room and disturbed everyone else on the labor and delivery floor.

The doctor gently insisted on administering a tranquilizer.

My daughter died the day after her due date. I gave birth to her the next afternoon. She was named Liala Ljunggren after two of her great-grandmothers. I never saw her breathe, never heard her cry, never saw her open her eyes or unclench her fist. Her seven-pound, eleven-ounce body had all its fingers and toes, perfect ears, a head of dark hair, her red lips shaped like her father's. Strips of her skin had begun to peel away after twenty-four hours of floating dead in amniotic fluid.

We called our parents from the delivery room. I didn't reach my mother, but my father was still at the office. He was short and stiff, his voice gruff, all business. "Well, Ginny, you win some, lose some. Sounds like you lost this one."

We spent the evening and the next morning holding our daughter, bathing and dressing her. She smelled sweet, not dead. Her fingernails needed trimming. Lost promise flaunted its victory, while we cuddled her, took pictures. We said our goodbyes, even though we never had the chance to say hello.

I had brought this disaster on myself, on my baby girl. The terrible truth gnawed me from the inside. I killed her, my Liala, with the ruby red lips waiting to be kissed, the chubby upper arms good enough to nibble, the tiny fingers with their too-long nails.

Dead and gone, thanks to me. Because I did not listen to my doctor when she insisted on bed rest during the last two weeks of my pregnancy. It didn't matter that she explained the risks of toxemia. It didn't matter that she showed me the graph of my blood pressure rising. Because who lies in bed during the middle of the day? I knew the answer to that question: Weak women. Crazy women. My mother. It was drummed into my psyche so deeply that I couldn't see it any other way. Of course I had to get up, soldier on, and fend off my mother's fate.

This voice of fear had governed my decisions for years. I believed it protected me from disaster.

I had listened to that voice the day after my daughter's due date when I went shopping at Keller Supply in Ballard, musing about plumbing fixtures and comparing prices instead of lying in bed. A rush of abdominal pain doubled me over and sent me scurrying into the ladies room to expel the gas I thought was cramping my insides. I sat on the toilet, needlessly I discovered, without relief. After a few minutes, my internal chaos subsided and all was quiet.

No alarm bells set off inside me, as I blithely ignored my doctor's orders, but my daughter died then. I mistook her death throes for an upset stomach, but I noticed her eerie quiet that evening. No soft bumping against me. No nudge under my ribs. The first feather of concern brushed across my thoughts, but its touch was gentle enough to ignore.

I woke up early the next morning to faint signs of labor, and still I insisted on going for a long walk. Again I ignored my doctor's orders; again I accepted the dominance of that fear-fed internal voice, yielding to the imperative for action at all costs. I wandered down the long, gently sloping hill from 42nd and Whitman Avenue North and stood in the middle of the Aurora Bridge, looking east at the Cascade Mountains. Leaning over the railing, I wondered if my daughter was finally ready for me, and I for her.

I didn't realize that my fear had hijacked sound judgment and taken her life in the bargain. It took an unimaginable tragedy to jolt me awake: I was listening to the wrong voice.

A week after her stillbirth, I received the call from the funeral home that Liala's cremation was complete: I could pick up her ashes. Then I went to the doctor: she should have been weighing my newborn and cooing over her good looks, but she only had my recovery to monitor. My blood pressure had returned to normal; my breasts were swollen with useless milk. My body was behaving on schedule in a world thrown off kilter.

And I could no longer keep the truth to myself. I began to sob, "It's all my fault."

"No, it is not your fault," Dr. Lardy said, her stern expression turning even more serious.

"It is." I regaled her with my litany of evidence; how many times I defied her advice, what a spectacular failure I was when it came to bed rest.

She defended me. "Normal stillbirth means they don't know what happened. The autopsy didn't reveal a specific cause of fetal death."

I shook my head and continued to sob.

"It's most likely that her cord got kinked. You had nothing to do with her death. Ginny, I mean it."

I knew better. I nodded: "Yes, I hear you." I certainly did not mean "Yes, thank you, I believe you."

Nothing I had lived through prepared me for this grief. I lay in bed every morning under the quilt my mother had sewn for me, wondering if I had any reason to drag myself up. Was this what my mother had experienced when her life changed overnight, when her marriage died without any apparent warning? The profound sense of dislocation from the life she regarded as normal, of being in freefall from what she knew, clueless about where she would land, or how; the surreal experience of walking through a world where everything looked ordinary, business as usual, while internally she felt ravaged, empty, and useless, with nothing to live for?

Every time the phone rang, a wild hope surged through me. It was the hospital! They had made a terrible mistake. They'd found my baby. She was fine. Please come get her, right away.

They told me healing would take time: two years was normal. There was nothing normal about losing my baby.

Life ground to a halt. I doubted my survival. I saw myself sliding toward my mother's escape hatch, the lure of a soft bed with pillows to burrow into, covers to crawl under. Impenetrable darkness surrounded me, as if I'd entered a bleak forest, the trees so thickly entwined that no sunlight could break through. I couldn't see a path forward, and I didn't care.

Lose your parents, lose your past. Lose your child, lose your future. I wandered through my days, crying constantly. I passed a church and realized I would never see my baby get married. A child running down the street reminded me that Liala would never graduate from preschool, much less college. Overhearing a daughter arguing with her mother, I understood I would miss every argument with my girl, who would never scowl and stomp out of a room muttering, "You've ruined my life." I would miss watching her grow, learn to read, kick a ball, do a cartwheel, pick up an oar. I would never hear her dreams whispered into my ear as we snuggled together. I would never, ever get to cheer her on from the sidelines and stand by her, win or lose. Everything. I would miss everything.

As for rowing, what was that? Who cared? The Olympics? Training? Tell me why propelling a flimsy manmade hull faster than anyone else mattered. Not to me. Not anymore.

Ten years of caring, gone. A decade of wanting, vanished. All those lessons learned of toughness and self-confidence were no match for my grief. A carefully constructed life, focused and purposed, was dead in the water.

PART IV

Recovery

17

The trait most commonly associated with rowing is that of extreme exertion, yet that's only half the story. Muscled might cannot alone create the beauty of a well-rowed shell. The drive and the recovery together make up a complete stroke, linked to each other by the catch and the release, the markers that signal the transition from one state to the other.

The recovery follows the blade's release from the water, a span of effortlessness when the boat flows forward on its own momentum. The quality of the recovery determines the fluidity of that forward motion. Imprecise synchronicity or rushing the return to effort can ruin the promise of these breaks in effort.

If the drive provides the boat's power, the recovery gifts its grace. The perfection of yin and yang gliding across the water, a pair of opposite yet equal, precisely balanced qualities gives birth to elegant boat speed.

Exhale, inhale, but keep moving. Gather yourself for the next effort, the start of another cycle, connected to its predecessor by this time to breathe.

The oar handle rolls along your palm to your fingertips, the oar turns in the lock, and the blade feathers flat, parallel to the water. Reverse the motions of the drive, starting with your hands moving away from your body. Your arms straighten as your hands pass over your knees. Swing your torso forward to claim your full reach. Only when your body is set does your seat move, allowing your legs to compress snugly against your chest, ready for their next explosion of energy. Not a rest, but a change of pace.

Without recovery, there is no progress. Extreme effort cannot be accomplished without respite, nor is propulsion possible without a gathering of energy. Arms, back, legs: that's the sequence of motion, a fluid, controlled process to get back into position from which you can explode with effort yet again. Recoil yourself into concentrated energy, step by step. Follow the established cadence. Exhale, create space for the next jolt of oxygen that's desperately needed. It's not anarchy, and it's not desperate, no matter how desperate you feel. Every movement is orchestrated, deliberate, and necessary.

Recovery takes time. Don't rush it.

I had to learn the hard way to slow down and breathe. Life gave me no choice.

My dreams of further Olympic glory died with my daughter. I leaned into the heaviness of Liala's loss and slowly learned to accept her absence. I grew accustomed to the pain, relentless and ever present. My capacity to swallow hard ebbed away. I could no longer buck up and shut up when it came to my grief. If only I could have coped in that old way, perhaps I wouldn't have felt so raw, but my well-honed muscles of denial had shriveled.

I tried to stay close to Josh. After all, he had lost his daughter too, but not only was I hurting, I was in the dark about myself. I wasn't just haunted by my daughter's death, but by the specter of my mother's long-ago psychological dissolution. I didn't know enough to confess that I was fighting off the past. All I knew was that I needed a partner in sorrow. I didn't trust Josh enough to allow him to fill that role, and Josh didn't know me well enough to figure out that he needed to fill that role. It was no surprise that our attempts to console each other fell short.

My mother tried to come to the rescue, but she could only travel so far, and I would only allow her to come so close. I met her at the airport following her flight to Seattle, six weeks after her first granddaughter's death, the trip planned when all was on track and left unchanged when everything went to hell.

We had spoken on the phone briefly a few times since Liala's still-birth, and she had groped for the right tone and the right words. I tried not to blame her for keeping her distance. I wanted to understand her fear of grief. I had to understand it, so that the same monster would not swallow me up as it had done her. I had long believed that I was destined to be my mother's daughter, that her impulses would be mine one day. She had viewed suicide as a viable option when life handed her seemingly overwhelming obstacles. I always assumed that I would respond the same way.

But now I wanted to chart a different course for myself. Rowing had provided me with a perfect training ground. On the water I learned to ignore my inner pleadings, perfected toughness, and became a champion at self-discipline. Now, all those races won and medals earned fell away. I faced the ultimate challenge, where my life was at stake, as surely as my mother's had been all those years before when she slumped over the dining room table, clutching her pill bottle, consumed by her pain.

I still longed for my mother's warmth, for a sense of connection. If she would only lead with her heart, I would abandon my reticence and my deliberate distance. This was a precious chance to erase our past, to redefine our relationship, and to reforge our connection.

But that wasn't to be. Her initial words were, "I almost didn't come," and when she hugged me, it was with her arms only, no full-body connection attempted or allowed, no place for us to sway together in our shared loss. As if distance could keep despair at bay.

She couldn't do it. I should not have blamed her for protecting herself, but I did. She gave me so little when I needed so much. It was the last time I would seek her out.

Oddly, I found myself calling my father, not once or twice, but regularly and often. He was the first parent to reach Seattle after Liala's stillbirth, the last one I would have bet on jumping on a plane and making the cross-country trek to confront grief eye to eye. He arrived with my stepmother two days after Liala's delivery. They spent a long weekend walking beside me as I took my first steps into the dark forest of deep sadness. They showed up at the worst of times. A priceless gift.

Long after that visit, when my sadness overwhelmed me to the point of near-total disconnection, I would dial Dad's office number and retain my composure long enough to identify myself to the receptionist.

"Hello?" At the sound of my father's voice, my throat would close up and my voice turn into a croak.

"It's Ginny." I could only whisper. Then I would cry. The minutes would flow by, my father on the other end of the phone, quiet, bobbing along in my flood of tears. He didn't know what to say, so said little, except "Hello. Goodbye. I love you." Sometimes he told me short stories about other people's losses. No lectures or put-downs, egging on or teasing, just searching for words that would help when there was nothing to say. He kept my head above water.

Was this the same father who had sounded so brusque when I called him from the delivery room, who acted so coolly professional? He apologized, unprompted, on one of those first hopeless, helpless calls. "Ginny, that day, when you called me from the hospital, I had someone in my office. Someone I was firing." He understood after all. His heart had broken, too. He would not run away.

Slowly, I began to understand my daughter's gift to me. I could learn to live with my sadness, even if it blocked out everything else: I did not have to poison myself by swallowing it. I could breathe by acknowledging its presence. I could survive feeling it. No more denial, no more pretending.

My mother buried her pain, only to have it detonate inside her; that didn't have to happen to me. In my quest for the Olympic podium, I honed my toughness and developed remarkable internal resolve, but only now did I learn I was my own person. I was not my mother. I didn't have her psyche, hadn't lived her life, and wasn't doomed to repeat her mistakes.

Instead of killing me, losing Liala released me.

Inhale. Exhale. Cry. Release. Repeat.

My days of pulling hard on and off the water were over. I sold my single in the spring of 1988, another Olympic year. I stored my last set of blades, painted in USA red, white, and blue, in the garage, wondering if anything could ever fill the emptiness.

The experts predicted it would take two years to work through my grief, and they were right. But finally I found myself at the edge of that pitch-black forest on a faint path, streaks of sunshine pointing my way forward. I learned that even sadness would run its course eventually and leave me standing bowed but not broken. And then I discovered I was pregnant again, this time with a son who would live to tell his own story.

She taught me so much, that first child of mine, who was too impatient to wait for life to begin and had to rush on to her next engagement. She left me heartbroken, but on a corrected course, guided by a new internal voice, confident, steadied by hope, and not driven by fear.

I may have set a new course, but I hadn't fully learned to row my own boat. I had conquered my fears of becoming my mother, but I remained my father's goody-goody daughter, still trying to please him. Still trying hard to please the world despite the high price of doing so.

How many thousands of strokes had I taken? How many countless hours had I spent on the water practicing hard strokes, perfecting technique, learning balance? Nonetheless, I had not yet mastered the most important lesson.

Ten years after Liala's death, I remained locked in a marriage that looked good on the outside but stank on the inside. Living the standard idea of happily ever after, I felt desiccated and desolate.

Not that life was all bad, by any means.

My dreams of motherhood came true not once or twice, but three times, each occasion filled with its own mystery and magic. Our first son, Gilder, made his appearance nearly three years after his older sister's fetal demise, a few days ahead of his due date, late in the evening, so quickly that I missed my chance for an epidural. To manage the pain, I pretended I was racing in the Head of the Charles and kept counting out ten-stroke pieces to stay focused and calm. Because I didn't know how long the delivery would take, I kept my imaginary racecourse progress measured, never allowing myself to travel beyond the first big turn by Magazine Beach. His live birth was a better reward than any medal.

Although fear of losing him plagued my entire pregnancy, Gilder's arrival more than compensated for the ups and downs of those nine months. He was alive and well, small but healthy. His blue eyes turned hazel within his first month and he grew off the charts quickly. His light birth weight doomed him to a protracted period of late-night feedings, so I became intimate with the peaceful hours of deep night. Rocking him in a quiet house swathed in a silent world, while he slurped milk in little gulps, I discovered what I missed with Liala. The joy of holding my little boy intensified while crystallizing and salving my grief for my lost baby girl.

Gilder was an articulate, active two-year-old when we adopted round-faced, pudgy Max from an agency in Philadelphia that was committed to giving children of color the same access to a life of opportunity that Caucasian and foreign-born babies enjoyed. As I sat with my second child that first day we met, he was all of six days old. I stroked his soft, chubby cheeks and let him grasp my fingers. He was nearly ten pounds, almost twice Gilder's birth weight, which gave me instant confidence. He was solid, my own little Buddha.

Nearly two months passed, while I held my breath and tried not to fall in love with Max, before a Pennsylvania court finalized the adoption on what would have been Liala's fifth birthday. By then, Max was a cheerful, active baby. He was on the go as soon as he learned to crawl, difficult to keep track of, and impossible to stop. Early on I could tell he would be a handful, strong willed and independent. When he woke in the morning, he switched on—there was no halfway with him—and he stayed in motion until he went to bed, when he switched off and fell asleep nearly instantly. Whereas Gilder took over eighteen months to sleep through the night, within six weeks of his arrival, Max slept like the dead.

I loved my boys, the observant towhead who was fascinated by shapes and loved to read, and the brown-haired barrel of energy who explored everywhere with a wriggling physicality. Already one-year-old Max wanted to wrestle with Gilder, who preferred calmer engagements. The pair often ran in opposite directions, one pulling pots out of the kitchen drawers to bang, the other pulling books off the living room shelf to devour.

Six weeks after Max's first birthday, a friend called with the news that she was pregnant. I took a deep breath. "What are you going to do?"

"Come on. I'm close to forty. I have two teenagers. I can't afford another child."

As we sorted through the options for an abortion, I heard the call-waiting signal sound on my phone line. I ignored it and kept talking with my friend until we worked through the details of what lay ahead for her.

We said goodbye and hung up. Another pregnancy would end at the wrong time, again.

I sat on a kitchen stool, thoughts of the unfairness of life pattering around me, soft raindrops of sadness.

Remembering I had missed a phone call, I picked up the phone and dialed my voice mail. The voice of the director of our adoption agency in Philadelphia spoke to me out of the blue. "Ginny, it's Chuck, from Option of Adoption. Would you please call me back as soon as you get this message? Don't worry, it's not about Max."

Of course it's about Max! I'm not going to give him up. I'll fight for him. Why do they want him back, after all this time?

Nerves jangling, hands shaking, I dialed. Chuck was waiting for my call and picked up the phone immediately, sparing me further agony.

"Ginny, I've spent the morning with Max's birth mother."

"What did she want?" I braced myself.

"She came in with another baby this morning."

"What?!" Is this for real?

"Look, we need to find a home for this baby quickly. I want to give you and Josh first choice. It's much better for Max if his sibling grows up with him, and I'm sure I can convince the birth mother to agree. You can have the weekend to decide, but we need to know by Monday morning."

And then, almost as an afterthought, he added, "By the way, it's a girl."

I had always wanted a daughter, maybe for the wrong reasons, but I couldn't lie to myself. Yes, I absolutely adored my two boys, but their presence in my life had not closed the gap I felt without a baby girl. I wanted to prove that a mother didn't have to raise a daughter the way my mom had, breaking my heart midstream. I wanted to validate my belief that, despite my mother's apparent experience with me, mothering a daughter, along with the inevitable hurts and upsets, could be filled with unquenchable love and a deep, unbreakable connection.

I dreamed of holding my daughter's hand and absorbing her experience, even if only vicariously and a generation removed, as I clasped her fingers and cupped her palm in mine: knowing she was lovable and belonged, trusting that, despite my own internal havoc, she could count on me, in good times and bad. Raising a daughter, I believed, would help heal the wounds my own mother had inflicted on me, unintentionally I knew by now, but still devastating.

My daughter finally arrived. Josh stepped off the plane a week later at 1 a.m., bringing her with him. I took my baby girl into my arms, our first embrace missed what would have been her older sister's sixth birthday by an hour. The moment I cradled Sierra, gazed into her brown eyes, and absorbed her serious expression as she examined my features, I knew she belonged to me, and I to her. I could tell we would forge our own bond, based on mutual trust and deep affection, and I would accompany her as she discovered the world and herself. From that day forward, I marveled at the universe's reversal of my daughter fortunes.

Josh and I ended up with three children less than forty months apart in age, all younger than age four, and life progressed from there. Outnumbered, often outwitted, we raised our three in a raucous household filled with music and sports. Two violinists, Gilder and Sierra, combined with Max the cellist. T-ball, soccer, and swimming filled afternoons, early evenings, and weekends.

Raising them took most of my energy and usurped all my patience. I never loved anybody the way I loved my trio. Snuggling together in the morning as they pounced on me, lying in their beds at night, reading, cuddling, talking, dozing off. Listening to their deep breathing at night and their chattering during the day, I felt the fullness of their presence in my life.

The memory of my first child made me grateful for all the moments the next three gave me, hard and easy. I rarely bypassed a chance to grab them for a hug or a kiss, and nestled them close when they sought me out for solace. They reawakened me to the little things, examining an ant on the sidewalk, discovering a turtle buried in the dirt, riding in the car with the wind blowing through our hair.

I convinced Josh to buy an eight-acre piece of high-bank, west-facing waterfront property on Lopez Island, one of the San Juan Islands that lies seventy-five miles northwest of Seattle, accessible only by private boat or ferry. We built our own summer cabin, raised a handmade flagpole with a tree cut from our property, fenced a square of land for a deer-free garden, carved out a baseball diamond, cobbled together a swing set and jungle gym, tucked a wood-burning hot tub at the edge of the woods, and constructed a fire pit at the far end of the wide front lawn where it sloped down to the high-banked shore. I convinced my big sister Peggy to come there, too, and she found a sprawling property less than two miles away where she brought her family for the summers. We even enticed our diehard East Coast siblings—the grown-up Littles, Miss Muffet, now Britt-Louise, and Richard III, whose only response to his old nickname "Dixie" was stone-cold, disgusted silence—to trek across the country now and then to our West Coast version of East Hampton, minus the warm ocean and wide sandy beaches. There we launched the next generation's accumulation of their own sweet memories of lazy summer days filled with nothing but exploration and pleasure.

The years ticked by. I poured myself into creating the happy family I had missed out on as a teenager and did my best to ignore the knot of tension that settled low in my belly. After a while I couldn't remember its absence and accepted my constant low-grade anxiety as part of me. If I could just maintain my focus on my children, I told myself, I'd be fine. I did my best to ignore the internal ache from building pressure and the accompanying refrain, "Is that all there is?" that I found myself humming in odd moments.

18

Rowing is fraught with the potential for disaster. For a sport so focused on command and control, it's really quite impressive how suddenly and completely a perfectly good row can go wrong. Little things happen, imperceptible to the casual observer, and all of a sudden, it's crisis. An oar digs into the water at the wrong angle, jerking the boat to port. You overcorrect and suddenly your shell is fighting a losing battle with physics and gravity. Unprepared and unprotected, far from shore, your options may be limited and extremely unsavory.

Imagine falling in love with someone else right before your husband's eyes. The irony is that my intentions were pure: I was trying to enliven my marriage, not kill it.

After fifteen years, our relationship had devolved to a framework for raising children, with nothing beyond it to bolster or inspire our interest in each other. I wanted more, but the odds were long. Although I wanted to want Josh, I didn't, and hadn't for a long, long time. Lack of desire was never a problem for me. But now my customary inner fire had lost its burn. As much as I knew I should want closeness with my husband, I couldn't go there. It was embarrassing.

I had made a promise when I married Josh, and I intended to keep it. What secret formula could I devise to awaken desire? Something new to give us a united focus, something to tussle with, discuss, care about, and share.

Predictably, I turned to sports.

We both liked tennis, regardless of our low skill levels. We played every summer when we gathered with Josh's family for a week of vacation by Bantam Lake in Connecticut. Something good seemed to happen when we stepped on a court together, a lot of positive energy. Whacking ground strokes and chasing after winners was fun. Even just playing against family, my competitive juices started oozing, and so did Josh's: with a racquet in his hand, he came alive. Maybe that was a place to begin. Maybe we could take lessons and get good together.

We showed up at the indoor tennis center in South Seattle on a day in late September. Dressed in ill-fitting, raggedy workout shorts and holey T-shirts, grayish white socks, and scuffed tennis shoes, Josh and I wielded racquets whose strings were more dead than alive.

The instructor walked in carrying a red-and-white tennis bag that looked big enough to hold half a dozen racquets, wearing a precisely color-coordinated outfit and pristine white tennis shoes. She had short, wavy, blondish-brown hair and freckles scattered across her cheeks.

Her name was Lynn.

She set us up on the court to attempt the first drill: standing half-court, tap the ball over the net to your opponent diagonally across from you at least a dozen times without a miss. I was instantly engaged. There were challenges to tackle, skills to master, asses to kick. Lynn got in the groove with us immediately, figuring out what to focus on and how to nudge our skill levels forward.

We had lucked into a good teacher. She knew the game and could translate her knowledge into beginner's language. She corrected our technique without offering criticism and was upbeat and enthusiastic without going overboard. She talked strategy, too, discussed the mental challenge of the game, and taught us to think about concepts like time and spacing. There was no hyperbole or false praise. She was matter-of-fact without being blunt. I liked that.

Lynn clearly loved the game. I could tell by watching her demonstrations, which she performed with alacrity and finesse. I was struck by her smooth movements and her easy, graceful ability to cover the court. She showed us how to move from serving at the baseline swiftly up to the net without losing control of our feet or our racquets. She looked completely comfortable tossing the ball in the air to serve and had no trouble demonstrating a spin serve, or a slice, or a flat hard ace. She could hit with top spin from baseline to baseline, or rush the net and slice a blooper that rebounded from her opponent's reach and died after a single, sorry half-bounce.

She counseled us not to play it safe at the baseline by whacking ground strokes ad infinitum, but to live dangerously and try something new. She encouraged us to work our way to the net so we could take control of a point and enjoy the satisfaction of slamming winners out of the air at our opponents' feet. She quoted statistics to cajole us out of our comfort zones, assuring us that our winners would more than compensate for our inevitable errors. She cheered us with her ready smile and positive feedback, noting our progress in attacking the ball, asserting control of the game, and diminishing focus on our mistakes.

Every lesson found Lynn weaving stories. She regaled her students with vignettes of matches she had played with her husband—usually to make a point of what not to do, laughing at herself and her own foibles. A good sense of humor loosens up any environment; she removed fear from the equation of learning before it snuck onto the court. She sounded as if her life worked off the court, too. I wondered about that, what it would be like to tell stories of a happy marriage.

The six weeks of lessons flew by. Josh and I had enjoyed ourselves and signed up for another series. Learning felt good, even though improvement seemed to come slowly. Josh was satisfied with the pace and didn't want to do more. But I was impatient: I wanted to be good, so I asked Lynn if she offered private lessons.

I didn't realize where I was headed.

After our first private lesson, Lynn and I left the tennis center together. We chatted as we walked to our cars and paused to finish our conversation before saying goodbye. That's when I first noticed her blue eyes and the shyness behind her smile.

Our twice-weekly meetings expanded beyond the seventy-five minutes of lessons. We followed Lynn's rigorous on-court instruction with meandering off-court conversation, which progressed into e-mails and phone calls. Starting with a sketch of our family lives—she was married eighteen years and counting, had a fifteen-year-old daughter and a twelve-year-old son—we branched into other topics. We covered a lot of ground quickly: family histories (her mom dead of bone cancer, three years past; her dad a retired engineer and sculptor, still living in the house she grew up in; from Houston; three much older sisters— she was a "mistake"); life stories (a settled housewife who liked vibrant colors, no pastels, enjoyed needlepoint, and played football with her son; UW graduate, psychology major); religious denomination and political preferences (avowed atheist, not overly liberal Democrat). The kind of details that new friends usually share in dribs and drabs tumbled out easily, a rivulet gathering force as it moved downstream.

I was caught totally off guard. In the span of ten days, my life turned upside down. I transformed from an earnest student, focused on improving my strokes, to an imagined home wrecker, wildly attracted to a sedate suburban housewife. And Lynn didn't exactly help matters. One day, she gave me some CDs to learn about the music she liked. Ever the obedient student, I drove home immediately and turned on the CD player. I lay on my living-room couch and listened. Phrases of longing and thrums of desire dominated the lyrics. Alanis Morissette sang of lust and betrayal, Melissa Etheridge of loves lost, and k.d. lang, with her talk of "how bad could it be?" and "release your sexuality" . . . Was she talking about illicit sex? Gay sex? I wriggled on the couch, now wide awake to the river of sexuality that ran through the depths of the music, wondering if Lynn was sending me a message. She's not sending you a message about anything, she's giving you music to listen to, you idiot. But I wasn't so sure.

I played cat and mouse with myself. We were new friends, wanting to get to know each other. There was nothing to worry about. She was cool, fun, a hint of the wild side peeking out from her neat, color-coordinated exterior. She drove her turquoise Mustang convertible like an Indy car racer, her hair rippling, with one hand on the steering wheel as she casually revved her speed toward 80 miles per hour, waving and smiling at me as she flew by.

Take me with you!

And then it happened: an apparently innocent invitation to visit her family's vacation getaway at Sun Cove in Wenatchee catapulted our lives into uncharted waters.

I found myself in a simple ranch house above the wide-open waters of the Columbia River, surrounded by the pale yellow and brownish hills of near-desert conditions, lying on the couch next to my new close friend. Josh stayed behind in Seattle to work, and my oldest was visiting his grandparents, so I had only Max and Sierra with me.

On the first day of the visit, I met Lynn's husband, daughter, and son. Within an hour of arriving, I landed on a tennis court, playing opposite the guy who'd starred in Lynn's instructional vignettes back in the fall when Josh and I first started lessons. The next morning, he returned to Seattle with their son, leaving me and Lynn with her daughter and my kids. We enjoyed an uneventful day. That evening we made pizza, ate with our children, played games after supper, and sent them off to sleep.

Now we lay talking with our heads at opposite ends of the couch, our legs stretched alongside each other, trying to remain still in the first-time rush of physical closeness. I brushed my hand over her foot as I played with the woven anklet her daughter had crocheted, pretending that nothing extraordinary was happening. I kept my eyes away from hers.

Our children slept deeply in a darkened bedroom down the hall. Our husbands puttered about in our respective homes a hundred miles away, secure in their ignorance. The buckles that tethered our pasts to our futures strained and rattled against the gathering force of our longing.

Trained long ago to ignore my body's pleas, I was surprised to succumb now. Determinedly married, happily ever after, with kids! I had sworn: no divorce for my children, no wreaking havoc on their lives. Those promises barely registered in the force of this moment.

I forgot to be afraid.

I felt the softness of her foot in my palm, cool and dry. I didn't want to stop stroking her. My hand crept up to her calf. I wanted more. I picked up my glass of wine and took a tiny sip. I was stone-cold sober. No alcoholic stupor could serve as my cover.

I craved intimacy with this woman. She was a tennis instructor, not a world titan; an ordinary person, just another mother living a normal life; cute yes, attractive yes, but not svelte and conventionally sexy. She sported a Venus figure, full breasted, a round middle, square hips, heavy thighs. Steady blue eyes that broadcast calm, not calamity; assurance, not arrogance; trust, not tension. Fabulous freckles, reminding me of a summer day; perfect teeth, and an easy smile. She had me totally going, hot and bothered.

The heart wants what the heart wants. It defies logic. It maintains its own calculus, follows its own rules. My body knew which way to go.

I listened to her talk. I watched her face closely. Her lips looked parched.

Heart pounding, unable to resist any longer, I stood and reached for the ChapStick on the kitchen counter. Pulling off the lid, I screwed the pale stick of salve out of its case and sat beside Lynn. With a steady hand, I applied it to her lips, while she sat quietly. Finished, I leaned over and put my lips on hers. They were warm and oh, so soft.

I closed my eyes as I felt her lips part slightly and invite me in. I met a mix of warm and wet, mystery and comfort. A passion absent for too long.

The buckles of our pasts unclasped, and our future blew wide open.

Things got hot on the couch; we progressed into the bedroom. First I had to shift my slumbering six-year-old into another bed in another room. Perhaps that interruption ruined the moment: all forward progress stopped cold. I tried to build on those first kisses, but Lynn's "no" was clear and insistent.

Was she kidding? In for a nickel, in for a dollar. She had already crossed the line with a kiss; the time to turn back had long passed. I had already broken my promise to be faithful. There is no such thing as half-pregnant or half-dishonest.

But she said no, so we lay next to each other all night. At least she allowed me to luxuriate in her embrace, warming me with her body, her deep sighing breaths whispering into my ear as we dozed. Lynn maintained her composure for the both of us. She had grasped the risks of flirting with impending chaos sooner than I, and insisted on pulling us both back to responsible sanity.

Of course, it was too late for that.

The next afternoon we drove to Wenatchee for groceries, leaving the younger kids with Lynn's daughter, Toni. "I'm falling in love with you," I announced. The windows weren't open, but I yelled my news flash.

Lynn was driving, so she couldn't look at me with more than a glance. She barely changed her expression. "Yes?" Given what had transpired the night before, maybe she thought it was obvious.

"But I'm a married woman!"

Now she started laughing. "In case you haven't noticed, so am I."

I kept silent for eighteen days following that first kiss. I knew how I felt, but didn't know what to do.

It was late. The kids were finally asleep. I lay on the bed, on top of the covers, still dressed. Josh staggered in, waking up from having read himself to sleep with a children's book again. He started undressing.

"Josh, I need to talk to you." I took a breath. "I think I'm falling in love with Lynn."

"That's okay. I'm falling in love with something new, too. All I want to do is practice acupuncture. It's good that we have outside interests."

"I don't think it's the same thing." I took another breath.

"Why not?"

"I want to sleep with her."

"What do you mean?"

"I want to, you know . . ." I squirmed as I spelled it out. "Have sex." I was whispering now, ashamed, yet driven to tell him. I couldn't hide any longer.

"What would that buy you?" And then, his face closed down, as if a blank expression could hide the bomb I had dropped into our life.

That was just the beginning. Summer started, my favorite time of year, with its escape from the demands of tight schedules, the duties of school and work. Ever since I was a little girl waiting on Manhattan's dirty gray concrete sidewalks for the bus to take me to school, I turned my face to the sunshine, happy to bask in its warmth. This time, my favorite season was hell.

Despite my attraction to Lynn, I couldn't up and leave Josh. Love her, but don't leave, love her, but can't stay . . . loves me, loves me not . . . My own twisted version of daisy-petal pulling ruined my summer as I contemplated ruining my family. Did I want to leave or simply experiment? Was I considering my course or preparing my exit? Memories plagued me . . . of that horrid Sunday afternoon nearly thirty years earlier when my mother announced she had tossed my father out, and all the chaos and disaster that followed. No. I wouldn't do that to my children. I couldn't kick them to the curb for my own satisfaction. I couldn't put myself first and them a considerably distant second.

Josh was a good man. He didn't deserve betrayal. Maybe he wasn't the best communicator, maybe the spark between us had never fully ignited, maybe he drove me crazy in myriad ways with his forgetfulness and sloppiness, but did I really have to detonate everything? Was it so very critical that I get my way? At everyone else's expense?

I had shorted the truth and never considered I would have to buy it back with interest, and now that moment arrived. I had avoided payment as long as I could, denied and evaded those impulses that threatened the life that the world expected of me, the life that would take me down if I allowed it to proceed unfettered.

Impulses? another voice inside me said. They weren't impulses but directives, calls from within. I had heard them when I fell for Strayer. And how had I responded? Derided them as momentary distractions to be waved away with a toss of the head, discounted in the name of putting away childish things, boxed and stored in the basement of my life to grow dusty with age and recede into memory. I conned myself into thinking denial would buy me safety.

And it did. I had a nice life, a lovely home, three fabulous children, and a husband who showed up every day and did his best, who didn't shrink from child-raising or household chores, who knew how to cook better than I did.

But I had disappeared. I had swallowed hard and succumbed to the dictum of my youth, to hide, hide, hide the messy, unacceptable truths that lay beneath my surface. Long before there was a Josh, or a Liala, a Gilder, a Max, or a Sierra, I buried myself.

All summer, I grabbed every secret moment I could to spend time with Lynn. We chose the most ordinary places for our trysts. She drove twelve miles from Shoreline to shop for groceries with me, with a pit stop by the Civil War cemetery to lie on the grass in the sunshine and nuzzle each other. A star-struck and rabid fan, I came to her tennis matches, tracked every point, and cheered for quick finishes, which gave us more time to make out in her convertible in random parking lots.

How can I live without this? I would despair as I lay in her arms.

The more time I spent with her, the more I longed for. I cried for the damage to my children if I left their father; I cried for the damage to myself if I stayed. I had landed in the middle of a zero-sum game where winning looked suspiciously like losing.

Josh didn't want to break up, despite the facts. He would stay the course if given the chance. The choice was mine.

Give up my safe straight life for an untested model? Didn't my life work perfectly well, filled with longtime friends who liked me mostly as I was, a family that counted on me to behave a certain way, and a role in my community that fit just fine? I was going to trade it all in for the chance to be a gay girl, a dyke, for the uniform of flannel shirts and baggy pants, greasy hair, and hiking boots? Really? I liked my male buddies, not to mention all my straight girlfriends. I loved flirting with boys. Was I supposed to stop that now? I didn't need a new slogan to adopt or another mantra to learn. No, forget the rainbow stickers, the new "lesbo" adjective to attach to my identity, the loss of my membership in the comfortably clueless majority, and by all means, don't assign me to that persecuted minority.

Nothing came easy. Stay married or leave Josh? Crush my kids or smother myself? How could I be gay? Nights found me sleepless and anxious, unable to lie down beside the husband I commanded myself to honor. Days found me weeping at the idea of raising my children on a part-time basis. As I stumbled through my confusion and confronted the choices that lay before me, I realized the old wisdom that used to guide me was dead. Of course, it wasn't wisdom, but fear—that familiar monster whose grip around my throat was stronger than my mother's fingers. By any means necessary, no holds barred, fear got the job done, saved me from myself, and heaved me back on the straight and narrow.

But something new was at work now, a force that wasn't to be messed with, one that wouldn't take no for an answer. It ripped through me and snapped my tough-girl, buck-up and shut-up stance like so many twigs in a twister. All the fear that kept me down for so many decades proved no match for what I felt when I was with Lynn. I couldn't resist her; I couldn't resist myself. The scent of her hair, the feel of her warmth, the touch of her hand, the sound of her voice, the sparkle in those oh-so-very-blue eyes when they stared into mine; it was all impossible to deny. I wanted her in my life, every moment, every day, by my side in the most intimate of ways. I could not live without her sarcastic sense of humor, her matter-of-fact pragmatism, her calm counter to my up-and-down dramas, her affection, her interest, and her devotion to us.

The heart wants what the heart wants. Long suppressed, kept corralled in a safe and sensible harbor, mine finally broke free and grabbed the rudder to steer me into wild waters. There was no turning back.

1 9

"My husband and I are struggling." I couldn't solve this problem by myself. I sought counsel from an expert, a therapist who specialized in children. Maybe she could terrify me back into behaving with her stories of kids ruined by divorce.

"Tell me what's happening."

Deep breath, hands clenched together, bracing for the lecture about selfishness and responsibility, I said, "I've fallen in love with someone else. A woman."

"Where did you meet her? Are you going to live together here? Seattle is a great place for gay couples."

"What? I haven't even decided whether I should leave my marriage. I just don't know if I can do that to my children."

"You'd stay in an unhappy marriage for your kids?"

This was not the conversation I had anticipated.

"I lived through my parents' divorce . . . barely. I don't want to do that to my kids. "

"Divorce isn't usually the problem. It's the parents' reactions that cause the most trouble."

Old memories stirred; I felt myself falling back into that familiar vortex, all alone. I swiped at my sudden tears. "I owe them an intact family life."

"Three years from now, do you think you'll be happy with that decision? Imagine what you'd think every time you looked at one of your children."

Sit quietly, close eyes, picture Lynn floating away from me, feel my joy ebb away, chasing her down the stream. "I'd probably resent them."

"How would that be for them?"

I looked out the window, blinking furiously. I didn't want to cry here. I needed information, not sympathy; facts, not emotion.

"Ginny," the therapist spoke more gently. "Your kids need a happy mother. Without that, their lives will be much harder. I can help you bring your children through this. It won't be easy, but they'll be okay."

What? I didn't have to choose between my children's happiness and my own? Wait a minute! I had blamed my mother for pursuing her happiness at my expense. Now I should forgive her just because a therapist suggested she did the right thing?

Memories crowded in, challenging the judgment and fury of my fifteen-year-old self. I scanned those faded images looking for signs of my mom's happiness. Nothing. I saw her curled up under the covers, crying alone in her bedroom between sips of cold coffee, castigating my father for having left her, stumbling through her days incoherently, losing her children, her apartment, her sense of purpose.

She didn't pursue her happiness; she barely survived. She tried to contain her agony and numb her pain. When she lost her footing, her problems magnified and multiplied. She could hardly hold on to herself; no wonder she couldn't attend to her children.

A way forward started to open up as I sat quietly. No one suggested I avoid my children's pain. But don't sell out in the name of loving them. I'd sold out before and look where I had ended up. Right here. My survival wasn't at stake, just my happiness. If my marriage ended, I wouldn't lose myself. The real question was what would happen if I stayed.

The sweetness of a life with Lynn beckoned. I couldn't deny how bright it looked, how much I wanted it. Maybe the future could unfold differently in this newest iteration of family if I took the leap.

Fear. It never stops. It's always jumping up and down to catch my attention, waving a red flag about the future. A major crisis lurks ahead. Duck and cover. I spent nearly thirty years warding off potential dangers, bracing for problems that never materialized, and protecting myself from nightmarish fantasies that may have had some basis in the past, but had no basis in the present. I had done enough push-ups by now. I had nothing more to prove to myself.

Enough already.

I wouldn't ignore my children's suffering. I would acknowledge their loss. I would sit with them when they wept—not sidestep or sugarcoat their pain, but hold their hands and listen. I would not leave them alone with their grief. And I would make my relationship with this marvelous woman work, not just for me, but for them too. I would do the hard work required to build a life with her, big enough to include and welcome them. They would live in a household headed by grown-ups who wanted each other, who sought and maintained connection. We would all learn the truth about love, its high-flying ups and messy downs, its bargains and trade-offs, its hugs, kisses, and bouts of yelling. We would thrive.

Despite all the uncertainty I had struggled through, the confusion I had battled, now that I could see the road ahead, I knew I would stay the course. There would be no second-guessing or turning back. Before, I had been tough enough to buck up and shut down; now I was tough enough to show my vulnerabilities and risk pain and loss. I would have the hand of the woman I loved to pull me up and calm me down, to steady me and hold me. She would show me the way if my steps faltered or my fear threatened me. I wouldn't have to negotiate this life alone, waste energy to keep a secret that only hurt and never helped. I would get to live out loud, and love it.

Within six months of picking up that ChapStick and daubing Lynn's lips, my marriage was over and Josh had moved out. Time played tricks on me during that period—everything happening so fast, yet slowly enough to allow way too much opportunity to weigh options and consider consequences. In retrospect, it all felt like a disconcerting dream, rushing down a corridor filled with open doors, a fierce wind chasing me and slamming each one shut before I could grab the handle and peek inside to decide whether to enter. It turns out there was only one route and one exit.

I broke my children's hearts. I destroyed my husband's trust in me and lost him as a friend. We hired lawyers and initiated our divorce proceedings. My friends knew our marriage was dead. Josh's parents and family heard the horrible news. I sketched the scene for my siblings, swearing Peggy, Muff, and Richard III to silence. The story of my affair rippled through the families in my daughter's kindergarten class; I heard the whispers and felt the stares at the school playground and in the classroom.

Three thousand miles lay between me and my parents. To them, I'd said nothing.

I looked in the mirror and imagined my father's affection and respect evaporating when I repainted his image of me with one bold stroke. I had avoided thoroughly disappointing him my entire life. I could see his downcast eyes and hear his voice in my head, and I didn't have to work hard to imagine his words, "I'm disappointed in you" and "I thought you would know better," challenging my resolve.

Was I ready to take this step, to let us both know that forever going forward, the force of his will was not going to trump mine?

It was now or never.

Late morning sunshine filtered in the kitchen window as I sat at the table with a pen and a notepad of yellow-lined paper. After a minute or two, I lay down along the cushioned window seat and stretched out in the sun, arms cradling my head, eyes closed. Words and phrases drifted in and out along with random thoughts. No guts, no glory. Birds chattered and twittered in the evergreens beyond the deck. Leave it all on the water. Jet engines rumbled above. Row your own race. I listened to the rhythm of my breathing as I thought of things to come. No pain, no gain. The waters ahead did not look particularly gentle; a slight wind had kicked up and small waves ran up against the current. Not quite whitecaps, but the going would be choppy. Time to turn into the wind and dig in.

I set the pad in front of me, uncapped the pen.

Dear Dad,

I've thought about writing you for a while now. I know I told you that my marriage wasn't going so well, but I didn't tell you the whole story. I've fallen in love with someone else. That someone else is a she. Her name is Lynn.

I don't know how it happened. All I can say is that she is worth all the pain of leaving my husband, hurting my children, and disappointing you.

I hope you can understand. I know this will be hard for you. You are very important to me; I love you. I want you to know the truth about me, even if it makes you stop loving me. It's been a long road, but I know I'm headed back on course.

2 0

Eight years later, on a gray and chilly January afternoon, I stand on the sidelines at the Starfire Soccer Complex in Tukwila, Washington, as my daughter tries out for the Olympic Development Program (ODP).

Fourteen-year-old Sierra is a forward, a player whose shots have a nose for the back of the net. The coach, inexplicably, has put her on defense. Why isn't he letting her show her stuff? But I know my mama bear instincts have no place here. I scrunch my chin into the collar of my pile jacket, shove my hands into my pockets, and clamp my teeth together. Sisi's doing fine. Her foot skills are sure, field vision excellent, and passing precise, no matter where she's put.

This tryout is merely a formality. Everyone has told Sierra she's a shoo-in for the team: her reserved and understated premier club coach, her soccer guide for the past three years; her high school coach, a rock star at hard ass; the mother of a current ODP player who has already added my name to the team's e-mail list.

The practice rolls to its end. Now the coach is talking to Sierra on the sidelines. Good! My hands clench and unclench in their respective pockets. Sierra nods okay and strides off the field, a girl on a mission, grabs her backpack lying near the bench, comes up to me, barely pauses, keeps on going. "Let's go, Mom."

I start to speak, but I can't. I fall in step with her.

Her expression impassive, she says quietly, "I didn't make it." I hear the break in her voice.

When the car door closes, the seat belts are clicked in, the engine started, her tears come: "I'm not good enough." The grief and pain of a lost dream.

Focus. Breathe. My daughter's dream has been derailed by a man who can't see how talented she is. My anger won't help. My tears won't help. I can't fall into the abyss that has just opened up within me; this is not the time.

Sierra is crying almost too hard to talk, playing back the coach's words between her guttural heaves. "He told me that I had to be a lot better than anyone on the team to get picked. I had to be better if he was going to cut someone. I'm not better."

She keeps going, slowed by her sobs. "I don't care. I didn't want to be on that team anyway."

I keep driving; Sierra is nearly choking with heartbreak, keening like a wild animal, injured and abandoned by its pack.

My memories come flooding back: the burn of wanting something so much yet being left behind; the agony of being labeled "not good enough"; the fear of what failure would mean about me.

Rowing taught me toughness and gave me the confidence to believe in myself. My beloved sport gave me a testing ground for standing on my own two feet, for discovering I could go my own way and my world would not disintegrate. After all, my father did not stop loving me when I ignored his advice and kept rowing after three years of being cut by National Team coaches. But ultimately, not even my ascent to Olympic heights could teach me my most fundamental life lesson: I was my own person with my own life to direct. Nothing, not fear or the prospect of loss should deter me.

No one had ever taken the time to assure me that I could not lose if I followed my heart. No one had ever realized how badly I needed to hear those words out loud.

I was an ordinary girl when it all began, with a mother who was ill and a father who needed distance from both his feelings and mine. Ordinary, that's what I was, a preteen whose understanding of the world was skewed, who mistrusted herself and her potential as a result, who had to fight the world harder because she thought she wasn't quite strong enough or good enough or lovable enough to win as she was.

That's what we all are in the beginning—ordinary—with the same ingredients poured into our psyches: the capacity to learn, to love, to stand up when we are shoved down hard by life, to persist in the face of agony, to listen to the quiet of our hearts when the world is shouting we are wrong, and to keep becoming ourselves. I reached the near-pinnacle of extraordinary by developing ordinary qualities, by honing my capacity for self-discipline and channeling my nearly debilitating fear into an imperative to go forward, regardless. I developed some of the muscles we are all given. I did it the hard way, alone and afraid much of the time.

I turn and look at my precious daughter, still sobbing. I will not leave her to draw her own wrong conclusions about the afternoon that has just ended. I cannot make her feel better, and that's not the point anyway, but maybe I can help her avoid the mistakes I made so long ago.

I say quietly, "Sierra, are you going to let one coach who watched you for one practice decide how good you are?"

No answer. She keeps sobbing. "You're going to let him have that much say about your future?"

She glances over at me. I continue, "One hour, that's all he saw. Does he know more about you than you do? Than the coaches who have worked with you for years?"

I take her hand and hold it, driving left-handed. Sierra knows I was an athlete; she grew up playing dress-up with my assortment of medals and knows that one of them is Olympic silver, hanging from a ribbon colored with the pastels of LA's 1984 Games. But she doesn't know everything.

"Have I ever told you about trying out for the Olympics?" She swallows and shakes her head. Her sobbing slows to crying. A half-hour drive home lies before us, more than enough time.

By the time I finish, we are nearly home. I pull in the driveway and turn off the ignition. Sierra has stopped crying. I reach over and take her hand again, pull her over to me, and cradle her head against my shoulder. I wish my love could salve her sorrow, but I know better. Then I take her hand and say, "Sierra, look at me."

Calm and quiet now, her usual rock-solid composure regained, she looks into my eyes.

"Don't ever let anyone tell you who you're going to be. Only you get to decide that. Okay?"

She nods. "Okay, Mom," she says. "I won't."

We get out of the car and walk to the top of the narrow path that leads to the front door. I envelop her in a mama bear hug. A circle completes itself. I know my baby girl is going to stay on course, regardless of the inevitable winds and waves that her own row will take her through and the currents that will buffet her.

I breathe deeply. I realize how far I've come; the young girl inside me, now well past forty, has fully claimed her future. I've never had any trouble dredging up painful memories, however measured—in years, in tears, in forgotten half-empty cups of bitter, cold coffee. But I often wondered what happened to my happy moments. Where were they? Why didn't they ever float into my thoughts?

The good of my past was there, burrowed deep inside, well beneath the expectations and the "shoulds," smothered by the buck-ups and shut-ups. Yet not lost; rather, I now realize, waiting for an invitation and a warm welcome.

Those good memories swell within me as I stand with my daughter. Here they come, like water from a stream finally undammed, a spigot finally unblocked; a dribble at first, and then I'm drinking from a fire hose . . .

Mom's piano tickle game, her goodnight kisses after a fancy night out, her perfume wafting sweetly while she gently pulled my thumb out of my mouth; Swedish meatballs with creamy gravy, mounds of thin pancakes, happy homes for butter and syrup; Christmas Eve parties rich with company, center-pieced with a groaning smorgasbord, stockings filled with silly gifts from Mrs. Claus; all those East Hampton summer days on Briar Patch Road, filled with days at the beach playing in the waves, sunbathing, building sandcastles; camping under the stars and waking up beneath dew-soaked blankets; swinging in the hammock with Dad; our underwater somersault contests; the penny doctor, invented by Dad to soothe a stubbed toe or salve a skinned knee; playing box ball, hand ball, and running bases on the city's sidewalks; my first-ever run around the reservoir, hot sun, barefoot, a long mile and five-eighths, inspired by Dad's patience and cheerleading to make it all the way without stopping, even though I was dead slow.

I remember that October day when I was sixteen and miserable, standing on the banks of the Charles, seeing those string-bean-slim boats for the first time. I remember falling in love with the oars splashing, the sunlight dancing, the synchronicity, and the power and control. I remember wanting to make it all mine.

Inside me, the river runs deep and clear now.

Standing by the shores of Lake Casitas, the desert sun reflecting off the shiny silver medal newly around my neck, I raise my head and see my family in the crowd, waving and cheering wildly. I feel the tug of my teammates' hands as we thrust our arms high above our heads. We did it. I did it.

"Let it run." Finish your stroke, let your hands come out of the bow in the first part of the recovery; pause on your slide, lower your oar handles into your lap so that the flat blades glide high above the water. Sit still as long as you can, balancing to prevent any oars from slapping the water. The boat will slow like a magnificent crane skimming over the water, until it finally comes to rest of its own accord.

Epilogue

Diana Taurasi, the undisputed star of the Phoenix Mercury in the Women's National Basketball Association, has just hit a trademark twenty-two-foot three-point shot on the run and is strutting down the court, tugging the upper corners of her jersey front in the classic "ain't I grand" gesture of athlete show-offs, smiling gleefully as the crowd roars its adulation and approval. I want to strangle her for gloating before the end of a game, rubbing in the drubbing.

But it's hard to dispute the facts: 3:21 left on the clock and we are down by 12, a big margin for a team that's far from home, playing in the Arizona desert. I'm not in the lineup myself. After all, basketball is a far cry from rowing, not to mention that I'm in my fifties now, but I am sitting in the visiting owners' seats, watching the action closely and willing my players to pull off a miracle.

There's no sniff of desperation from my Seattle Storm players. They look focused as they switch to offense. Swin Cash starts the Storm's comeback attempt by hitting an eight-foot running bank shot, drawing a foul by DeWanna Bonner, and making her free throw. Taurasi misses her next three-point attempt, Lauren Jackson's jump shot from nine feet out swishes in, and our defense kicks in, forcing a pair of turnovers, including a steal by Camille Little, which culminates with her being fouled and going to the line for two, which go in. Down by five now. Another couple of Mercury misses (suddenly Taurasi has gone stone cold, oh sweet!), sandwiched by another Jackson bucket and one, courtesy of another Mercury foul. With thirty-two seconds left, Swin ties the score at 88 with an effortless lay-up, but it's the Mercury's ball and they call a time-out.

I watch my team huddling with their coaches by the visitors' bench, the WNBA franchise I purchased with three other women two-and-a-half years earlier when the then new owner of Seattle's men's and women's professional basketball franchises, the Seattle Supersonics and Storm, respectively, decided to move his teams to Oklahoma. While our group could do nothing to avert the loss of the men's team, we succeeded in keeping the women's team in the city. It wasn't like any of us had dreamed of owning a professional sports team, but this opportunity offered so much upside that pursuing the purchase proved irresistible: contributing to our community by keeping one of its gems safe and sound at home; helping to build the nation's only women's professional team sports league; showcasing top women athletes as leaders and role models; and promoting the concept of women as successful leaders in any business domain. Prior to the WNBA's inception, only two women had bought majority stakes in professional sports teams instead of inheriting them. (Joan Payson was founder of the New York Mets in 1961; Marge Schott purchased a minority share of the Cincinnati Reds in 1981 and assumed majority ownership in 1984.) Who wouldn't relish the idea of helping to bust the glass ceiling of professional sports team ownership? What better use of our dollars than to assume the financial risk for a business endeavor that married our shared love of sports with our commitment to social justice?

We were playing for the Western Conference title. One step outside the arena, the weather, cloudless blue sky, 107 degrees, made me grateful that basketball was not an outdoor sport. The arena was cool and dark, but the players sweated visibly nonetheless.

The year? 2010. The players on the court were all born at least ten years after Title IX's passage. They grew up shooting hoops, earned full rides to play in college, and now were living their dream: playing basketball for a living. As for me and my co-owners—who grew up in the decade preceding Title IX and pioneered the legislation's application to force the first changes in college sports venues—views on girls' participation in sports had differed from community to community, college scholarships for female athletes didn't exist, and the idea of playing sports for a living was a pipe dream for women. Now, sitting courtside at a game televised live by ESPN, our ownership group was in the hunt to claim the first championship in professional sports history by a franchise that was not just owned, but purchased by women.

Time out over, the Mercury set up and Temeka Johnson attempts a jumper, which our star point guard, Sue Bird, blocks. She then grabs the rebound and signals another time-out. The clock shows 23.7 seconds left.

I haven't always known where to steer, but I've consistently pursued ways to express the passion that emerged from my years as a top athlete, increasing access to opportunity for marginalized populations. I probably wouldn't have used that fancy phrase to explain my decision to participate in the Yale Women's Crew strip-in or to rationalize my drive to make an Olympic team despite my shorter stature, but my wake offers proof of the course I've taken over the decades.

My favorite occupation is to incite people not just to dream, and dream big, but to shrink the divide between imagination and reality to their point of convergence, setback by setback, step by step. My efforts focus on removing the barriers—cultural, situational, and financial— that narrow the route to a meaningful life, and I've dedicated myself to addressing those in the realm of sports. I didn't exactly follow a straight line from my involvement in the sports world as an athlete to that of a business woman. I worked in a variety of domains on both the non-profit and for-profit sides of the business aisle, usually as an entrepreneur, before I found my way home to sports. But that's another story for another day. What's important is that I landed where I belong.

I own the Storm not because it's a basketball team, but because it's a professional sports team that offers the best female basketball players in the world the opportunity to do what they love as a career. Far from the college campus and Joni Barnett's office where I stood with my teammates nearly forty years ago, our backs stained with Yale blue ink, now I stand with different partners, engaged in another sport, promoting the same ideal on a different stage: male or female, people deserve the same chance to reach for greatness.

Fair or not, access to opportunity is never given freely. I am one of the lucky ones and one of the determined ones. I was in the right place at the right time to help challenge the status quo that relegated women athletes to secondary status, and I have chosen to set my course on realizing the ideal of parity between the sexes in sports. Perhaps this dream is fantastic and will always remain beyond our reach. Miracles do happen, however, although never by accident and never without extreme effort.

Tanisha Wright receives the inbound pass that ends the Storm's time-out, dribbles deliberately to reduce the time on the clock and ensure that the Storm's last shot attempt will be the game's last shot . . . under twenty seconds to go, now under ten. She passes to Sue, who catches the ball outside the three-point arc and puts it up immediately, not a hint of hesitation, but an instant's evidence of the beauty that comes from being in the zone. Mercury players jump to deflect the ball, arms reaching high and flailing. As the ball swishes through the net, there are 2.8 seconds left. Phoenix calls one more, now desperate, time-out, and Taurasi takes the last shot, her third miss in a row. Game over in a whoosh of poetic justice. One of my partners, Lisa Brummel, envelops me in a gigantic bear hug. Damn, after all these years, winning still feels incredible; there's nothing else like it.

I strive to keep on course, still applying the life lessons that started accruing the first day I stepped into a rowing shell. My Storm players may have learned their lessons on a basketball court, my daughter on a soccer field, but, no matter what sport, the take-aways are fundamentally the same: never give in to your fear or up on your dream, go the extra mile, planning and hard work consistently pay off, and the power of teamwork is tough to beat. Simple phrases, trite off the tongue, yet tough to traverse in real time.

Ready all, row.

Acknowledgments

This endeavor's beginnings go way back, so I will begin by acknowledging my parents. Along with loving me as best they could and providing for me in nearly every way possible, they set me up with all the curiosities that make up my personality and well supplied me with grist for my mill.

Jumping forward fifty years to 2008, Dara Torres, whom I have not had the pleasure of meeting, nonetheless inspired me to question my assumptions about my own limits. Her willingness to challenge accepted boundaries related to age and peak athletic performance on the world stage set me on course to write this memoir, by igniting my desire to train for the Olympics again. Michael Gervais, PhD, took the hand-off from Dara. He didn't laugh me away when I first asked him to help me train for the 2012 Olympics, but took me seriously, advising that "something unexpected will likely come out of this adventure." He was right; my return to the water as a competitive rower opened the memory floodgates that flowed not to London, but right here.

Thanks to Lisa Wogan, who didn't snicker when I first shared my dream to write a memoir but directed me to Hugo House, Seattle's Mecca for those seeking their muse, where I immersed myself in the world of writers and writing and luxuriated in the experience of learning as a fresh-faced (okay, not really) novice.

Without Kelley Eskridge, I would still be stuck on page 100, unable to figure out where and how to go. Kelley served as my writing coach and editor, first helping me figure out what story to tell and then coaxing and cheering me through every paragraph, period, and page. Realistic, yet supremely knowledgeable, compassionate, and patient, she took my initial draft down to its foundation and guided me from there. A champion of the writing process, which in my case meant a seemingly endless loop of rewriting, Kelley buoyed me through writing's rough waters in every way possible and, in doing so, floated into the realm of trusted confidante and friend. Without Kelley, you would not be reading this sentence.

My beta readers agreed to peruse an early draft of the manuscript and provide unalloyed feedback, likely wincing in anticipation. To Ester Bailey, Susan Coskey, Nicola Griffith, Cathy Harvey, Charlie Stevenson, Ed Taylor, Joanie Warner, and Andrea Wenet, thanks for donating your only chance to read this book for the first time to the improvement of a version that needed your help to find its full self.

My Yale Women's Crew posse searched their memories and their files for various tidbits pertaining to our college years on the water and off and engaged in spirited e-mail exchanges to help me recall various incidents: Chris Ernst, Sally Fisher, Jenny Kiesling, Margaret Mathews, Elaine Mathies, Mary O'Connor, and Cathy Pew. Thanks also to Nat Case and Barbara Chesler at Yale University for generously making source materials available. Thanks to David LaBarge for affectionately reminiscing with me about why he stayed so adamantly in the closet while he was at Yale, and to Ann Strayer, who so generously allowed me to share part of her story without shortchanging the truth.

Kelley Eskridge and Nicola Griffith merit double mention, Kelley for introducing me to her wife and well-reputed author, Nicola, and Nicola for thinking her agent might like *Course Correction* and then introducing us. Stephanie Cabot, no doubt influenced by her experience with the world of rowing, courtesy of her two oldest children, both Division I collegiate athletes, stepped up to the not inconsiderable challenge of finding a publishing home for a new author writing about a minor sport. Of course, Stephanie got her job done, for which I will be eternally grateful. Without her optimism and dedicated follow-through, my dream of becoming a published writer would be wallowing in the muddy backwaters of bitter longing.

Thanks to my always upbeat editor, Joanna Green, who sold my story to her compatriots at Beacon Press and helped me wend my way through the publication process with a minimum of angst. I appreciate the efforts of the entire Beacon Press team, including Susan Lumenello, managing editor, and Beth Collins, production coordinator, whose expertise improved my manuscript at every step. Pam MacColl, Beacon's director of communications, led the way on the marketing front, aided by Lucinda Blumenfeld of Lucinda Literary, who coaxed me out of the shadows into social media's sunshine. Together, Pam and Lucinda worked assiduously to get the word out about my story, with great spirit and keen eyes for opportunity. My executive assistant, Jennifer Harshbarger, handled logistics of every stripe with aplomb, allowing me to spread myself thin enough to get everything that needed doing accomplished.

Last, and of course not least, there's my family. I owe deep thanks to my siblings: Britt-Louise, who read the completed manuscript to discern the depths of upset to which the rest of my family might descend and, encouraged that this was no *Mommy Dearest*, gave me the emotional approval to proceed; my prickly brother and Latin scholar extraordinaire, Dr. Richard Gilder III, who debated declensions and precise meanings to arrive at the perfect phrasing of my dedication; and last but so not least, Peggy, who has protected me as often as she teased me, keeping me safe and toughening me up for well over five decades now.

To my three children, Gilder, Max, and Sierra, whom I did not ask permission to mention, much less, in Sierra's case, to share part of her story, I love you forever, no matter what. And, finally, to the person who read every word of every draft in between her full-time job and her graduate studies, who heard (and may be excused for not listening intently to) every passing concern and complaint about the writing and publishing process and managed to convey sincere interest and patient support every time, my wife, Lynn, thank you. Without you, I would not have the amazing life I have.

Bibliographic Essay

In writing this book, I relied on a number of secondary sources to paint the picture and progress of both the women's and the gay liberation movements from the 1950s to the present. In addition, I occasionally relied on the memories of my Yale Women's Crew teammates to bolster my own.

CHAPTER 4
I had several wide-ranging conversations with Chris Ernst on several dates, including June 9, 2009, October 1, 2009, October 18, 2009, and March 20, 2014, during which we discussed which Yale programs rowed at the lagoon, for how long, and the events that led to her decision to arrange a team protest in Joni Barnett's office.

I engaged in an e-mail exchange with Jennie Kiesling on March 14, 2014, regarding Nat Case's immediate reaction to the strip-in and surrounding events.

Joe Ristuccia, in an e-mail dated May 12, 2014, confirmed Tony Johnson's financial support of the nascent Yale Women's Crew program. Conversations with Joyce Majure and Janet Klauber on April 26, 2014, and follow-up e-mails on May 8 and 9, 2014, provided details on the history of the Yale Women's Crew and the beginnings of the EAWRC.

See also:

Steve Wulf, "Title IX: 37 Words That Changed Everything," *ESPN Magazine* online, April 12, 2012, http://espn.go.com/espnw/title-ix/article /7722632/37-words-changed-everything.

In addition, the official US Olympics Committee books proved valuable in detailing various Olympics-related statistics; see *United States Olympic Book 1980* (Colorado Springs: US Olympic Committee, 1980); and Dick Schapp, *The 1984 Olympic Games* (New York: Random House, 1984).

For details on the beginnings of the Eastern Association of Women's Rowing Colleges and the first women's rowing regattas in the early 1970s, see Paula D. Welch, *Silver Era Golden Moments: A Celebration of Ivy League Women's Athletics* (Lanham, MD: Madison Books, 1999).

See also:

Kathrine Switzer, "The Real Story of Kathrine Switzer's 1967 Boston Marathon," *Marathon Woman: Running the Race to Revolutionize Women's Sports* (New York: Carroll & Graf, 2007), http://kathrineswitzer.com/about -kathrine/1967-boston-marathon-the-real-story/.

Women in Higher Education, "The Real Story of the Passage of Title IX 35 Years Ago," http://wihe.com/the-real-story-behind-the-passage-of-title-ix-35-years-ago/.

Iram Valentin, "Title IX: A Brief History," WEEA Equity Resource Center, 1997, http://www2.edc.org/womensequity/pdffiles/t9digest.pdf.

Barbara Winslow, "The Impact of Title IX," Gilder Lehrman Institute of American History, http://www.gilderlehrman.org/historynow/03_2010/historian6.php.

US Department of Education, "Title IX: 25 Years of Progress," 1997, http://www2.ed.gov/pubs/TitleIX.

CHAPTER 7

For the history of women's engagement in sports from the early twentieth century, with a specific emphasis of the impact of social attitudes on the choices made available to girls and young women who wanted to play sports, see Welch, *Silver Era Golden Moments*.

I spoke with Chris Ernst on March 20, 2014, about how she handled being gay in the 1970s when she was at Yale, specifically in her role as captain.

CHAPTER 8

On May 28, 2014, David LaBarge and I had a long conversation about his homosexuality and slow progression to living as an openly gay man in the early to mid-1970s.

CHAPTER 10

I used standard and commonly accessed online sources to obtain details related to the above, as well as the Soviets' invasion of Afghanistan, President Jimmy Carter's decision to boycott the Moscow Olympics, and Anita DeFrantz's challenge of his decision.

DeFrantz v. United States Olympic Committee, http://www.leagle.com/decision/19801673492FSupp1181_11510.

I obtained details regarding the celebration and associated events the US government hosted for US Olympians in the wake of the boycott of the Moscow Olympics from *United States Olympic Book 1980* (Colorado Springs: US Olympic Committee, 1980).

CHAPTER 15

I used standard and commonly accessed online sources to obtain statistics on the growth of women's participation in the Olympics.

International Olympic Committee, "Fact Sheet: Women in the Olympic Movement," update May 2014, http://www.olympic.org/Documents/Reference_documents_Factsheets/Women_in_Olympic_Movement.pdf.